THE INVISIBLE BAR

THE INVISIBLE BAR

THE WOMAN LAWYER IN AMERICA 1638 TO THE PRESENT

KAREN BERGER MORELLO

BEACON PRESS   BOSTON

Beacon Press
25 Beacon Street
Boston, Massachusetts 02108

Beacon Press books
are published under the auspices of
the Unitarian Universalist Association of Congregations.

95 94 93 92 91 90 89 88   1 2 3 4 5 6 7 8

Library of Congress Cataloging-in-Publication Data

Morello, Karen Berger, 1949–
The invisible bar.

Bibliography: p.
Includes index.
1. Women lawyers—United States—History.   I. Title.
KF299.W6M67 1988   340'.023'73   87-42851
ISBN 0-8070-6741-5 (pbk.)

Cover design: Richard Adelson
Left photo: Alice G. McGee, Warren County Historical Society
Middle photo: Julia Radle Kline, Dickinson School of Law
Right photo: Tiera Farrow, Wyandotte County Museum
Bottom photo: Sandra Day O'Connor, AP/Wide World Photos

CONTENTS

INTRODUCTION

Shortly after Sandra Day O'Connor was nominated to the United States Supreme Court in September 1981, she appeared at confirmation hearings held by the Senate Judiciary Committee. Senator Robert Dole of Kansas, noting the age of the Supreme Court and the significance of her appointment, welcomed O'Connor by saying, "Better one hundred and ninety years late than never—you are among friends." While obviously intending to put O'Connor at ease, Dole's remarks pointed up the uneasy fact that for most of our history women have been excluded from participation in the legal system and from attaining positions of importance within the legal profession.

Justice O'Connor is destined to have a place in history, but the names of few, if any, of the women lawyers who came before her are widely known. Although women have practiced law in America since Colonial times, little more than a hundred years ago the United States Supreme Court ruled that a female's natural "timidity and delicacy" made her unfit for many occupations, most particularly the law. The giants of the legal profession, men like Harlan Fiske Stone, Roscoe Pound and Clarence Darrow, consistently opposed the entry of women into the law and sought to keep them on the fringes of the profession. Darrow is reported to have told a group of women attorneys in Chicago:

You can't be shining lights at the bar because you are too kind. You can never be corporation lawyers because you are not cold-blooded. You have not a high grade of intellect. You can never expect to get the fees men get. I doubt if you [can] ever make a living. Of course you can be divorce lawyers. That is a useful field. And there is another field you can have solely for your own. You can't make a living at it, but it's worthwhile and you'll have no competition. That is the free defense of criminals.

Women who nevertheless insisted on seeking a career in the law were regarded as oddballs and misfits who in not accepting more traditional feminine roles were destined for failure. In 1890 a woman lawyer from Massachusetts bitterly complained that "newspapers publish and republish little floating items about women lawyers along with those of the latest sea-serpent, the popular idea seeming to be that the one is about as real as the other." Nearly a century later, with record enroll-ments of women in the nation's law schools and with Justice O'Connor seated on the nation's highest court, the press still finds women lawyers unusual. Recent headlines such as THE CASE OF THE PREGNANT PROSE-CUTOR, D.A.'s MINISKIRTED AIDE MAJORS IN CRIME CASES, and THE Ms. WHO KEEPS PICKING ON THE BOYS help to keep the sea-serpent theory alive. Part of the reason may lie with the fact that so little is known about women who have practiced law in this country that the old myths were bound to survive as long as they have. Unless women attorneys were highlighted in offbeat newspaper items or were spectac-ular "firsts" who battled courts and legislatures to gain admission to the bar, they consistently have been ignored.

The reasons for the resistance to women lawyers can never fully be explained, but it is likely that it has to do with the law's close relation-ship to power in our society. When Barbara J. Harris studied nine-teenth-century professional women in *Beyond Her Sphere*, comparing the difficulties women had in entering the legal and medical profes-sions, she found that women faced greatest opposition from the bar. Harris and others who have examined the role of women in the legal system note that while entry into the medical profession might be justified as a natural extension of women's nurturing role, the law clearly was an all-male domain, closest to the center of power, that was not to be invaded or changed by females.

In the fight to keep women out of that domain, bar associations claimed women lacked the physical strength to handle heavy case loads, and newspapers charged that attractive women would unfairly sway juries. Law business was conveniently discussed in men-only private clubs, bar groups restricted their memberships for such "practical" reasons as not having adequate bathroom facilities, law schools operated on a quota system if they admitted women at all, and interviewers for law firms routinely told female applicants, "We're not hiring any women this year." Even when the clients and cases were rewarding, women faced so much opposition to their participation in the law that for many it proved to be a difficult and lonely profession.

Just fifteen years ago when I decided to pursue a legal career, the resistance to women lawyers was still substantial. In college my prelaw adviser suggested that as a woman, I was better suited for marriage than for law school. A law professor I once greatly admired boasted that he placed all the women students in one of two classes so he could enjoy teaching the other one. A county prosecutor's office in New York City hired male students for criminal law internships but offered me, then a third-year law student, a typing job. After I passed my bar examination a prominent New York attorney suggested hiring me at a salary considerably lower than what the men were earning. When I refused, pointing up the difference in pay, he asked, "Are you married?" I said I wasn't. "Well then, what's a single girl need with all that money— let the guys buy you dinner." Throughout much of the 1970s I found myself conspicuously the only woman lawyer in the courtroom. On several occasions I was told to sit down and wait for my lawyer to show up. Once, when I approached the bench for a pretrial conference, the presiding judge refused to believe I was a lawyer. A crowded and noisy courtroom fell silent as he demanded to know the date and place of my admission to the bar. When I gave the information the judge winked at me and said, "Okay, I'm sorry, honey," then he and the spectators exploded with laughter.

I have no reason to believe that I was singled out for difficult treatment, and in speaking with many other women lawyers, I learned that their experiences were remarkably similar to mine. Fortunately, with increasing numbers of women entering the legal profession in the 1970s and 1980s, women began to refuse to accept the notion that hostility and humiliation were the price you paid for joining a "man's profession."

Sandra Day O'Connor's appointment to the United States Supreme Court in 1981 was undoubtedly the most visible symbol of the changing status of women in the law. O'Connor's background and stated commitment to such women's issues as reproductive rights, equal pay and equal opportunity meant she was a woman with whom most of us could identify. O'Connor had managed a household and a family, had been a state legislator and had served as a trial and appellate judge. She brought a wide range of experiences with her to the bench and she freely admitted that as an honors graduate of Stanford Law School, she could not find a job with any California law firm except as a stenographer. As Justice O'Connor took her oath of office I could not help but wonder why it had taken so long for women to reach this highest level of the profession. If many other women had tried, what had happened to them? If there was a pool of prominent women attorneys who through the years might have been considered for the job, why couldn't I name more than a handful of them?

Coincidentally, 1981 was the year I served as historian of my local women's bar association in New York. The Queens Women's Bar had been formed fifty years earlier when women were being refused membership in the "regular" county bar. It was not until the 1960s that the Queens County Bar Association admitted women, and it took a lawsuit by attorney Marie Beary to bring about the change. As historian, I maintained our association's archives, which contained some wonderful photographs and clippings about members dating back to the 1920s. Although these lawyers had active practices and in most cases families, they somehow managed also to visit women in prison, give free legal aid to the poor, participate in equal rights forums, and counsel families of servicemen. The photos ranged from the serious (the admission of several members to practice before the United States Supreme Court) to the silly (a ceremony in the 1940s at which the most glamorous "Queen of the Lady Lawyers" was crowned). The recipient of that "honor," Fortune Vecchiarelli, was, ironically, one of the organization's strongest proponents of a national Equal Rights Amendment.

After reviewing these old records, I decided to prepare a fiftieth anniversary datebook joining together our photographs with important dates in the history of women lawyers in America. The project was enthusiastically supported by the other members, and those who worked on it began telling me about their lives and their careers. Whether it was Bessie Geffner describing her defense of a murder trial in the summer of 1925, dressed all the while in an overcoat to hide her pregnancy, or Geraldine Ferraro discussing the frustrations of trying to get congressional colleagues to support women's issues, I was fascinated with the stories these gifted women had to tell.

The recorded history of women in the law proved much more elusive. While there are some fine books and articles touching on the history of women in our profession, I could not find one book that dealt exclusively with the subject. Women had been practicing law for centuries and yet we had no written history. In order to complete the datebook I culled as much information as I could from the existing literature, contacted a number of historical societies, and continued talking with members about their experiences in and out of the courtroom. Meanwhile, I realized I had the rough beginnings of a much-needed book and decided to continue with my research. Almost immediately, I began receiving calls and materials from interested librarians, historians, law professors, attorneys and private individuals who had had women lawyers in their families. Through their clippings and stories I discovered women lawyers who rode circuit on horseback, who crossed the West in covered wagons, and who held court in log cabins. While their names were not well known, some proved to have been able statesmen, orators and legal publishers. Quite a few were eccentric and outlandish, most practiced law for the love of it, and all worked to support causes they believed in.

In the course of my research I was also to discover that the history of women lawyers in the United States remains controversial. In 1981, Columbia Law School asked me to write an article for its alumni journal about the school's first women law students, who enrolled in 1927. I found that Harlan Fiske Stone, while dean of Columbia Law School, vigorously opposed the admission of women. It was only after he left Columbia and joined the United States Supreme Court that women were permitted to register for law classes. I also discovered that despite some extremely hostile reactions from faculty and male students, women graduates of Columbia Law School were convinced that they had received a superior education. The article I wrote for Columbia contained all these observations, but shortly after I submitted it, I was asked by members of the law school administration to reword the section on Harlan Fiske Stone. I refused to do so. A request was made a second time. Again I refused. Then, though the article had already been set into type and given a publication date, it was hurriedly withdrawn at the direction of one of the school's deans, I was told, who deemed it "downbeat and not necessary." I later learned that Cynthia Fuchs Epstein, the noted sociologist and author of *Women in Law,* a study of the current status of women in the legal profession, also had an article rejected by Columbia because of what she had to say about the law school's early treatment of women.

Shortly after the Columbia incident, Harvard Law School asked me to write a piece about its first women students. Although the distinguished Soia Mentschikoff had been a visiting professor of law at Harvard in the 1940s, Harvard Law School did not admit women until 1950, almost the last law school in the country to do so. In my research for the article I interviewed Kenneth Weinberg, a graduate of Harvard Law School's class of 1948, who vividly recalled for me the day the legendary Roscoe Pound threw a woman visitor out of his class because he did not believe in teaching law to women. I had no trouble getting the *Harvard Law School Record* to print the story, but again a storm of controversy arose. Weinberg told me that after the article was printed he received numerous calls from enraged alumni who asked him to write to the *Record* and claim my information was incorrect. He declined to do so. Letters also began pouring in from graduates who believed I had vilified Professor W. Barton Leach, the man most closely identified with "Ladies Day," the practice at Harvard in which women students were called on to recite on one specially selected day each semester and then only for the amusement of the professor and the male members of the class.

While I can well understand the embarrassment certain administrators and alumni might feel about their institutions' discriminatory policies in the past, their misguided efforts in the 1980s to change history naturally made the uncovering and reporting of these events all the more important to me.

In order to complete this history of women lawyers in the United States I have interviewed several hundred women attorneys and read about hundreds more. I have come away with a tremendous sense of pride for what they have accomplished. Their perseverance made it possible for those of us who follow in their footsteps to use our full capabilities in the law and to make real choices about our lives and our careers. It was in the late 1700s that William Sampson, a prominent New York lawyer, criticized attempts by Colonial attorneys to imitate the style and thinking of the British barristers. "Must we tread always in their steps, go where they go, do what they do, and say what they say?" he asked. Sampson urged his fellow lawyers to create instead a distinctly American legal system, one that would be responsive to the needs of a new nation. Nearly three hundred years later women lawyers are adopting similar views, insisting that their contribution to the law be not as associate males but as independent actors who by their very presence are changing the nature of the legal profession and our system of laws as well. It is for them, and for the women who preceded them, that this book has been written.

THE INVISIBLE BAR

1

THE FIRST WOMEN LAWYERS

The first woman lawyer in America, Margaret Brent, arrived in the colonies in 1638. She was a master negotiator, an accomplished litigator, and later, because of political circumstances, she proved to be a respected leader as well. Shortly after settling in St. Mary's Parish, Maryland, Brent amassed some of the largest real estate holdings in the New World, while getting herself appointed counsel to the governor. She broke through all the existing restrictions facing seventeenth-century women and clearly had no equal in the province—male or female. Because the colonists did not quite know what to call such a formidable woman, they frequently addressed her, in person and in court records, as "Gentleman Margaret Brent."

Most of what is known about Brent begins with her arrival in St. Mary's Parish four years after it was founded. Brent was a cousin of Lord Baltimore's and she came from a wealthy land-owning family in England. Before setting sail with relatives and servants for America, she obtained two letters from Lord Baltimore directing Governor Calvert of Maryland to give her the right to acquire land on more favorable terms than other recent settlers. In part Lord Baltimore wrote:

I would have you pass to Margaret Brent and her sister Mary and their heirs and assigns for and in respect of four maid servants, besides themselves, which they transport this year to plant in the Province of Maryland, a grant of as much land in and about the Town of Saint Maries and elsewhere in the Province, in as ample a manner and with as large privileges as any of the first adventurers had.

Brent used the letter to buy up sizable tracts of land, at first for herself and her family to use, later for political and investment purposes. In a message to England one colonist complained: "Margaret requires far more room than we can afford." Land meant power in the colony, not only because it represented wealth but also because it was a source of political strength: voting in the province was conditioned on the owner-ship of real property.

Brent's shrewd intelligence and ability to make and execute deals soon made her indispensable to the governor. According to Mary E. W. Ramey, a historian who in 1915 wrote the *Chronicles of Mistress Margaret Brent* between the years 1639 to 1643

there is frequent mention of Mistress Brent. . . . The court records show where she recovered judgments against the Irish fugitives, O'Sullivan and others, and helped to run them out of the province. The land records show her demands for grants of land, her assignment of portions thereof to the men she transported from time to time, proving that she was doing what she could to build up and strengthen the Colony.

Brent also managed to look after the welfare of some of the children in the colony and was appointed guardian of a young Indian girl she named Mary Brent Kitomagund.

In 1643, while civil war was raging in England, Governor Leonard Calvert was called home. Two Virginia colonists, William Claiborne and Richard Ingle (who in many accounts is referred to as a pirate), had been stirring up resistance to the Calvert government. With Calvert gone they were able successfully to take control of the province. When he tried to return, Calvert was forced into exile, but with Margaret Brent's help he was able to raise a force of men to retake St. Mary's. Part of the recapture plan they devised had Calvert pledging his and Lord Baltimore's estates, promising to pay the soldiers with

corn and tobacco. Calvert's forces won and immediately he was returned as head of the province, but he lived only a little while longer.
On his deathbed Calvert summoned Margaret Brent to his side. In the
presence of witnesses he named Thomas Green to be his successor and
directed Margaret to "take all and pay all." Brent declared herself
Calvert's executor on the strength of that statement and claimed she
was now the Lord Proprietor's attorney. No one disagreed. In fact,
when the colonists learned of Calvert's deathbed decision, many said
his order should have been reversed—that Brent would have made a
better governor than Green.

Ten days after Calvert's death, the Maryland Assembly ratified
Brent's claim and issued letters of administration to her. Under oath
she agreed to bring in an inventory of Calvert's possessions and she
fulfilled her promise. But as one writer was to note a good many years
later, "To any one accustomed to modern luxury there is a startling
incongruity between the high-sounding title of Governor of Maryland
and the details of this inventory." Some of the items Brent recorded
were:

Two prs-new Holland shoes; 3 oz. sweet head powder; 3 small bits silver plate;
1 silver sack cup; 1 old Bed and Bolster; 1 old green rug; 1 very old bed; 1
empty case without bottles, and another old case with four bottles, a blew juge;
a white box without lock or key; a very little Trunk; a red leather letter case;
an Iron Pott; a kneeling desk and picture of Paules; an old frame of a chayre
—2 combs and 1 hatt-brush . . .

Because most records were destroyed under the Claiborne-Ingle siege,
an unusual number of claims were being made against Calvert's estate.
Brent was forced to defend these lawsuits and to institute actions of
her own against those who had been in debt to the governor. With little
documentation to support or refute claims, it was an especially demanding job. Greatly complicating matters was the promise of payment
Calvert made to his troops when he was plotting to retake the province.
The soldiers still had not been paid and they were hungry and hostile.
Records reveal that officially the troops ". . . declared under oath, taken
in open Assembly that Governor Calvert had pledged his own and Lord
Baltimore's estate for their pay." Unofficially they were threatening a

mutiny. Governor Green could not cope with the situation but Brent, sensing the gravity of the circumstances, quickly took charge. She ordered as a first step that her own cattle be slaughtered to feed the soldiers until more suitable arrangements could be made, then pressed for some payments to be made as a way of staving off riot.

In the middle of the crisis Brent continued to handle claims for and against Calvert's estate and received formal recognition of her work from the court. "The administrator of Leonard Calvert," the Court directed, "should be received and looked upon as his Lordship's attorney." Brent's caseload was considerable. According to Ramey's *Chronicles,*

In many cases Mistress Brent prayed a jury trial. Each juror received fifteen pounds of tobacco ($1.80) per day, the cost to be charged to the person demanding the jury. She was evidently convinced that she could better protect the interests of those she represented in the court by incurring this additional expense.

Court records also indicate that "her name was one of the most frequently appearing . . . she figured in one hundred and twenty-four court cases in eight years . . ."

In politics, as in everyday life, Margaret Brent chose to ignore the status of other women in the colony. She believed she had not only a right but a duty as attorney for the governor to have a "vote and voyce" in the Maryland Assembly. The records of Assembly proceedings for 1648 indicate what happened when she formally made that demand:

ffriday 21st. January came Mistress Margaret Brent and requested to have vote in the House for herself, and voyce allso, for that att the last Court, 3rd. January, it was ordered that the said Mistress Brent was to be looked uppon and received as his Lordship's Attorney. The Governor denied that the said Mistress Brent should have any vote in the House. And the said Mistress Brent protested against all proceedings in this present Assembly unless she may be present and have vote as aforesaid.

More than two hundred and fifty years later, *Harper's* magazine in an 1898 article noted: "By this action Margaret Brent undoubtedly placed herself on record as the first woman in America to make a stand for the rights of her sex. It is surprising to find how little this fact is known."

Despite the setback in the Assembly, Brent continued to handle the estate of Leonard Calvert. A final accounting showed what Brent had long suspected—Calvert had not left an amount sufficient to pay the soldiers despite his promise to do so. Brent realized that unless she paid the troops out of Lord Baltimore's estate as Calvert had also pledged to do, there would be full-scale riots in the province. But when Brent announced her intention to begin paying the soldiers, Lord Baltimore became furious and decided to attack her publicly. Again Governor Green sidestepped the controversy. Brent ignored Lord Baltimore and by her actions successfully prevented the threatened mutiny. Only later would she be recognized for her quick thinking and integrity.

Lord Baltimore sent written charges against Brent to the Maryland Assembly, hoping that they would rebuke her again as they had when she sought representation in the House. But this time the Assembly sided with Margaret Brent. In answer to Lord Baltimore it said:

As for Mistress Margaret Brent undertaking and meddling with your estate, we do verily believe and in conscience report that it were better for the colony's safety at that time in her hands than in any man's else, in the whole province after your brother's death; for the soldiers would never have treated any other with that civility and respect, and though they were ever ready at several times to run into mutiny, yet she still pacified them, till at last the things were brought to that strait, that she must be admitted and declared your Lordship's Attorney, by order of the court, or else all must go to ruin again, and the second mischief had doubtless been far greater than the former; so that, if there had not been any sinister use made of your Lordship's estate by her, from what it was intended and engaged for by Mr. Calvert before his death, as we verily believe she has not, then we conceive from that time she rather deserved favor and thanks from your Honor, for her so much concurring to the public safety, than to be justly liable to all those bitter invectives you have been pleased to express against her.

Brent should have felt vindicated, but she remained bitter about the Assembly's refusal to let her vote and was resentful about Lord Baltimore's accusations. At the age of fifty-six Brent moved to Virginia and spent the rest of her life quietly on a manor in Westmoreland County, which she called Peace. She died in 1671.

Three hundred years later the Baltimore *Evening Sun* listed her remarkable accomplishments and wondered why by 1971 so little had been done to recognize Brent's achievements:

In 1926, a 16-inch doll dressed in colonial costume as Margaret Brent was sent to the Philadelphia sesquicentennial exhibition by the Maryland Federation of Women's Clubs. A Margaret Brent doll won first prize for Maryland in a fashion show conducted by the National Women's Democratic Club in Washington in the 1950s . . . one shudders at Mistress Brent's probable reaction to the picture of women politicians playing with dolls while the boys in the smoke-filled rooms ran the party.

History records no other women lawyers until 1869, although a number of women, among them Gertrude James of Maryland, Sarah Bland of Virginia, and Anna Meyanders of New York pleaded their own cases in Colonial courts. While most of these efforts concerned property or estate settlements, an interesting constitutional argument was raised by Mumbet, a slave woman who preferred to use the name Elizabeth Freeman. In 1783, on her own initiative and with assistance of counsel, she entered a Massachusetts court and demanded her freedom, claiming that key provisions of the Massachusetts Bill of Rights made her, as a native-born American, free and equal. The court was both surprised and impressed by the argument and Elizabeth Freeman was granted the relief she sought.

In 1795, Lucy Terry Prince, a black woman who had tried without success to gain admission for her son to the Williams College for Men, was successful in defending a land claim that went all the way to the United States Supreme Court. Historian Barbara Wertheimer in her book on working women, *We Were There,* claims that surviving records indicate Prince was the first woman ever to have addressed the Supreme Court.*

During this period, Abigail Adams, not a lawyer but indisputably a feminist, was concerned about the effect formal government and laws had on women. She had warned her husband, John, that "in the new

---

*Also reported is the instance in which Myra Clark Gaines of New Orleans, who spent years in litigation over her inheritance, argued and won her own case in the U.S. Supreme Court against the formidable Daniel Webster.

Code of Laws which I suppose it will be necessary for you to make I desire you would Remember the Ladies, and be more generous and favourable to them than your ancestors. Do not put such unlimited power into the hands of the Husbands. Remember all Men would be tyrants if they could. If particular care and attention is not paid to the Ladies, we are determined to foment a rebellion, and will not hold ourselves bound by any Laws in which we have no voice or Representation."

But bound they were, so much so that well into the nineteenth century married women could not vote, serve on a jury, get a professional education, hold elective office, enter into a contract, obtain custody of their own children, or control their own money, even when they had earned it. Abigail Adams, for all her intelligence and strength, was cast in the role of an adviser, not an activist. Women leaders throughout this period would write about the injustices and would urge that there be full equality, but none realistically were in a position to effect change. Society had become so formal, particularly in the large cities in the northeast, that restrictions on race, sex and class prevented the emergence of any successors to Margaret Brent.

But by the early part of the nineteenth century a number of factors combined to offer women some hope of professional achievement. Industrialization had taken many working-class women out of their homes and into the factories. By 1828 the first women workers participated in a labor strike in Dover, New Hampshire, and the first woman is recorded as having addressed a mixed public audience. Education was becoming more of a possibility, particularly for upper-class young women who were encouraged to attend seminaries protecting them from outside influences and training them for their proper roles as wives and mothers. Significantly, westward expansion in the 1830s and 1840s contributed to breaking down gender and class distinctions. As women succeeded at traditionally male jobs, all kinds of opportunities suddenly became available. And, as the abolitionist movement emerged during the pre–Civil War period, a number of women used it as a focus for their talents, emotions and energies. Angela Davis points out in *Women, Race and Class* how the antislavery movement offered middle- and upper-class white women the opportunity to prove their worth outside their traditional roles.

The link between equality for blacks and equality for women was being emphasized by many participants in both movements. Sarah and Angelina Grimke, for example, were passionate in their support of both abolition and feminism. Sarah Grimke, much like feminist leader Elizabeth Cady Stanton, had wanted to become a lawyer and went so far as to begin studying law with her brother Thomas. But she and Stanton were a generation too early to accomplish these career goals. Nevertheless their activism, and that of such feminist leaders as Lucy Stone and Lucretia Mott, inspired Sarah Grimke in the 1830s to write the document "The Equality of the Sexes and the Condition of Woman," in which she boldly stated: "But I ask no favors for my sex. I surrender not our claim to equality. All I ask of our brethren is, that they will take their feet from off our necks and permit us to stand upright on that ground which God designed us to occupy."

Political unrest in Europe in the 1840s may have been an additional factor touching off women's interest in fighting for equality. It was difficult for American women to ignore the daily newspaper reports of happenings on the Continent, for 1848 was a year of manifestos and proclamations evincing the European's willingness to fight for equality and justice and to overthrow the established order. Not surprisingly, that same year, for the first time in the nation's history, a group of women gathered together in Seneca Falls, New York, to talk about their condition and to actively seek changes in the role of women. The storm that Abigail Adams warned would come if laws did not reflect the needs of women finally was here. Out of the convention came a "Declaration of Principles," which essentially was a rewrite of the Declaration of Independence: "We hold these truths to be self-evident, that all men *and women* are created equal . . ." Delegates pointed out the disturbing absence of women in the fields of law and medicine and reiterated demands for equality in education and justice under the law.

Disliking the prevailing mood, a writer for the New York *Herald* complained about these feminists whose demands were capturing the attention of the public and the press:

They want to fill all other posts which men are ambitious to occupy, to be lawyers, doctors, captains of vessels and generals in the field. How funny it would sound in the newspapers that Lucy Stone, pleading a cause, took suddenly ill in the pains of parturition and perhaps gave birth to a fine bouncing boy in court!

The feminists somehow ignored the ridicule to which they were subjected and continued to write and rally.

The Civil War and westward expansion provided women with opportunities to serve in occupations that previously had been closed to them. And the farther away women were from the restrictions of northeastern society the better able they were to strike out in areas of their own. As early as February 1869, we know that a woman was practicing law in a small town in Iowa. The *Chicago Legal News* reported under the headline FEMALE LAWYER that "in North English, Iowa County, there may be seen in front of a neat office a sign with the following inscription in gilt letters, 'Mrs. Mary E. Magoon, Attorney at Law.' We understand that Mrs. Magoon is having a good practice and is very successful as a jury lawyer." Since law practice on the county level often did not require admission to a state or territorial bar, it is possible that Mrs. Magoon practiced only locally. She is not on record with the State of Iowa as having been admitted to its Supreme Court. But her mention in the *Chicago Legal News* leaves open the question of how many other women lawyers were practicing in small towns throughout the Midwest and West without having been admitted on the state level and consequently without having been recognized by history.

Iowa appears to have been the most progressive of all the states in accepting women in to the legal profession, so it is not surprising that Mrs. Magoon was able to thrive in a pioneer practice. In June 1869, Belle Babb Mansfield, a twenty-three-year-old woman from Mt. Pleasant, passed the Iowa State bar and officially became recognized as the first woman lawyer in the United States. Mansfield had taken advantage of the Civil War slump in college enrollments and registered for classes at Iowa Wesleyan College. She quickly became known as a skilled debater and a brilliant student of the classics. At commencement Mansfield gave the valedictory address. After graduation she joined her brother's law firm, Amblers & Babb, and began an apprenticeship in the law. In 1868 she married college professor John Mansfield, who not only encouraged her to continue her legal studies but supported her efforts for women's suffrage as well.

The following year Belle Mansfield made formal application for the Iowa bar examinations, well aware of the provisions of the Iowa Code of 1851, Section 1610, which specifically limited admission to the bar to "any white male person, twenty one years of age, who is an inhabitant of this State," and who satisfies the court that "he possesses the requisite learning . . ." Because of her proven ability in the law Mansfield hoped to secure admission to the bar in spite of these gender restrictions.

Belle Mansfield was permitted to take the examination. The attorneys who conducted her interview reported:

Your committee takes unusual pleasure in recommending the admission of Mrs. Mansfield, not only because she is the first lady who has applied for this authority in this state, but because in her examination she has given the very best rebuke possible to the imputation that ladies cannot qualify for the practice of law.

The matter came before Justice Francis Springer, then one of the most liberal and progressive judges in Iowa. Springer agreed that Belle Mansfield had the necessary qualifications of intellect and character to practice law but felt limited by the wording of the admissions statute. In order to circumvent the gender provisions, Springer relied on another Iowa statute which held that "words importing the masculine gender only may be extended to females." Then Judge Springer went one step further. He declared that when a statute contained an affirmative declaration of gender, as the Iowa admissions statute had, it could not be construed as an implied denial of the right to females. This interpretation of the law, which clearly was intended to support women who were seeking admission to the bar, would be challenged by courts in a number of states and by the United States Supreme Court itself.

Because Judge Springer was more progressive than most other jurists of his time, in June 1869, Belle Babb Mansfield became the first woman in the United States formally admitted to the bar. The following year the Iowa state legislature ensured the admission of women to the profession by removing the restrictive gender language in its admissions statute.

Regrettably, Belle Mansfield never practiced law. She once explained that she studied law because of her "love of it," and when she was admitted to the bar, fully intended to practice. But she postponed her law career to accompany her husband to Europe. There she used her time to continue studying law, taking a course of law lectures on such varied subjects as Hindu and Muhammedan law, conveyances, equity and the science of jurisprudence. When not attending classes, she visited courtrooms in London and Paris, hoping to gain a better perspective on Continental practice and laws.

But when Belle Mansfield returned to Iowa she accepted a faculty position at Iowa Wesleyan rather than make a career in the law. Historian Louis A. Haselmayer noted that during this period she and her husband, John, "were without question the most distinguished members of the Iowa Wesleyan faculty and important leaders of thought and action in the community." In addition to her academic work, Belle Mansfield traveled throughout the state of Iowa to promote the aims of women's suffrage. She was one of the founders of the Iowa Women's Suffrage Society and served as an officer of that organization for many years. Billed as "Belle Mansfield, Esq." she was popular on the lecture circuit for her speeches on government and women's rights. One reviewer called Mansfield "deep and earnest, . . ." showing "a well-balanced, well-stored mind, in its close analyses and excellent applications." Another noted, "Mrs. Mansfield is the first lady that has ever been admitted to the bar in Iowa, and in her lecture last evening showed in forcible and conclusive language that she was a master of her situation. Her lecture was a brilliant, foreasic [forensic] display, her words coming with force and vehemence, and, although speaking entirely without reference to her notes, it was a plain and suggestive argument as to 'what women should do' and pointed very clearly to their social and public sphere. Taking it all in all it was indeed a rich literary treat."

In 1881 the Mansfields moved to Indiana to accept faculty positions at DePauw University. John was a professor of chemistry and Belle served first as dean of women and later as professor of history. Within three years John Mansfield suffered a nervous breakdown from which he never recovered. He was committed to an insane asylum in Napa

Valley and died there in 1894. Belle Mansfield never discussed her husband's condition in public, but she continued to work and to pay his medical and living expenses. When she retired, Belle Mansfield was dean of DePauw's Schools of Music and Art and was still an ardent supporter of women's rights. Lelia J. Robinson, at the end of Mansfield's career, noted that although Belle never practiced law, "her interest in law and women lawyers has never been lost, and she is glad that her pioneering along this line has helped open up the way in which others are now achieving success." Belle Mansfield died in 1911.

Two months after Belle Mansfield was admitted to the Iowa State bar, Myra Colby Bradwell, wife of Cook County Court Judge James B. Bradwell, took and passed the 1869 Chicago bar exam. The previous year Bradwell had begun publication of the *Chicago Legal News,* the first law journal printed in the West. She served as editor and business manager of the weekly and in her opening editorial said her paper would be devoted to "legal information, general news, the publication of new and important decisions, and of other matters useful to the practicing lawyer. . . . It will give abstracts of the points decided in our local courts, comment freely, but fairly, upon the conduct of our judges, the members of the bar, officers of courts, members of congress and our state legislature in their administration of public affairs." Almost immediately the *Chicago Legal News* was a critical and financial success. After the first issue Bradwell added a column called "Law Relating to Women" in which she reported on developments—or the lack of them—in laws relating to women. In a two-column attack on those who opposed women's suffrage editor Bradwell wrote:

Have not some of the greatest, richest and most prosperous of nations in ancient and modern times been governed by women under the name of Queens.

We are asked is not the *News* neutral in politics? It is. We do not regard this as a political question but as a reform. In fact, we do not know which of the two great parties of the day will be for or against it. We have never said anything in the columns of the *News* and never intend to, from which any person could tell whether we were in favor of the Democratic or Republican party—the Methodist, Baptist, Universalist or Catholic churches. But one thing we do claim—that woman has a right to think and act as an individual —believing if the great Father had intended it to be otherwise—he would have placed Eve in a cage and given Adam the key.

With the same intensity, Myra Bradwell went after the established bar, citing the need to "decrease the vast number of incompetent persons who are yearly admitted to the bar," and sparing neither lawyers ("Newel Pratt, one of the divorce attorneys of this city, died last week. It was the liquor killed him"), nor judges ("A judge has no more right, morally speaking, by his tardiness to take an hour from the time of a lawyer than he has to put his hand in the attorney's pocket and extract five dollars").

It had not been Myra Bradwell's early intention to become a lawyer. While she had worked in her husband's law office before the Civil War, her purpose was simply to assist him in researching and writing briefs. When the Civil War came, Myra Bradwell focused her attention on soldiers' relief groups and programs that were helping new immigrants adjust to city life. Her creation of the *Chicago Legal News* reflected her interest in the law just as her involvement in Chicago's first women's suffrage convention that same year reflected her concern for the rights of women. It was then that Myra Bradwell decided to make a formal application for admission to the Illinois bar.

In August 1869 she was examined by Judge E. S. Williams of the Seventh Judicial Circuit and by Charles H. Reed, the State's Attorney. They certified that they examined Mrs. Myra Bradwell as to her qualifications to practice law "and finding her qualified therefor, recommend that a license should be issued to her." Bradwell filed her certificate of examination with the September term of the Third Grand Division of the Illinois Supreme Court and petitioned for a license to be given. In her supporting statement, she said, "Your petitioner suggests that the only question involved in her case is—Does being a woman disqualify her under the laws of Illinois from receiving a license to practice law —and claims that the Legislature has answered this question in the negative."

Bradwell's argument on the point essentially was the same one Belle Mansfield had used in Iowa. Relying on Section 28, Chapter 90 of the

Revised Statutes of Illinois, Bradwell claimed that the legislature had already provided that "when any party or person is described or referred to by words importing the masculine gender, females as well as males shall be deemed to be included." But Myra Bradwell did not have the benefit of a Judge Springer to liberally interpret the Illinois statutes. To support her argument further she cited instance after instance where the words "he" and "him" by necessity included women: "Section 3 of our Declaration of Rights says 'that all men have a natural and indefeasible right to worship Almighty God' etc. It will not be contended that women are not included in this provision." Bradwell went on to quote the statutes pertaining to the rights of defendants to trial by jury, the laws of public domain and the laws of forcible detainer, all of which were written in the masculine gender only, but which certainly pertained to women as well.

On October 7, 1869, Mrs. Bradwell received the following notice from the court:

Madam:

The court instruct me to inform you that they are compelled to deny your application for a license to practice as an attorney-at-law in the courts of this State, upon the ground that you would not be bound by the obligations necessary to be assumed where the relation of attorney and client shall exist, by reason of the disability imposed by your married condition—it being assumed that you are a married woman.

Applications of the same character have occasionally been made by persons under twenty-one years of age, and have always been denied upon the same ground—that they are not bound by their contracts, being under a legal disability in that regard.

Until such disability shall be removed by legislation, the court regards itself powerless to grant your application.

Very respectfully, your obt. serv't.

          N. L. Freeman
          Clerk's Office

Bradwell was incensed by the court's decision and printed it on the front page of the *Chicago Legal News*. She quickly submitted a supplemental brief in which "your petitioner admits to your honors that she is a married woman (although she believes that fact does not appear in the record) but insists most firmly that under the laws of Illinois it is neither a crime nor a disqualification to be a married woman."

The distinction between married and single women had to do with the common law doctrines of *feme sole* (unmarried) and *feme covert* (married). Under the French and English law from which it was adapted in the United States, once a woman married she lost the right to inherit property on her own, to enter into contracts on her own and to independently obtain goods and services. Decisions about her property and her style of living belonged exclusively with her husband. Feminists in the early part of the nineteenth century fought with some success to revise the law so that married women had some greater independence than existed under the common law. Nevertheless, by relying on the doctrine of *feme covert* in denying Myra Bradwell a license to practice law, the court was reaching back to the old standards. Bradwell said that by referring to "the disability imposed by your married condition," the court was striking "a blow at the rights of every married woman in the great state of Illinois who is dependent on her labor for support and say to her, you cannot enter into the smallest contract in relation to your earnings or separate property that can be enforced by you in a court of law."

Backed into a corner by Mrs. Bradwell's argument the Illinois Supreme Court extended its objections to her admission to the bar. It was not just that she was a married woman—this time the rationale was simply that she was a woman.

In its decision, dated February 5, 1870, the court said:

It is to be also remembered that female attorneys-at-law were unknown in England, and a proposition that a woman should enter the courts of Westminster Hall in that capacity, or as a barrister, would have created hardly less astonishment than one that she should ascend the bench of Bishops, or be elected to a seat in the House of Commons . . .

That God designed the sexes to occupy different spheres of action, and that it belonged to men to make, apply and execute the laws, was regarded as an almost axiomatic truth . . .

We are certainly warranted in saying, that when the Legislature gave to this court the power of granting licenses to practice law, it was with not the slightest expectation that this privilege would be extended equally to men and women . . .

Whether, on the other hand, to engage in the hot strifes of the bar, in the presence of the public, and with momentous verdicts the prizes of the struggle, would not tend to destroy the deference and delicacy with which it is the pride of our ruder sex to treat her is a matter certainly worthy of her consideration. But the important question is, what effect the presence of women as barristers in our courts would have upon the administration of justice . . .*

Myra Bradwell was anxious for her readers to see the court's full opinion. In a small paragraph after the printed text she wrote:

We have not the space to review the opinion in this issue, but shall do so at some future day, and will simply say now, that what the decision of the Supreme Court of the United States in the Dred Scott case was to the rights of negroes as citizens of the United States, this decision is to the political rights of women in Illinois—annihilation.

As for the argument made by the court that women in England could not practice law, Bradwell wrote in one of her lively editorials: "According to our Canadian and English brothers it would be cruel to allow a woman to 'embark upon the rough and troubled sea of actual legal practice,' but not to allow her to govern all England with Canada and other dependencies thrown in. Our brothers will get used to it and then it will not seem any worse to them to have women practicing in the courts than it does now to have a queen rule over them."

Myra Bradwell was not about to let stand the decision of the Illinois Supreme Court. She filed a writ of error to the United States Supreme Court and asked Senator Matt H. Carpenter of Wisconsin, an expert in the field of constitutional law, to represent her.

Carpenter had no adversary when he appeared before the United

In re Bradwell, 55 Ill. Sup. Ct. Rep. 535.

States Supreme Court to argue *Bradwell*.* He insisted that under the Fourteenth Amendment and Article IV of the United States Constitution, Bradwell was entitled to the same privileges and immunities as citizens of all other states and that the state of Illinois lacked the power to limit admission to the bar to a class of citizens whether it be because of their race or sex:

Now Mrs. Bradwell is a citizen of the United States, and the State of Illinois, residing therein; she has been judicially ascertained to be of full age, and to possess the requisite character and learning.

Still admission to the bar was denied her, not upon the ground that she was not a citizen; not for want of age or qualifications; not because the profession of the law is not one of those avocations which are open to every American citizen as a matter of right, upon complying with the reasonable regulations prescribed by the legislature; but first upon the ground that inconvenience would result from permitting her to enjoy her legal rights in this, to wit, that her clients might have difficulty in enforcing the contracts they might make with her, as their attorney, because of her being a married woman; and, finally on the ground of her sex, merely.

The objection arising from her coverture was in fact abandoned, in its more full consideration of the case, by the court itself: and the refusal put upon the fact that the statute of Illinois, interpreted by the light of early days, could not have contemplated the admission of any woman, though unmarried, to the bar. But whatever the statute of Illinois meant, I maintain that the fourteenth amendment opens to every citizen of the United States, male or female, black or white, married or single, the honorable professions as well as the servile employments of life: and that no citizen can be excluded from any one of them. Intelligence, integrity, and honor are the only qualifications that can be prescribed as conditions precedent to an entry upon any honorable pursuit or profitable avocation, and all the privileges and immunities which I vindicate to a colored citizen, I vindicate to our mothers, our sisters, and our daughters.

The Supreme Court held on to the case for nearly two years. When it finally rendered its decision in 1873, seven of the eight members of the Court ruled against Myra Bradwell. The majority disagreed with Carpenter's argument that the privileges and immunities clause of the Constitution guaranteed her right to practice law. Justice Samuel F.

*16 Wall. 130.

Miller, speaking for the Court, said of that argument, "We agree with him that there are privileges and immunities belonging to citizens of the United States, in that relation and character, and that it is these and these alone which a State is forbidden to abridge. But the right to admission to practice in the courts of a State is not one of them."

Justice Joseph P. Bradley wrote the concurring opinion and in doing so was joined by Justices Field and Swayne. Bradley said it could not be assumed "that one of the privileges and immunities of women as citizens is to engage in any and every profession, occupation, or employment in civil life." He went on to give the Court's views on the rights of women:

The civil law, as well as nature herself, has always recognized a wide difference in the respective spheres and destinies of man and woman. Man is, or should be, woman's protector and defender. The natural and proper timidity and delicacy which belongs to the female sex evidently unfits it for many of the occupations of civil life. The constitution of the family organization which is founded in the divine ordinance, as well as in the nature of things, indicates the domestic sphere as that which properly belongs to the domain and functions of womanhood. The harmony, not to say identity, of interests and views which belong, or should belong, to the family institution is repugnant to the idea of a woman adopting a distinct and independent career from that of her husband. So firmly fixed was this sentiment in the founders of the common law that it became a maxim of that system of jurisprudence that a woman had no legal existence separate from her husband, who was regarded as her head and representative in the social state; and, notwithstanding some recent modifications of this civil status, many of the special rules of law flowing from and dependent upon this cardinal principle still exist in full force in most States. One of these is, that a married woman is incapable, without her husband's consent, of making contracts which shall be binding on her or him. This very incapacity was one circumstance which the Supreme Court of Illinois deemed important in rendering a married woman incompetent fully to perform the duties and trusts that belong to the office of an attorney and counsellor.

It is true that many women are unmarried and not affected by any of the duties, complications and incapacities arising out of the married state, but these are exceptions to the general rule. The paramount destiny and mission of women are to fulfil the noble and benign offices of wife and mother. This is the law of the Creator. And the rules of civil society must be adapted to the general constitution of things, and cannot be based upon exceptional cases.

While waiting for the Supreme Court's decision, Myra Bradwell suffered still another, albeit a lesser, defeat. Although sixty prominent lawyers in Chicago had petitioned Governor John M. Palmer to appoint Bradwell a notary public, he refused to do so, saying he regretted that a married woman could not execute the bond required by statute.

By the time the United States Supreme Court rendered its opinion in 1873 it had little or no effect in Illinois. The previous year Alta M. Hulett, an eighteen-year-old girl studying law with a Rockford attorney, had applied for admission to the Illinois bar. Despite the fact that Hulett was single, she too was denied her license. Hulett decided to challenge the decision in the courts and to take her case to the legislature as well. She drafted a bill providing that no person could be precluded or debarred from any occupation, profession or employment, except the military, on account of sex. Through the efforts of Ada H. Kepley, who also had been denied admission to the bar on the basis of her sex, Myra Bradwell and countless readers of the *Chicago Legal News*, Hulett was successful in getting her bill passed by the Illinois legislature. In March 1872 it was Alta M. Hulett, not Myra Bradwell, who became the first woman lawyer in the state of Illinois. The *American Law Review*, hailing the news, said, "If the State . . . has overcome its prejudices so far as to admit to equality the hated black, the time can not be far distant when women will also find the victory won."

Hulett lived only several years after her admission to the bar. Lelia J. Robinson, in a turn-of-the-century article on women lawyers, noted that from the date of Hulett's admission to the bar "till that of her death in the spring of 1877 she had a lucrative business following general lines of work without limiting herself to any specialty and succeeded marvelously well both in handling her cases and disarming prejudice."

Myra Bradwell continued to work for women's suffrage and continued to publish the *Chicago Legal News*. In 1890 the Illinois Supreme Court, on its own motion, granted Bradwell her license to practice law. Two years later she was admitted to practice before the United States Supreme Court but she never did. When she died in 1894, Myra Bradwell was survived by a son and a daughter, Bessie Bradwell Helmer. Both her children were lawyers.

·   ·   ·

The United States Supreme Court's refusal to overturn Illinois's prohibition against women practicing law in *Bradwell* meant that women, by necessity, would be engaged in a state-by-state struggle for admission to their individual bars. In some areas all that was needed was the "requisite learning and good moral character," but in others, protracted lawsuits and long legislative campaigns characterized the struggle for equality within the law.

Only a few years after the *Bradwell* case came *In re Goodell,** or more formally, *In the Matter of the Motion to Admit Miss Lavinia Goodell to the Bar of this Court.* Lavinia Goodell was the daughter of abolitionist William Goodell, a well-known New York writer and editor. Her first job, after graduating from a ladies seminary in Brooklyn Heights, was helping her father edit the antislavery magazine *Principia.* In 1866 she joined the editorial staff of *Harper's Weekly,* and an editor there described her as "a shrewd, quick-witted girl, full of humor, studious and argumentative. . . . She was of medium height but looking tall from her slender, erect figure, blue-eyed and with light brown curling hair." Goodell had told him that her life's ambition was to become a lawyer but that she realized it was not a realistic goal for a woman.

In 1871, Lavinia Goodell's parents retired to Janesville, Wisconsin, and tried to convince their daughter to join them. Janesville held little attraction for a young woman who was making a career in publishing, but it did offer Goodell one possibility not available to her in New York —she could go there to study law. If she would agree to relocate, her parents promised to help her find attorneys who would allow her to study and practice law with them. Goodell agreed and began working toward her bar admission as an apprentice in the firm of Jackson & Norcross, a partnership of two young men who were known in the area for their interest in social reform. Goodell quickly proved her ability in the law and was soon permitted to handle a full caseload. In June 1874 she was formally admitted to practice at the local level in the Circuit Court of Rock County, Wisconsin.

*In re Goodell, 39 Wis. 232.

That same year Lavinia Goodell opened up her own law office in Janesville. Her clients for the most part were women and old people, and her work consisted mostly of drafting papers and appearing at hearings in local courts. But in 1875 one of Goodell's cases was appealed to the Wisconsin Supreme Court; and since Goodell had not been admitted to the state bar, she was unable to argue the case at that level. She immediately made application for admission so that she could represent her client but was told she would need legal representation on her application—the justices would not let her argue her own motion for admission. Goodell hired I. C. Sloan, a Janesville attorney and former congressman, to appear on her behalf. In doing so, Sloan let the court know that Goodell had prepared all the legal briefs in the case.

The matter came before Justice Edward Ryan of Milwaukee, an avowed antifeminist. At issue were the gender references in the Wisconsin admissions statute that read, in part: "To entitle any such person to practice as such attorney . . . he shall be first licensed by order of one of the judges thereof made in open court, and no such order shall be made . . . unless such person be a resident of this State, more than twenty-one years of age, and of good moral character." There were no prohibitions or restrictions in the statute, there simply were the words "he" and "his" referring to the applicants.

As was argued in *Mansfield* and *Bradwell*, Goodell pointed out in her brief that Wisconsin's statute provided that "every word importing the masculine gender only may extend and be applied to females as well as males." Further, she claimed that by the 1867 act of the state legislature the University of Wisconsin was admitting females to the law department. She argued that if the legislature approved of women studying law in its state educational system, surely it approved of their practicing law upon graduation. Moreover, Goodell mentioned her success as a practicing attorney at the local level and indicated her belief that she was competent to practice in higher courts.

One of Goodell's most ardent supporters was Myra Bradwell. The *Chicago Legal News* published information about the case on page one, and Sloan's argument in the Wisconsin Supreme Court was printed in full. Bradwell found the Goodell case worthy of editorial comment and told her readers:

Miss Goodell comes from a family that was never known to give up when in the right. The question is, shall Miss Goodell, who has spent years of her life in preparing herself for her profession, has passed the required examination, has a paying practice, be allowed to continue it, or be financially ruined because she is a woman?

There was little doubt how Judge Ryan would decide the case. In 1846, as a delegate to the Wisconsin Constitutional Convention, Ryan had heatedly opposed women's suffrage. In the years preceding the *Goodell* decision he frequently made known his view that women belonged in the home. But if there was any question as to how Ryan might decide this case, he answered it with the opening statements in his opinion:

This is the first application for admission of a female to the bar of this court. And it is just matter for congratulation that it is made in favor of a lady, whose character raises no personal objection—something, perhaps, not always to be looked for in women who forsake the ways of their sex for the ways of ours.

While Ryan acknowledged that other courts in other states, Iowa for example, had given liberal interpretation to gender-restrictive admissions statutes, he insisted that "if we should follow that authority in ignoring the distinction of sex we do not perceive why it should not emasculate the Constitution itself." As for Goodell's argument that the legislative intent was indicated by its approval of women studying law at the University of Wisconsin, Judge Ryan claimed he did not have to consider that issue, since Lavinia Goodell had not been a student there. He then went on to give his views about women and the law. It was an opinion that would rival Supreme Court Justice Bradley's in *Bradwell.*

We cannot but think the common law wise in excluding women from the profession of law. . . . The law of nature destines and qualifies the female sex for the bearing and nurture of the children of our race, and for the custody of the homes of the world, and their maintenance in love and honor. And all lifelong calling of women, inconsistent with these radical and social duties of their sex, as is the profession of law, are departures from the order of nature, and when voluntary, treason against it. The cruel chances of life sometimes battle both sexes, and may leave women free from the peculiar duties of their sex. These may need employment, and should be welcomed to any not derogatory to their sex and its proprieties or inconsistent with the good order of society. But it is public policy to provide for the sex, not for its superfluous members; and not to tempt women from the proper duties of their sex by opening to them duties peculiar to ours. There are many employments in life not unfit for female character. The profession of law is surely not one of these. The peculiar qualities of womanhood, its gentle graces, its quick sensibility, its tender susceptibility, its purity, its delicacy, its emotional impulses, its subordination of hard reason to sympathetic feeling, are surely not qualifications for forensic strife. Nature has tempered women as little for the judicial conflicts of the court-room as for the physical conflicts of the battle-field. Womanhood is modeled for gentler and better things. And it is not the saints of the world who chiefly give employment to our profession. It has essentially and habitually to do with all that is selfish and extortionate, knavish and criminal, coarse and brutal, repulsive and obscene in human life. It would be revolting to all female sense of innocence and sanctity of their sex, shocking to man's reverence for womanhood and faith in woman, on which hinge all the better affectations and humanities of life, that woman should be permitted to mix professionally in all the nastiness of the world which finds its way into courts of justice; all the unclean issues, all the collateral questions, of sodomy, incest, rape, seduction, fornication, adultery, pregnancy, bastardy, legitimacy, prostitution, lascivious cohabitation, abortion, infanticide, obscene publication, libel and slander of sex, impotence, divorce—all the nameless indecencies. . . . Reverence for all womanhood would suffer in the public spectacle of woman so interested and so engaged. . . . Discussions are habitually necessary in courts of justice, which are unfit for female ears. The habitual presence of women at these would tend to relax the public sense of decency and propriety. If, as counsel threatened, these things are to come, we will take no voluntary part in bringing them about.

The reaction of the press and the bar to Ryan's decision was swift, and indicated how much had changed in the generation after Seneca Falls. The Wisconsin *State Journal* wrote: "If her purity is in danger, it would be better to reconstruct the court and bar than to exclude the women." The Chicago *Tribune* described Ryan's decision as "a libel on the character of women." The Milwaukee *Sentinel* said: "The prejudice of the sex is the most imbecile, the least excusable, of all prejudices—and yet it is one of the strongest. Long after the opponents of 'woman's rights' have ceased to present an argument; long after every argument has proved fallacious, the prejudice remains in full force, and the intolerance of woman workers in the fields assumed to be out of their sphere is as bitter and almost as widespread as ever."

Judge Ryan's decision had the unintended effect of helping his opponents gather the support they needed to change the restrictions of the Wisconsin admissions statute. Through Lavinia Goodell's efforts and testimony the legislature on March 8, 1877, revised the Wisconsin statute by adding the following: "No person shall be denied admission or license to practice as an attorney in any court of this state on account of sex." After passage of the bill Goodell again petitioned the Supreme Court for admission. This time, on June 18, 1879, Judge Orsamus Cole, citing the intent of the legislature, admitted Lavinia Goodell to the bar of Wisconsin. Judge Ryan dissented.

Goodell continued her law practice in Janesville, forming a partnership with Angie King, who had been a student at the University of Chicago Law School. They advertised frequently in Wisconsin newspapers as "Goodell & King, Business attended to with promptness and dispatch." One reporter noted: "They have fitted up a cozy office over Britton & Kimball's store, and will be found there ready to attend to the wants and wishes of clients. The new firm embraces ability, industry and enterprise, and is bound to meet with success."

Probably their most famous case was their appeal on behalf of a Thomas Ingalls, who had been charged with stealing goods from a local merchant. Ingalls was found guilty by a jury in Rock County and was sentenced to five years in prison. In Goodell's appeal to the Wisconsin Supreme Court she claimed that the evidence at trial showed Ingalls to have been so drunk at the time the crime took place that he could not possibly have committed it. The Supreme Court agreed and in 1880 reversed the conviction. The Janesville *Gazette* gave the victory page-one coverage and noted exuberantly that with both Goodell and King handling the appeal "it is a case with women in it throughout."

Just when Goodell's career was flourishing, she was stricken with sciatic rheumatism and died. The Chicago *Times*, reporting on her death in 1880, called Goodell "the best practical exponent of what a woman can accomplish and the position she may attain in the profession of law." The Chicago *Journal* was not as kind. Its editors claimed Lavinia Goodell's death at the age of forty-one "suggests the query whether women are able to endure the hard usage and severe mental application incidental to a legal professional career." In answer, the Chicago *Independent* wrote: "Henry Armitt Brown, the noted young lawyer of Philadelphia, died recently at thirty-two. We would like to suggest the query whether men are able to endure the hard usage, etc. One swallow does not make a summer."

Probably the most notorious of the pioneer women attorneys was Mary Gissen Leonard, the first woman lawyer in both Oregon and Washington. Mary Gissen was a Swiss immigrant who moved to the Northwest Territory sometime after the Civil War. Little is known about her until her marriage to Portland innkeeper Daniel Leonard in 1875. Theirs was a stormy relationship that ended two years later in a bitter divorce. Mary claimed to have been swindled by Daniel's promises of support. Daniel countered that Mary was an adulteress who abused him both mentally and physically. The Leonard divorce was a source of great interest to Portland society. While the case was pending, the court approved a settlement worked out by lawyers for the parties that temporarily provided for Mary's maintenance. But shortly afterward Daniel balked, refusing to honor the terms of the court order. Mary, finding herself almost penniless, bitterly expressed her outrage in a letter to her estranged husband:

To expose what a brute you are I am willing to suffer punishment—if you make it necessary . . . do you think you still can have over me your tyrannical sway . . . have I not suffered insult and abuse enough in all those unhappy days—so don't rejoice. . . . I have the spirit to get even with you—do your worse and it will com [sic] home to you—I swear it by my life . . . don't fool with a woman like me . . . my soul cried out of the debth [sic] of pain and asked for vengeance—beware I say once more . . .

As far as is known, Mary Leonard did not receive her money. Three weeks later Daniel Leonard was found dead in his bed from a gunshot wound to the head caused by a very small gun. There were no witnesses to the shooting, no indication of a struggle or an attempted burglary and no one with a motive to kill him—except for Mary Leonard. Mary, who had been seen in the neighborhood the night of the killing, was arrested and jailed for a period of five months before the grand jury finally indicted her for "unlawfully feloniously purposely and of deliberate and unpremeditated malice," killing Daniel G. Leonard. Also charged in the murder was Nathaniel Lindsay, a man delicately described by historian Malcolm H. Clark, Jr., as a little known figure in Portland "save that his relations with Mary were alleged to have been close in the extreme . . ."

Mary Leonard did not go on trial until eleven months after the murder. Yet despite the sensational allegations and the extensive newspaper coverage of the case, Leonard was acquitted. Through her attorney she was able to convince the jurors that the angry letter was not enough to link her to the murder. Under these most unusual circumstances Leonard had won what was to be her first case.

Because Leonard was acquitted she was entitled to inherit Daniel Leonard's estate. Once she was financially solvent she moved to Seattle and decided to study law under an apprenticeship with Colonel J. C. Haines, a prominent Washington lawyer. After only eighteen months she passed the local bar exam. The following year, she was admitted to practice in the Washington Territory and in the federal court in Portland. But when she sought admission to the Oregon Supreme Court she was denied a license to practice. In 1885 the court held:

The applicant has produced a certificate of admission to the courts of Washington Territory, which, under the practice referred to, would ordinarily be regarded as sufficient to entitle a person to admission as an attorney. But the applicant being a woman, the court is in doubt whether it has the right to admit her. . . . This is the first application of the kind in this State that the court has any cognizance of, and it is very generally understood that women are disqualified from holding such positions. The legislative assembly has not manifested any intention by any act it has adopted to confer such a right upon them, and it would be highly improper for the courts of the State to take the initiative in so important a movement. . . . The court is of opinion that it has no authority under the existing laws of this State to admit women as attorneys of this court, and the application is therefore denied.*

Mary Leonard would not be discouraged. She persuaded state senator J. M. Siglin to introduce a bill in a special session of the legislature that would permit women to practice law in Oregon "upon the same

*In re Leonard, 12 Ore. 93.

terms and conditions as men." The bill passed and was signed into law on November 20, 1885.

Leonard once again applied for admission to the Oregon Supreme Court, but now the court raised another objection: it claimed that Leonard failed to meet the one-year residency requirement. Leonard, outraged that this technicality was being used against her, asked for and received permission to argue the point on her own behalf. The full text of her argument was reported in the Portland newspapers:

It appears that this stringent rule has not been applied or enforced in a single instance, although since the adoption thereof twelve attorneys have been admitted—five of those since the rule was published in book form. If in its discretion the court saw fit to treat these men with such consideration, then may I ask who is entitled to more consideration than I am? Since I have been deprived of practicing my profession for the last twelve months, having made my arrangements and calculations under the old rule, and knowing nothing else until a month ago, when the rules were published. I am now pleading to this court not to impose upon me a hardship which the court deems too hard for a strong, free and unfettered man to bear. I am not a free man, but since I belong to the protected sex, or oppressed sex, whichever you please, and since the legislature with almost unanimous voice has agreed to relieve me from the cruel shackles placed upon my wrists, I stand before this court a woman thrown upon her own resources, and beseachingly [sic] I reach out my imprisoned hands and ask to have these shackles removed. I am asking for the pitiful privilege to be allowed to obtain a livelihood as best I can which is a natural and a God-given right and my right in law.

The Supreme Court, impressed with Leonard's argument, granted her application for admission, making her Oregon's first woman attorney. It was the beginning of a career that would both amuse and embarrass the Portland legal community.

Mary Leonard was decidedly eccentric. She had a reputation for being both a drinker and a fighter and insisted that she be called "Judge" Leonard. She practiced mostly in the low-level police courts and it is said she ran a combination boarding house/bordello in the heart of town. The landlord of Richelieu Rooms, as this establishment was called, tried on many occasions to evict Leonard, claiming she never had any right to possession of the premises. In 1897 landlord William Ballis had Leonard arrested, saying that she had threatened his life by producing "from the folds of her garment" a small caliber pistol. In light of the circumstances surrounding Daniel Leonard's murder this was a shocking allegation. Mary Leonard, who had fought not only with Ballis but with most of her tenants and neighbors as well, managed to turn her trial into something of a circus. The *Oregonian* reported that "the trial was highly amusing at every stage, as it developed all the tribulations this lone female member of Oregon's bar has suffered for a long time past . . ." The newspaper went on to report:

Mrs. Leonard took the stand in her own behalf. When the case commenced she had three counsel, Messrs. McMahon, Davis and Mendenhall, but later this coterie of legal talent was increased by the aid of George C. Stout. Mrs. Leonard told the story, weaving into the narrative a multitude of affairs that have been aired in the police court. The four counsel labored jointly and severally to have the witness confine her tale to the case in hand, but each interruption gave her new breath, and caused her to commence a little farther back than where she left off. The four counsel appealed to the court for assistance and with the judge's aid, and the surplus bailiffs present, finally got the witness to cease letting off private grievances and to testify in regard to the pistol.

The judge in the case dismissed the charge of carrying a concealed weapon, despite Leonard's admissions, and instead held her "in $100 bonds to keep the peace." Leonard declared it a victory and went so far as to issue a statement to the press in which she wrote: "The lady is not young or stylish withal she is comely and attractive possessed [*sic*] of sparkling wit and her company pleases young attorneys."

But it was not to be the end of Mary Leonard's lively encounters in court. Clark notes that she was arrested three more times—once for suborning perjury, once for threatening bodily violence, and once for embezzlement because she refused to pay $1.40 in witness fees to her client's mother. Judge Frank Hennessey fined Mary Leonard $18 on the embezzlement case and ordered her jailed, but in fact it was true that she had the friendship and support of a number of young attorneys. They brought a writ of habeas corpus, which the court granted on the grounds that since the minimum fine for the offense was $25, Judge Hennessey's imposition of a lower amount was error. No sooner was Mary Leonard released than she told a reporter that the release saved her life and very possibly Judge Hennessey's.

Mary Leonard's last appearance as an attorney in court proved to be a disaster. She had tried to break up a spendthrift guardianship that had been imposed upon her client. Leonard began making frivolous motions as her client's "next friend," tying up the courts with litigation for several years. It was apparent to courtroom observers that neither Mary Leonard nor her client was competent, and in fact before the proceedings were completed, her client was declared insane. Now broken and incoherent and close to seventy years of age Mary Leonard in defeat asked the court for permission to withdraw her motion. The court, which had been considering disbarment, quickly permitted her to do so.

Admission to the federal courts turned out to be just as difficult and frustrating for women lawyers as their state experiences had been. The first woman to try was Belva A. Lockwood, known in Washington, D.C., for her unorthodox views, her unequaled ability in the law, and for the tricycle she used to travel from her office to court.

After graduating in 1873 from the National University Law School in Washington, D.C., with much difficulty because of prejudice against women students, Lockwood built up a practice in the Capitol area. She handled cases in police and probate courts, filed divorce and support proceedings and tried to specialize in claims against the United States government. Her interest in this area of the law began with a visit from a client who wanted representation in a suit against the government for infringement of her husband's patent on the design of a torpedo boat. Lockwood was not admitted to the United States Court of Claims, but she filed her power of attorney and a certificate with the court and asked attorney A. A. Hosmer to move her admission. When the five-man court convened, Belva Lockwood's admission was the first matter on the calendar. After Hosmer completed his oral argument, Chief Judge Charles Drake looked Lockwood over, then said, "Mistress Lockwood, you are a woman." Silence. Then, "This cause will be continued for a week. The court will recess for ten minutes." Lockwood, who never forgot the incident, remarked, "For the first time in my life I began to realize that it was a crime to be a woman, but it was too late to put in a denial, so I pled guilty." The following week Lockwood returned to the Court of Claims, and on the advice of counsel she was accompanied by her husband, Ezekiel Lockwood. This time Judge Drake sternly noted, "Mistress Lockwood, you are a married woman." Sensing the implication that she was barred from practicing law because of the doctrine of *feme covert*, Lockwood answered, "Yes but may it please the court, I am here with the consent of my husband." Drake replied, "Madam, women do not speak in this courtroom. You will sit down." The case was continued for another week. After several more adjournments, attorney Charles W. Horner filed an application for admission on Lockwood's behalf. But Horner had no better results than Hosmer or Lockwood herself had had—Judge Charles Nott, in delivering the decision of the court, said, "The position which this court assumes is that under the laws and Constitution of the United States a court is without power to grant such an application and that a woman is without legal capacity to take the office of attorney. The request is denied." Lockwood was not prepared to give up entirely. Unable to represent her client in court she schemed to win the case another way. Lockwood prepared the legal briefs in the case, then trained her client, Mrs. von Cort, to read them in open court, since no judge could prevent a citizen from pleading her own case. But Lockwood knew this method of practicing law could not continue. Ahead of her were countless cases needing to be argued in court— among them *Webster Raines* v. *United States*.

Mr. and Mrs. Raines had disagreed about whether Belva Lockwood should represent them. Mrs. Raines was determined to hire Lockwood as their attorney, but her husband thought their case might be seriously jeopardized by the restrictions placed on Lockwood in the Court of Claims. Lockwood managed to convince them that it would be only a little while longer before she would be eligible for admission to the federal courts. The wording of the federal statute for admission to the United States Supreme Court was the basis for her assumption. It held that "any attorney in good standing before the highest court of any State or Territory for the space of three years shall be admitted to this court when presented by a member of this bar." With no restrictions in the statute regarding gender Lockwood was certain she would be able to take her clients' case all the way up to the Supreme Court. In the meantime she would try her luck again with the Court of Claims—this time with client Webster Raines close at her side.

When the *Raines* case was called, Judge Nott was amazed to see Lockwood daring to make another appearance before him. "Madam," he asked, "what are you doing in my courtroom?" But he apparently did not want to hear the answer because when Lockwood attempted to explain her reason for being there Nott cut her off: "Mrs. Lockwood, if you dare speak, I shall hold you in contempt." Webster Raines tried to intervene, even demanding that the judge let him proceed with the attorney of his choice, but Judge Nott ordered Raines to go out and get himself a "capable" lawyer.

Making no secret of her annoyance, Belva Lockwood conferred with her clients and realized they would have no other choice but to hire substitute counsel for the oral argument. After her replacement finished presenting his case before the court, Lockwood complained that "he said very badly in three days what I could have said well in one hour." Worse yet, they lost. The only optimistic note was that on appeal Belva Lockwood might possibly argue the case before the United States Supreme Court, since its admissions statute was not gender restrictive.

The opportunity arose in October 1876. Lockwood retained attorney Albert G. Riddle to move her admission to the Supreme Court and expected to have little difficulty in getting through the process. But as soon as Riddle stated his purpose, Chief Justice Morrison R. Waite announced that the matter of Mrs. Lockwood's admission would have to be taken under advisement. One week later the Chief Justice delivered the opinion of the Court:

By the uniform practice of the court, from its organization to the present time, and by the fair construction of its rule, none but men are admitted to practice before it as attorneys and counselors. This is in accordance with immemorial usage in England, and the law and practice in all the states until within a recent period; and the court does not feel called upon to make a change, until such change is required by statute, or a more extended practice in the highest courts of the States. . . . As this court knows no English precedent for the admission of women to the bar, it declines to admit, unless there shall be a more extended public opinion or special legislation.

News of the Supreme Court's decision outraged Lockwood and supportive members of the bar. Myra Bradwell was the first to ridicule Chief Justice Waite in the pages of the *Chicago Legal News:*

The opinion delivered by Waite, C.J., refusing Mrs. Lockwood a license to practice in the Supreme Court of the United States . . . was unsound, and contrary to the practice of the court in every case since its organization. The same reasoning which the Chief Justice used to exclude Mrs. Lockwood, would compel every attorney who appears in the Supreme Court of the United States to wear a gown and wig. Women have never been admitted to practice in Westminster Hall, and therefore Mrs. Lockwood is denied the right to practice in the United States Supreme Court. Counsellors have never been allowed to practice in Westminster Hall, and other superior courts in England, unless they wore gowns and wigs, and therefore it follows that they should not be allowed to practice in the Supreme Court of the United States without these necessary articles.

Belva Lockwood realized she would have to take the matter to Congress. She drafted a bill specifically providing for the admission of women to the federal courts and persuaded Representative Benjamin F. Butler to submit it to the House Judiciary Committee. The bill, and a second one she drafted, never got to the floor of the House. But finally, in April 1878, the House did pass Bill No. 1077—"An Act to Relieve Certain Legal Disabilities of Women," which gave women attorneys access to the federal courts. Lockwood knew the battle would be even more difficult in the Senate and she publicly urged women to "get up a fight all along the line." She buttonholed senators in the corridors of the Capitol and cultivated the interest of the courthouse reporters who had always found Belva to be a lively source for articles. The favorable publicity she received in turn brought in more mail and more supporters.

Senators Aaron Sargent of California and Joseph McDonald of Indiana proved to be the greatest supporters of the bill in the Senate. In an impassioned argument, Sargent said:

Mr. President, the best evidence that members of the legal profession have no jealousy against the admission to the Bar of women who have the proper learning, is shown by that document which I hold in my hand, signed by one hundred and fifty-five lawyers of the District of Columbia, embracing the most eminent men in the ranks of that profession [exhibiting a petition in support of the bill].

Where is the propriety in opening our colleges, our higher institutions of learning, or any institutions of learning to women and then, when they have acquired in the race with men the cultivation for higher employments, to shut them out? There certainly is none.

Some excellent lady lawyers in the United States are now practicing at the Bar, behaving themselves with propriety, acceptably received before courts and juries; and when they have conducted their cases to a successful issue, or to an unsuccessful one in any court below, why should the United States Courts, to which an appeal may be taken, and where their adversary of the male sex may follow the case up, why should they be debarred from appearing before those tribunals.

On February 7, 1879, the "Lockwood" bill passed the Senate; shortly thereafter President Rutherford B. Hayes signed it into law. The Washington *Star* said: "The credit for this victory belongs to Mrs. Belva Lockwood of this city, having been refused admission to the bar of the United States Supreme Court, appealed to Congress and by dint of hard work has finally succeeded in having her bill passed by both houses."

Belva Lockwood continued to be successful at practicing law, earning as much as $300 monthly—an enormous sum for a lawyer to be making in the last decades of the nineteenth century. The first woman lawyer to argue a case before the United States Supreme Court, Lockwood went on to obtain a $5 million settlement for the Cherokee nation after having filed massive claims for the Indians against the United States government.

Belva Lockwood had one additional passion—women's suffrage. At the June 1884 Republican convention she tried to get a plank for women's rights on the platform, but was unsuccessful. Writing to a suffrage group in California, she noted: "If women in the states are not permitted to vote, there is no law against their being voted for, and if elected, filling the highest office in the gift of the people. . . . It is quite time that we had our own party, our own platform, and our own nominees. . . . Act up to your convictions of justice and right and you cannot go far wrong." The California women agreed. They wrote from San Francisco telling Lockwood they were forming the Equal Rights Party and placing her name in candidacy for President of the United States. Lockwood ran with Marietta L. Stow on the Equal Rights ticket. Their opponents were Republican James G. Blaine and Democrat Grover Cleveland. Newspapers—especially their cartoonists—loved the idea of women candidates to liven up the campaign. With accompanying caricatures the Lockport *Daily Union* wrote:

> My soul is tired of politics
> Its vicious ways,
> Its knavish tricks;
> I will not vote for any man
> But whoop it up for Belva Ann.

Although women were not permitted to vote in the election, the women candidates obtained 4,149 votes in six states.

Four years later Belva Lockwood ran again on the Equal Rights Party ticket and again inspired poetry. This time the Washington, D.C., *Morning Journal* wrote:

> When our votes for you are cast,
> Belva, dear; Belva, dear;
> Will you tax the bustle vast,
> Belva, dear; Belva, dear?
> Will you place a tariff high,
> On the hosiery we buy?
> We await your calm reply,
> Belva, dear; Belva dear!

Belva Lockwood continued to practice law and to work for women's rights, prison reform and suffrage. She died before seeing women get the vote, but at the time of her death in 1917 women were admitted to practice law in all but four states in the union.

These firsts were:

Alabama	Luelle L. Allen	1907
Arizona	Beatrice Hopson;	
	Vivian Hopson	1903
California	Clara S. Foltz	1878
Colorado	Mary S. Thomas	1891
Connecticut	Mary Hall	1882
District of Columbia	Charlotte E. Ray	1872
Florida	Louise R. Pinnell	1898
Georgia	Mary C. Johnson	1916
Hawaii	Almeda E. Hitchcock	1888
Idaho	Helen L. Young	1895
Illinois	Alta M. Hulett	1873
Indiana	Elizabeth Eaglesfield	1875
Iowa	Belle Mansfield	1869
Kansas	J. M. Kellogg	1881
Kentucky	Ruby J. Gordon	1912
Louisiana	Betty Runnels	1898
Maine	Clara H. Nash	1872
Maryland	Etta H. Madox	1902
Massachusetts	Lelia J. Robinson	1882
Michigan	Sarah Kilgore	1871
Minnesota	Martha Dorsett	1877
Mississippi	Mrs. L. H. Greaves	1914
Missouri	Lemma Barkaloo	1870
Montana	Ella J. Knowles	1890
Nebraska	Ada M. C. Bittenbinder	1881
Nevada	Laura Ray Tilden	1893
New Hampshire	Marilla M. Ricker	1890
New Jersey	Mary Philbrook	1895
New Mexico	Catherine Mabry	1917
New York	Kate Stoneman	1886
North Carolina	Tabitha A. Holton	1878

North Dakota	Helen Hamilton	1905
Ohio	Nettie C. Lutes	1873
Oklahoma	Laura Lykins	1898
Oregon	Mary A. Leonard	1886
Pennsylvania	Carrie Kilgore	1883
South Dakota	Nellie A. Douglass	1893
Tennessee	Marion S. Griffin	1907
Texas	Hortense Ward	1910
Utah	Phoebe W. Couzins	1872
Vermont	Ellen M. M. Hoar	1914
Virginia	Belva Lockwood	1894
Washington	Mary A. Leonard	1885
West Virginia	Agnes J. Morrison	1896
Wisconsin	Elsie B. Botensek	1875
Wyoming	Grace Hebard	1899*

Each of these pioneers knew that by her determination and example she was helping the others who were bound to follow. Perhaps Belva Lockwood best expressed their spirit when late in her career she said, "I never stopped fighting. My cause was the cause of thousands of women."

*Later firsts were Mildred Herman, Alaska (1950); Sarah Jobe Shields, Arkansas (1918); Evangelyn Barsky, Sybil Ward, Delaware (1923); Ada L. Sawyer, Rhode Island (1920); Claudia J. Sullivan, South Carolina (1918).

2

THE FIRST WOMEN
LAW STUDENTS

Westward expansion to the territories in the 1800s brought with it substantial changes in the law and in the status of women. The aristocratic British-based legal style adopted by the wealthy, well-educated eastern bar by necessity gave way to a strikingly different system that at times depended greatly upon circuit-riding judges and shotgun justice. As historian Frank L. Ellsworth noted in his book *Law on the Midway,* the elitism of the late eighteenth- and nineteenth-century bar collided with Jacksonian democracy to form an amalgamation that eventually evolved into our current system of law. "During no previous period in the country's history had the nature of the law and the role of the lawyer changed so dramatically."

Western law grew out of a combination of influences: the military court-martial, Indian tribal justice and the ad hoc development of community "squatters courts" that sprang up in response to an immediate need for settlement of boundary disputes. While these claims tribunals had no statutory authority, they proved to be an effective means of bringing law and order to the wilderness and of convincing settlers that disputes might be settled peaceably. Not only were working conditions crude in these makeshift courts but often they were held in cabins, sod-houses and, when necessary, in a field out of doors, but research facilities were virtually nonexistent. Written opinions were rare and when they were delivered in writing seldom cited laws or precedents. Richard Lingeman in *Small Town America* noted that too often lawyers were "only a few books more learned than non-lawyers. They practiced by their wits and common sense, plus their volumes of Blackstone, Espinasse's *Nisi Prius,* and Peak's *Evidence* with the pages turned down at the most frequently consulted sections."

Paul E. Wilson, a professor of law at the University of Kansas, illustrates the informality of law in the West with the story of Chief Justice Samuel LeCompte, who bravely reversed his own decision in the district court. "This decision was made by me in the hurry and turmoil incident to a district court in this territory, without argument and without presentation of authorities or even a reading of the petition; but I am fully convinced that I committed an error in overruling the demurrer. It gives me sincere pleasure to give my view in its correction."

Judge LeCompte's mea culpa was only slightly less embarrassing than the admission of Kansas judge David J. Brewer, who perhaps best demonstrated the candor that marked law in the West. Brewer was the presiding judge in the case of *Harris* v. *Harris* in the First District Court. When his term as judge expired, Brewer agreed to serve as counsel for the plaintiff in error in *Harris* on appeal. As Kansas Supreme Court justice John F. Fontron, Jr., noted in retelling the story about Brewer, "Standing there to complain of his own decision, he seemed to feel that the situation was somewhat awkward and in half apology the Judge said that he could not see why he should not complain of his decision as everybody else had done so." The Supreme Court agreed with Counsel Brewer and reversed Judge Brewer's decision.

This kind of makeshift justice brought with it the problem of slackening standards for members of the legal profession. While it may have been true that litigation on the frontier was crudely simple, competent practitioners and members of the public believed attorneys should be professionals, no matter how informal the setting. By the last half of the nineteenth century, complaints about lawyers and the lack of intellectual and ethical standards in the profession were becoming wide-spread.

Julius Rosenthal, a legal scholar of the period living in Illinois, complained that "not even a fundamental knowledge of the three R's is necessary for admission . . ." In Kansas a bar association committee reported that professional standards had reached an all-time low: "If the stories of lawyers are to be believed, many are the attorneys who have been admitted with the distinct understanding that they were to practice law in some neighboring state." The Board of Law Examiners warned Kansans that stricter admission standards would have to be adopted: "Any state which resists, will get into the position of Indiana where it is said that any man who can tell two funny stories, one of them for men only, tell one lie and drink two glasses of whiskey can be admitted to the bar." In Iowa the situation was much the same. "The usual practice was to appoint a committee of three from the local bar to examine the candidate. It was sometimes said that one of the requisites for admission was the price of an oyster stew for the committee."

The less-than-professional lawyer was not strictly a phenomenon of western or rural areas alone. In 1876 the Grievance Committee of the Chicago Bar Association looked at its work and at its members and decided it had achieved the following: $8,625 for dues and fees and $1,500 for three annual dinners. "For all this, what do we have to show? A little furniture, rarely used; a few legal periodicals, never read; one divorce lawyer disbarred and pursuing his nefarious traffic with more brazen impunity than before; three dinners eaten in the past; and the absolute proprietorship of a janitor *in praesenti* and *in futuro*. This, and nothing more." Myra Bradwell suggested in the *Chicago Legal News* that "the crude and vulgar course of study pursued in law offices has been the means of placing the names of many very poor lawyers upon the roll of the profession who, if they had taken a thorough and well-digested course of reading, might have been numbered among its most useful members." In keeping with this view, lawyers and judges started reexamining the practice of apprenticing, the most common method of learning the law, and began recommending law school education as a prerequisite for admission to the bar.

At the same time this was happening, western expansion was playing an important part in changing and expanding the roles of women. While educational opportunities for women in the East seemed to be more readily available, in fact they were in institutions that did more to perpetuate the distinctions of sex than to eliminate them. Few men, or women for that matter, agreed with Matthew Vassar, the founder of the prestigious women's college that bears his name when he said that women were intellectual equals of men, and therefore were entitled to equal opportunities in education. The more prevalent view was expressed by Judge Horatio Davis in the remarkable commencement address he delivered in 1898 to the graduating class of the East Florida Seminary for Women in Gainesville:

And now young ladies . . . although you may have no desire to be orators, statesmen or scientists, a well-stored mind will be a most valuable companion in your journey through life. The circle of woman's sphere is rapidly extending. Within the last month, for the first time in the history of Florida, young ladies have been examined and licensed to practice law. Whether they will make a success of it is yet to be determined. Law is said to be the perfection of reason and Shakespeare says that when one of your sex was asked for a reason she replied, "I have no other but a woman's reason. I think it so because . . . I think it so." And I must acknowledge that when a woman thinks a thing so it is very apt to be so—at least in her own family . . .

If the practice of law was confined to drawing deeds and wills you would be a success, but if a man wanted to get rid of his wife or to keep his wife from getting rid of him I don't believe that you would be impartial.

History is full of the noble deeds of your sex. Isabella sold her jewels to enable Columbus to discover America—a woman came forth in the time of her country's need and took charge of a demoralized army and Joan of Arc became immortal.

But publicity is not your true sphere. It is a sun that while it warms, scorches and blisters.

"Seek to be good, but aim not to be great,
A woman's noblest station is retreat . . ."

The harsh life of the frontier and the inevitable shortage of resources required women to share in the backbreaking labor of building homes, towns and schools. When Sojourner Truth, the former slave, gave her now-famous speech about black women to a feminist convention in Akron, Ohio, she might just as well have been speaking for pioneer white women too:

The man over there says women need to be helped into carriages and lifted over ditches, and to have the best place everywhere. Nobody ever helps me into carriages or over puddles, or gives me the best place—and ain't I a woman?

Look at my arm! I have ploughed and planted and gathered into barns and no man could head me—and ain't I a woman?

The egalitarian development of these new towns and the need that new territories had for women settlers contributed to a more balanced view of women and their abilities than existed back East. Women were still very much second-class citizens, but the myth that they were faint-hearted and in need of special protection could not be perpetuated on the frontier.

One immediate and substantial change from the eastern academic system was that schools in the West were from the outset coeducational. Ruth A. Gallaher, writing early in this century on the status of women in Iowa, pointed out that "like all the northwestern or north central states, the Territory of Wisconsin made no discrimination against girls and women in the matter of education . . . their boys and girls worked and played together on the prairies . . . when the public schools were first organized the Legislative Assembly declared that they should be open and free for every class of woman citizens between the ages of 4 and 21 years."

However, there were other, more cynical explanations for coeducation. Barbara J. Harris claims that state universities in the late nineteenth century were open to women simply because males did not enroll in sufficient numbers to support them. Political and financial reasons dictated that women students be admitted.

But whether it was because their abilities were recognized or because western areas acted out of economic self-interest, in the 1800s women were better able to obtain university and professional training in the Midwest and West than anywhere else in the country. It is not surprising then that when the impetus came for more and better law schools in the West and for higher standards for admission to the bar, women not only supported these concepts but sought to take advantage of the opportunities they provided. Out of these combined movements came the first women law students and lawyers in the United States.

The nation's first woman law student—and Missouri's first woman lawyer—was Lemma Barkaloo, described as "a large heavy built, cheerful looking woman of twenty or thereabouts . . . who gives a rather pleasing impression." Born into a wealthy Dutch family in Brooklyn, New York, Barkaloo was a highly educated and serious student of music who performed under the tutelage of the then famous Madame de Tasson of New York City. In 1868, when Barkaloo came into a large inheritance, she unexplainably abandoned her career in music in hopes of obtaining a legal education. No woman in the United States had yet been admitted to a law school or to a state bar, so this was no ordinary undertaking. Yet within two years Lemma Barkaloo not only completed her studies but became the first woman to try a case in court. These honors should have been obtained in her native northeast, but when Barkaloo applied for admission to Columbia and Harvard Law Schools she was soundly rejected. "What a sad chapter upon the intelligence and progress of the age," a prominent Midwest lawyer was to remark, "that the regulations of our best colleges [can] admit to their halls and lectures rooms only those of the male sex."

Barkaloo began searching for schools in the West that would be amenable to having a female student. On writing to Dean Henry Hitchcock of the Law Department of the Washington University in St. Louis, Missouri, she learned that her application for admission would be considered. On October 1, 1869, Lemma Barkaloo arrived in St. Louis and was given permission to enter the incoming law class. Little is known about Barkaloo's experiences at Washington University, but from W.H.H. Russell, a distinguished member of the Missouri bar who at Barkaloo's death delivered her eulogy, we learn that "while in St. Louis she made but few acquaintances owing to the fact of her incessant application in the arduous studies of the profession. She availed herself of both the junior and senior course of lectures at the last term of the law school and was always found to be in her seat at the lecture hour. In literary parlance, she was a 'hard student,' ever ready and willing to undertake what might seem insurmountable objects, but with a lofty purpose and a fixed determination to overcome all. And upon examination for admission to the bar before Judge Knight, she passed the most creditable examination of a class of five, among which was an experienced lawyer who had practiced in the State of Wisconsin for fifteen years."

Professor William B. Napton, who taught at the Washington University Law School and who took particular delight in writing disparaging remarks about his students in a private diary, claimed that while Lemma Barkaloo was attending the law school she "seemed to enjoy the embarrassment of the young men very much." His was an unlikely description of the woman depicted by a variety of other sources as "an honor to her class" and "an example of self-reliance, of intellectual labor and of courage." Yet despite her high marks, Barkaloo never completed law school, choosing after the first year to take and pass the Missouri bar examination instead.

Tragically, in 1870, only a few months after passing the bar, Lemma Barkaloo contracted typhoid fever and died. Judge Wilson A. Primm, addressing a meeting of the St. Louis Bar Association, told his audience:

In the very opening and bloom of life Miss Barkeloo [sic], the deceased, in a strange land, entered upon a profession for which very few are qualified morally and intellectually, which very few men dare to approach, and which before her no woman to my knowledge, had ventured to aspire. It must have been a brave soul that could thus face the prejudices of society, depart from the usual employments of her sex, devote for years the energies of her mind to the mastery of a science, the dry intricate details of which present nothing of amusement or attraction, and finally to enter into an arena in which men, oft times rude and ungallant, are the gladiators.

Before her death Lemma Barkaloo gave an interview to the Sedalia, Missouri, *Daily Bazoo* in which she said that "she expects to have to bear slurs from the press but has brought patience to the work." Barkaloo could not have predicted how serious those slurs would be. Eight years after her death from typhoid, the *United States Biographical Dictionary* gave this remarkable account of her funeral:

Mr. Russell, it is said, is one of [the] ablest jury advocates and orators at the bar of St. Louis. His eulogies on Miss Barkaloo, the promising young lady who came to Missouri from New York to study and be admitted into the profession and died of *over-mental exertion* . . . were all published in full and are said to have been among the most eloquent ever delivered at the bar of the State.

Joining Lemma Barkaloo at Washington University was Phoebe Couzins—the law school's first woman graduate. In 1868, the same year Lemma Barkaloo had requested admission, Couzins wrote to Professor John M. Krum, an instructor in Washington University's Law Department. Krum referred Couzins's letter to the deans of the law faculty to determine whether the Law Department was intended to include female as well as male students. The faculty agreed it appropriately was a matter for the board of directors, but decided to openly declare its own view:

If the question were left to them to decide, however, the Law Faculty see no reason why any young woman who in respect to character and acquirements fulfilled the Conditions applicable to male Students, and who chose to attend the Law Lectures in good faith for the purpose of becoming acquainted with the laws of her country, should be denied that privilege.

The board of directors unanimously agreed, paving the way for admission of both Barkaloo and Couzins.

Instead of the hostile or chilly receptions women would receive at other institutions, the professors of the Washington University Law School seemed to have welcomed women to their classes and to have been especially gracious in their dealings with them. At a formal dinner to mark the completion of her studies, Phoebe Couzins was given an opportunity to speak about her experiences:

Two years ago I entered upon the study of law with many forebodings, with many conflicts and doubts as to its expediency, yet, actuated solely by a desire to open new paths for women, enlarge her usefulness, widen her responsibilities and to pleade her cause in a struggle which I believed was surely coming. . . .

To the Washington University which has thus conferred this honor upon [me] . . . let me return thanks for all true men and women. The law faculty and board of directors by unanimous action, signified their willingness to open the doors of this institution to woman, nobly declaring that sex should be no barrier to those who desire to acquaint themselves with the laws of their country. . . . To Judge Krum I am especially indebted for my introduction in the school and substantial aid in the loan of legal works throughout the term. To Judge Reber I tender the gratitude of a sincere woman's heart for the words spoken in behalf of her sex at the graduating exercises. To one whose soul has been sadly torn and bruised by endless friction with the carping spirits and narrow minds of today, this kind and fatherly anointing oil fell upon troubled waters.

Couzins also wanted it to be known that the male students never showed any objection to her being a member of their class.

After graduation Phoebe Couzins was admitted to practice in the courts of Missouri, Kansas and Utah and the federal courts, but in her lifetime she handled only a few cases. For a time she served as United States Marshal, completing her father's unexpired term. Couzins's true passion was women's rights, and she traveled throughout the country making speeches in support of suffrage and equality. She was a particularly well-known speaker in the West and was as much a part of the suffragist scene as were her friends and contemporaries Susan B. Anthony and Elizabeth Cady Stanton. Couzins's work on behalf of women's suffrage took her to most of the major cities in the United States, and she and Susan B. Anthony stood together in Philadelphia to present the Declaration of Women's Rights.

Couzins was a stirring writer and speaker who brought audiences to their feet. In Augusta, Illinois, her lecture in 1878 was called "elevated and pure, far above drivelling sentimentalities, and an eloquent plea for the broader, fuller intellectual and physical development of her sex. Devoid of the stiffness of set speeches, or a prim array of glittering periods, it was a fresh and logical dissertation upon the evils that afflict society in its compass of the woman problem, and every idea was presented with a bristling point that stuck fast to the mark." In Whitewater, Wisconsin, her speech was called a combination of "sweetness and power." In St. Louis there was an editorial saying that "St Louisans feel a pride in her bright face and brilliant talents, and they like to hear of her successes." Adding to the accolades, suffragist Elizabeth Cady Stanton noted:

Phoebe Couzins on "Woman as Lawyers" was ably written and well delivered. It was rich in illustration, logical, keen, witty, pathetic, moving her audience alike to laughter and tears. Fine-looking, well-dressed, straight as an Indian girl, head erect, her whole appearance was pleasing. In a deep, rich voice, she told her audience what she had seen, and felt, and believed, with a calm, dignified, self-assertion that seemed to say the earth is the Lord's and the fulness thereof, and I am one of the rightful heirs to this inheritance.

As a result of her respected reputation and no doubt because she was the first woman lawyer in Utah, in 1882 it was suggested that President Chester Arthur appoint Couzins to the commission that was then regulating the affairs of the Utah territory. The St. Louis *Spectator*, which disliked both feminism and Couzins, ridiculed the idea:

The *Spectator* has a very high respect for Miss Phoebe Cozzens [*sic*], a lady who has earned a wide reputation as a strenuous advocate of a doctrine that is as absurd and impractical in sociology as it is in politics. The *Spectator*'s respect for Miss Cozzens is founded on the earnestness with which she has pursued what she believes to be a genuine mission of disenthrallment and emancipation of her sisterhood. Earnest people are always deserving of respect, although there were cases on record where one was so earnest that he went crazy . . .

There has been a vast amount said about the capabilities of women as lawyers, and it is unquestionably true that they may become very learned in the theory of the law, as they may become learned in any science, but they are totally unfit to enter into the courts and practice law; and the very fact Miss Cozzens and the others of her sex who have attempted it do not meet with any encouragement or success is the best proof that can be afforded. They have the privilege but they make no use of it for the very simple and plain reasons that the general public does not want them in any such capacity and because such work is repugnant to their own habits and tastes.

Couzins failed to get the job. She tried writing for a while, but that career never materialized. In 1893, when Phoebe Couzins joined her associates at the Women's Pavilion of the Chicago World's Fair—or the Columbian Exposition as it was called—her disappointment and bitterness were starting to show. She told a number of people she resented the attention being paid to the young and wealthy women who had recently joined the suffrage movement, when pioneers like herself were being ignored. Couzins, once the most powerful speaker in a room, began to snipe from the back of lecture halls, bringing up previous slights and generally refusing to cooperate with the new order. At the age of fifty-one Phoebe Couzins was at the edge of poverty and sanity, arguing with old friends and forcing new acquaintances to choose sides. In 1898 Dr. Anna Shaw, the prominent temperance leader, is reported to have warned mutual friends that "Phoebe Couzins has been crazy for the past six years." Couzins's mental state was such that in 1909 she repudiated a lifetime of hard work and bitterly announced to the press that she no longer believed in women's suffrage: "I have come to see that woman's greatest responsibility is homekeeping . . ." Newspapers loved the irony of the situation, but those who knew Phoebe Couzins were saddened by this turn of events. Probably the last mention of Couzins appears in a small item in the *Women Lawyers Journal* of 1913 in which readers were told Couzins was destitute and "desperately looking for business." That same year, when Phoebe Couzins died, there was nobody left who cared enough about her to mark the grave.

Couzins was not the first woman law graduate in the United States, although at the end her life sadly paralleled that of the woman who was —Ada H. Kepley. Kepley, who was from Effingham, Illinois, studied law in her husband's office before enrolling in the Law Department of the University of Chicago. She graduated in June 1870.

After earning her law degree, Ada Kepley applied for a certificate to practice: "I went with others of the class to the Honorable Charles Reed, State's Attorney of Cook County, who was qualified to issue licenses to practice law, but he very politely and with many apologies refused me, saying the law in Illinois at that time did not permit women to enter the learned professions. Women might be cooks, wash women, floor scrubbers and do any sort of menial labor at that time, but they were barred from the so called learned professions." Ada Kepley and her husband, Henry, campaigned vigorously for an amendment to the Illinois statute that barred the admission of women. Their work and that of others, particularly Chicago's Myra Bradwell and Alta Hulett, led to an eventual end to the restriction. Kepley finally was admitted to the Illinois bar in 1881. In the years that followed her graduation from law school, she assisted her husband in his law practice, but spent most of her time working on suffrage and temperance issues.

Noting the commotion her graduation from law school had caused, she said, "The matter was novel and new and it travelled around the whole civilized world, for it seems I was the first woman to graduate from a law school in the world, and in addition, America, which boasted to the rest of the world to be 'the land of the free and the home of the brave,' gave no freedom to her women . . ." Later she wrote: "I have been a suffragist all my life because I have a strong sense of justice. I have friends who are Democrats and Republicans politically, but I would never belong to a political organization that did not declare for the ballot for women, for it is rank injustice to them, and to join with those who are unjust is wrong . . ." The inequities in the tax system as they related to women led her to complain, "I work as hard as a man; I earn money like a man. I bear the burdens of Community like a man. I am robbed as a woman. I have no voice in anything or in saying how my money, which I have earned, shall be spent."

Ada Kepley was a determined organizer for the Women's Christian Temperance Union, conducting parades through the center of Effingham so that children would be involved in the movement at the earliest possible age. Late in life she wondered if "the little boys who wielded the drum sticks with such gusto and determination in the cause of Temperance 'remembered' those happy days." Kepley was a spirited speaker who when not campaigning for temperance and suffrage spoke out on the evils of politics and corruption: "Government officials can be sure of trouble if they break laws where I am and I find out."

But when Henry Kepley died, Ada Kepley's life began to fall apart. As had happened with Phoebe Couzins, Kepley in later life was a broken woman—both poor and eccentric. Citizens of Effingham could not help but notice the strange sight she presented while wandering the streets of her town:

A lawyer said that she wore "outlandish clothes." Her long dresses of expensive brocades and velvets had once been highly fashionable but by the 1920s were badly worn and quite out of style. That didn't bother Ada, though. Most of her dresses had big pockets in which she carried candy for children, food for dogs and other things she might need during the day. In winter she wore a long black fur cape and on the farm she had worn men's boots. Her outfits were always topped with unusual hats which she trimmed herself with feathers and other things. She often carried a large carpet bag.

With her money having run out, Ada Kepley tried to maintain herself by writing. Her efforts amounted to not much more than a World War I song called "My Sweetheart Over the Sea Who Fought for Liberty," and a book about temperance called *A Farm Philosopher*. She peddled copies of the song on street corners. By 1923 Kepley was so deeply in debt that she was forced to sell her family home. She begged friends to buy copies of her book to keep her from further disgrace:

Dear Friend,

I let the only piece of property I owned or could have held go to pay a debt I did not make. All I had left out of plenty was a gift that was given me by a man who got the bulk of my stuff and a small sum from the sale of some personal belongings of my own. I built with this a cheap little place to call home but there was, and still is, an encumbrance on it . . . If my friends will buy the five hundred (500) books still on my hands I would come out clear. . . . I do not beg. So kind friend, I appeal to you to buy the book. Secure me against the loss of my little home and relieve me from the humiliation of the debt. Mr. Kepley hated debt. So do I. I have sacrificed and suffered . . . relieve me of deep trouble . . .

Yours sincerely,
Ada H. Kepley

Two years later, the woman who said of herself "I could not help being a reformer—it was born in me," died a charity case at St. Anthony's Hospital in Illinois.

Many of the midwestern states accepted women at their law schools and a few actively encouraged their enrollment. The Law Department of the State University of Iowa, when it was featured in a national law magazine in 1889, pointedly mentioned:

It is not to be understood that the advantages of the Law Department are limited to men. The University of Iowa, from the first, has admitted women on equal footing with men, obeying in this the growing sentiment for equality which has abolished distinctions between the sexes as to property rights and has admitted women to practise at the Bar. No objection whatever has appeared to the admission of women to the Department; they have made excellent students. But there seem to be obstacles to the practice of the profession by women, inherent in the nature of the occupation, which have discouraged the study of law by them so that few have availed themselves of the advantages of the Department.

Whatever the disadvantages may have been in practice, enrollments of Iowa women in the law school increased dramatically. It was reported that women in Iowa society were so determined to see young females obtain law degrees that they accompanied them to class in an effort to make their assimilation more comfortable. Mary B. Hickey, the first woman to graduate, did so in 1873. By 1880 five more women had received their law degrees; by 1890 another twenty-one had; and at the turn of the century an additional fifty-three held bachelor of law degrees.

In a survey of women lawyers written in 1890, it was noted that the law school of the University of Michigan located at Ann Arbor "has graduated more women than any other in the country." Yet nearly thirty years earlier the Regents were debating whether to permit women at the university at all. According to historian Elizabeth Gaspar Brown, while President Haven had at first opposed the idea, setting forth his views in the president's report for 1867, he eventually altered his opinions. In the report filed by the acting president Henry Frieze for 1870–1871, Frieze wrote:

At the beginning of the present year women were received for the first time into all the departments of the institution. The whole number of female students registered is thirty-four; two in the Law Department. . . . One has already graduated in law . . .

The Law Department encountered no difficulty in the admission of women to the course of lectures, already organized for men. No separate lecture course is found necessary, or desirable . . ."

In Ruth Bordin's history of the university she notes that resistance to women at Michigan came from a variety of sources—not the least of which was the president's wife. Bordin notes that "to begin with intellectual girls were something of an oddity. The faculty wives saw them as not quite proper and it took a couple of decades before they became desirable boarders." But once they arrived, women law students seem to have been well received and their participation in law school activities was encouraged. Sara Kilgore Wertman became the first woman to graduate from the law school. She had studied one year at the Chicago Law School before transferring to Michigan, earning her LL.B. in 1871. Wertman went on to become an expert in real estate law, practicing in partnership with her husband.

Probably the best glimpse of what life was like for women law students at Michigan comes from the diary of Lettie Burlingame, a member of the class of 1886, whose greatest complaint was that one professor would "arouse my indignation by picking out easy questions to ask us women."

November 1. Since last Tuesday, September 29, when I took my examination, I have scarcely had time for anything but steady study. I passed the examination successfully and entered the Senior Class. . . . I spend considerable time in the Law Library. I am working now on a Moot-Court case for the 10th of January. As soon as I get through with that I shall go to work on my Thesis.

November 12. At table we got to talking about divorce, and that subject is always a disagreeable one to me. Miss H. and I thought there ought not to be any divorces *a vinculo,* but the rest disagreed. But Prof. Rogers took up the subject of divorce this morning, and he spoke of Gladstone's views on that subject. I was delighted to find that they coincided with my own.

January 20th. Friday afternoon we had our Club Court, and I had to preside. I was rather nervous, but got along all right I guess. I have determined to make a specialty of Equity. It is very interesting to me, and a very nice subject for a lady to pursue. We have had afternoon quizzes right along since

the second semester began. I have been copying last year's lectures which Mr.
H. kindly furnished me.

October 6th. There are seven ladies in the Law Department this year and
as Miss P. and myself were here we, with Mrs. W., determined to have
a banquet for the new ladies. We had it at our house. It was of course
quite informal. We spent the evening very pleasantly in conversation and
music. . . . Then as previously agreed, I proposed that we should form a local
organization for the purpose of bringing about a National Congress of Lady
Lawyers to be held in Ann Arbor in the near future . . . to be called the Equity
Club.

Lettie Burlingame went on to develop an active law practice. The
Equity Club, which she helped to found while in Law School, continued to thrive:

February 2d 1887. Last Saturday afternoon the Equity Club met, our
subject was What is Our Duty as Women Lawyers in Society? Some said: to
peg along at our business, that is, the Law, I suppose; but I believe that as
Women Lawyers who profess and certainly ought to be of broad and liberal
mind that we must make a special effort, also, outside of our profession, for
other women besides ourselves. . . . While I was in a jewelry store waiting for
my purchase to be boxed up, a Lawyer came in to get the Jeweler and his wife
to sign a deed. When the lady signed it, he asked me to sign it as a witness.
But the Jeweler said: "Oh, no! here's a man; let me get him." But the Lawyer said: "This lady will do as well—just for a witness you know." Well, I
signed my name and after it wrote 'Att'y.' You should have seen the look of
astonishment and heard the emphatic 'Thank you,' of the lawyer, and I
heard the Jeweler tell him afterwards he did not know a lady could be an
attorney. It did me good all over. The idea: 'here's a man,' and 'just for a
witness.'

In his report to the Regents for 1899–1900, Michigan's President
Angell stated that at the university

the number of women in the Law School is always small. Of those who
graduate only a few engage much in practice in court. Some study the profession for the express purpose of assisting their fathers in office work. A few have
taken the course in whole or in part with a belief that a knowledge of law would
enable them to be more efficient teachers of political economy, civil government, and history in academies, high schools, or colleges. It seems improbable

that any considerable number of women will find it congenial or remunerative to follow the profession of law.

Lettie Burlingame's account of her own law practice is in direct contrast with President Angell's impressions. In her letter of May 17, 1888, to the Equity Club, she wrote:

I opened my Office on the first Monday in May and the first week I took three cases, besides having a number of collections given me to make. I don't expect to fare as well as that every week, still I feel very hopeful.

I was surprised at Prof. R's letter to Mrs. B. in which he hinted that women were unfit for the Forum, because I am just wicked enough to prefer court-room work. Skillful questioning, and honest logic, have charms for me that filling in prescribed forms, with parrot-like precision never could have. I think women ought to go into the court-room. Where are they needed more? If your heart, O woman, versed in the Law, fails you at the threshold of the Forum, what of her, whose all, and often, more than all, is there at stake? Shall not your courageous dignity sustain her in her hour of trial?

A year later Lettie Burlingame shared her thoughts with members on how the law practice was doing:

As I write this letter, my first year of legal practise draws towards its close; and rich has it been to me in new and delightful experiences. I opened my Office alone, and wholly independent of others, borrowed the money with which I bought my books and furnished my office, and with no capital but courage and patience, faced the future.

I have had the full conduct of only one jury trial, that resulted in a victory for my Client to the full amount demanded, $1,507.00. The defendant appealed, but finally paid over the full amount, with damages for delay. So I lost my chance to win a case in the Appellate Court. I was pleased with my treatment in this strange Court where kind Judge B. and all the officers of the court vied with each other in courtesy. The defendant, being one of the wealthiest citizens of La Salle county, was represented

*by five lawyers. I fought the fight alone . . . my practise has come solely
through my own efforts.*

The next year she wrote to Rebecca May, who had been a fellow law
student at Michigan, and asked her to consider a partnership, since
Burlingame now had more work than one lawyer alone could handle.

*You ask me, "If I meet people who treat me coldly on account of my
profession." I am often asked that question. I can truly say: Never, outside of my own Church doors. A very few there seem to expect me to dis-
solve beneath their frigid coldness. This "better I than thou," I admit,
has often chilled my best resolves. Still I trust that time will obliterate
these things which are so hard for my sensitive nature to bear now.*

Despite the heavy workload, Burlingame spent a portion of her time
working for women's suffrage. Most of her efforts were in the form of
poetry or music such as "Put on the Orange Ribbon," the suffrage song
she wrote in 1890:

> Put on the Orange Ribbon
> The suffrage emblem bright;
> Come join our growing army,
> For truth and justice fight.
>
> One sex without consent
> The right to vote denied
> Forbidden voice in making,
> The laws by which she's tried
>
> Deprived of every weapon
> Of civil self defense,
> Yet, taxed full rates for meeting
> The government's expense.
>
> So we've girded on our armor
> of resolution steel;
> We pause not till we conquer
> And unjust laws repeal.

That same year, Lettie Burlingame contracted "la grippe," as it then was called, and died at the age of thirty-one. One newspaper, in reporting her death, said: "So successful was she that she won every case entrusted to her, much to the surprise of the older attorneys who were not yet accustomed to seeing their profession invaded by a woman." Another noted: "Although she fought off the insidious disease as heroically as she had hewn to the mark of her early years, she was forced to lay aside her textbooks, perfectly aware as she often expressed it, that her work was finished, and that her next great suit would be plead before the bar of Almighty God."

As midwestern and western areas became more prosperous, their citizens tried to introduce the civility of the eastern states they had left behind. Cultural and educational institutions played a key role in lending real or imagined respectability to western towns. In 1878 when Justice Serranus Clinton Hastings announced the University of California would be opening a law school that would strive for a reputation of excellence, the judge reminded his audience that the general standing of the bar in California "is not perhaps as high as it ought to be." Hastings emphasized that this would be the only law school west of Des Moines and only one of three law schools in the nation requiring a three-year course of study. What he did not mention was that like those other prestigious law schools in the East, the Hastings College of the Law would be closed to women.

The first meeting of the school's board of directors took place on June 6, 1878. Four months later when the board again convened, it was given word that Mrs. Clara S. Foltz was applying for admission. Without explanation the board tabled her application for its next meeting, scheduled for January 10, 1879. This seemingly minor procedural matter was to have a lasting effect on all of the parties involved.

Clara Shortridge Foltz was stubborn, passionate and smart. Born in the Midwest, she became a schoolteacher at the age of fifteen. Against everyone's advice she eloped with "a young Pennsylvania Dutchman of wandering disposition and slight promise." Eleven years and five children later she divorced Jeremiah Foltz, taking work wherever she could find it—as a seamstress, a speaker on women's suffrage, and a campaigner in support of local community issues.

Whether it was the influence of her father, a lawyer and minister who stumped the state of Indiana campaigning for Abraham Lincoln, or her own interest in legislative reform, by 1876 Clara Foltz decided she wanted to become a lawyer. There were no women attorneys in the state of California and only a handful in the entire United States. Nevertheless, Clara Foltz made the round of law offices, trying to find a lawyer who would let her apprentice with his firm. The standard answer was that she ought to stay at home and that women could not be admitted to the California bar anyway:

My dear young friend,

Excuse my delay in answering your letter asking permission to enter my law office as a student. My high regard for your parents, and for you, who seem to have no understanding of what you say you want to undertake, forbid encouraging you in so foolish a pursuit—wherein you would invite nothing but ridicule, if not contempt.

A woman's place is at home, unless it is as a teacher. If you would like a position in our public schools I will be glad to recommend you, for I think you are well-qualified.

> *Very respectfully,*
> *Francis Spencer*

But C. C. Stephens, a lawyer in San Jose, agreed to let Foltz join him. No sooner was she in his office than Clara began a campaign to amend the California statute that prohibited women from practicing law. According to historian Thomas G. Barnes, Foltz's fight to change the words "any white male citizen" to "any citizen or person" in the admissions statute took two years and she was "not home free until Mrs. Foltz, by her own account, stormed past the sergeant-at-arms into the governor's chambers, and persuaded Governor William Irwin to fish S.B. 66 out of a pile of discarded bills and sign it just as the clock struck midnight and the legislative session ended."

Assisting Clara Foltz in her fight for the Woman Lawyers Bill was the formidable Laura De Force Gordon. Gordon, reported to be the first white woman to settle in White Plains, Nevada, later moved to Sacramento, where she was a vigorous speaker and campaigner for women's rights. At the first meeting of the California Woman Suffrage Society in 1870, Laura warned the assembled women to "not sit like mummies but open their mouths and vote audibly: This disinclination to do business in a business-like way, is discreditable."

Gordon decided to run for the California State Senate, and newspapers, when they printed accounts of her campaign at all, ridiculed the effort. This typical item appeared in the Stockton *Daily Evening Herald*:

While Mrs. Gordon was delivering her last great speech of the campaign, last night, a white male victim, over 21 years of age, was away back of the crowd, pacifying the baby as resignedly as could be expected, while its mother was listening to the arguments of the champion of her rights.

Not unexpectedly, the election results were disastrous.

Gordon turned next to journalism, buying out a succession of defunct and bankrupt newspapers and becoming editor of the Stockton *Daily Leader*, which was, according to one source, "the only daily paper in the world edited and published by a woman." Eventually she took over the Oakland *Daily Democrat* as well.

In 1878 Gordon flirted with politics again, this time campaigning for a seat at the Constitutional Convention. Her old newspaper, the *Daily Evening Herald*, covered the election, noting her "splendid gift of female oratory," and her ability to state her case with "as much precision and force as anybody," but in the end the paper and the voters rejected her. "Laura is only having a little sport, and does not entertain the remotest idea of being elected. The accident of sex cannot be overcome by the gifts of oratory." When Clara Foltz introduced her Woman Lawyers Bill to permit women to be admitted to the bar, the California Suffrage Society endorsed it and suggested a lobbyist— Laura De Force Gordon. Thus began a long and remarkable association.

In 1878 the board of directors of the Hastings College of the Law was deliberating the issue of admitting women to the law school. With no action having been taken on her application, Foltz, and now Gordon, decided to strike out on their own. At the start of the law school's second semester, the two women began attending classes. Foltz later described the experience:

The first day I had a bad cold and was forced to cough. To my astonishment every young man in the class was seized with a violent fit of coughing. You would have thought the whooping cough was a raging epidemic among the little fellows. If I turned over a leaf in my notebook every student in the class did likewise. If I moved my chair—hitch went every chair in the room. I don't know what ever became of the members of that class. They must have been an inferior lot, for certain it is, I have never seen nor heard tell of one of them from that day to this.

With Foltz and Gordon attending classes, the board realized the issue could not be ignored. Two days later it met and unanimously resolved "that women be not admitted to the Hastings College of the Law," and directed the registrar to throw them out. In fact, it turned out to be the janitor who did. An editorial in the Stockton *Herald* correctly predicted that "those Directors will repent of their rash reconsideration before those two ladies die."

No longer able to study law, Foltz and Gordon started practicing it. Clara Foltz applied to Judge R. F. Morrison, of the Fourth District Court in San Francisco for leave to practice. In order to do this she presented the certificate of admission she already had obtained from her hometown's Twentieth District Court, which had made her the first woman lawyer in the state of California. The Barnes history of Hastings College of the Law reports that Foltz's intention was probably less to practice in San Francisco (since she was well-settled in San Jose) than to be admitted to plead *in propria personna* in the action she meant to file in the Fourth District Court against Hastings. Judge Morrison denied the application, but he appointed a committee of three prominent attorneys to examine her qualifications. One member of the committee was W. W. Cope, a former Supreme Court Justice —and a director of Hastings. The committee reported favorably and Judge Morrison permitted Foltz to practice in the Fourth District.

Foltz and Gordon quickly developed their plan of action. Gordon would sue Hastings in the California Supreme Court, applying for a writ of mandamus to compel the board of directors to admit women, while Foltz would bring an identical action in the Fourth District Court in San Francisco. The Supreme Court of California remitted Gordon's petition in the Fourth District Court for consolidation with Foltz's case. Meanwhile, Hastings' board of directors selected two of its own directors to defend the school: T. B. Bishop and Delos Lake.

Judge Morrison, presiding in the Fourth District, reviewed Foltz's petition for a writ of mandamus and ordered Hastings to admit her "upon the same terms and conditions as other citizens of the State of California" or show cause why it could not; a hearing date was set for February 24, 1879.

The issues in the case seemed at first clear-cut. Foltz's position was that the 1868 act creating the University of California contemplated affiliation of medical and law colleges with the university in which the standards of admission for all departments would be the same; that the University of California did not exclude women from any of its other departments; that the 1878 act creating the Hastings College of the Law made no explicit qualifications for admission nor did it permit the board of directors to exercise discretion in making rules governing the law school that were inconsistent with the rules that governed the university as a whole; that the law college, being a department of the University of California, was bound by the university's rules and was therefore without authority to exclude her on the basis of her sex.

Lawyers for the board of directors argued that the Hastings College of the Law was not subject to the general university rules because it was privately founded and funded and thereby governed by a special trust in which authority was placed with the board of directors; that the courts therefore did not have the power to review the decision of a private board, and accordingly lacked the power to issue a writ of mandamus. Noting the "weakness" of Hastings' case, "director Delos Lake felt compelled to go further, arguing against the 'enlargement of woman's sphere,' and conjuring up the spectre of how a woman's beauty might make an 'impartial jury' impossible if she appeared as counsel for a criminal!"

The newspapers took delight in reporting on the litigation. The San Francisco *Chronicle*'s reporter covering the oral argument noted: "The hearing excited great interest. The room was filled with lawyers, the younger and more gallant members of the profession being present in large numbers. The aggressive female sex was well-represented . . ."

Clara Foltz was portrayed as a woman whose "hands were not lacking in bone and muscle." Laura De Force Gordon "wore a stylish black dress with some suggestions of masculinity in the make." The characterizations did not stop there. Clara Foltz had "profuse hair done in braids which fell backward from the crown on her head like an Alpine glacier lit by a setting sun." Laura Gordon had "curls enough to supply half the thin-haired ladies of San Francisco with respectable switches."

Occasionally the *Chronicle* got down to reporting events in the courtroom:

When the Court convened, and some trivial business had been disposed of, Mrs. Folz [*sic*] rose, flushed with excitement, and erect with the dignity of a great cause, and read her simple and straightforward prayer for a writ of mandamus. It set forth succinctly the facts that she, being of good moral character, past 21 years of age, well-qualified in all respects, and rightfully being entitled to the privilege of the institution, being a branch of the University of California, had been excluded from the Hastings College of Law, after having for a week or two, enjoyed the great advantages it afforded.

Hastings countered by claiming once again that the law school had been privately founded and therefore was not subject to public scrutiny. It argued that there was in effect a private trust and that the university had no control over the school except to furnish diplomas; it insisted that the board of directors had an absolute right to exclude all persons whose presence would be "useless to such persons themselves, or detrimental to said college, or likely to impair or interfere with the proper discipline and instruction of the students . . ." (Clara Foltz later claimed she was told that "the rustle of the ladies' garments would distract the attention of the young gentlemen," and therefore women had to be excluded.)

The tennis-match style continued. Foltz talked about the burden women had paying taxes without benefit. Hastings cited the "disabilities . . . troubles and impossibilities of women practicing law." Laura De Force Gordon moved in to argue that if the law school could admit "a Chinaman," how could it possibly exclude "respectable women" like them? Rather than being shocked by the crassness of the assertion, the lawyer for Hastings countered by proudly claiming the Hastings board had thrown "the Chinaman" out, too.*

The hearing finally ended with one of the Hastings lawyers saying that if he was obliged to meet "the fair ladies at the Bar," he would rather have them "as associates than as opponents," to which Judge Morrison "politely begged leave to suggest a partnership." When the laughter in the courtroom died down, Judge Morrison said the hearing was over and he would take the matter under advisement. One week later he delivered judgment for petitioners Foltz and Gordon.

Hastings' board of directors was stunned. Justice Hastings did not favor an appeal. He felt the law was with the petitioners and he did not want to contest the matter further. But his own board of directors strongly disagreed and took the case up to the state's highest court. Not surprisingly in that appeal, *Foltz* v. *Hoge et al.*, † the Supreme Court of California affirmed Foltz's position, holding that mandamus was the proper and only remedy; that Hastings was not a private law school but in fact was part of the University of California; that discretionary power to regulate and manage could not be used to exclude one class of citizens while remaining open to another and that the rules and regulations of such institutions may not be inconsistent with the laws of the state.

Defeated in the courts, the Hastings board of directors still would not let the matter pass and decided to find other ways to exclude Foltz and Gordon from the law school. Since Foltz was the first woman lawyer in California, and Gordon the second, the board unanimously passed a resolution barring the admission to the law school of anyone who already had been admitted to the California bar, except by special order of the board of directors. Had they thoroughly read the *Foltz* v. *Hoge* decision, they would have known that the California Supreme Court expressly provided for the admission to Hastings of those already

*The student referred to in court is mentioned in the San Francisco *Chronicle* as Cain Mook Sow, but Thomas G. Barnes, in his history of the law school, believes him to have been Sit Ming Cook of Hong Kong, who although listed as a member of the law school's junior class of 1878–79, subsequently was rejected by the board. Citing then existing prejudice against Asians in California, Barnes noted "it would be a long time before another Chinese name appeared on the College's student roll."
†*Foltz v. Hoge et al.*, 54 Cal. 28.

admitted to practice. Two years after the janitor had showed them to the door, Foltz and Gordon were back at their seats at the Hastings College of the Law. Their return was more a matter of principle than of need, for each in her absence had developed remarkable skills as a practicing lawyer. A justice of the California Supreme Court, after listening to Foltz's arguments in the *Foltz* v. *Hoge* case, is said to have remarked, "I have never heard a better argument, for the first argument, made by anyone."

Both Foltz and Gordon continued to actively practice law and work for women's suffrage. Laura De Force Gordon had no particular specialty, but began taking on a number of criminal cases after successfully defending a murder trial two months after her admission to the bar. Her most celebrated case, *The People* v. *Sproule,* was a murder trial that appealed to the sensational appetites of California newspapers and readers. After Sproule discovered that his wife had been "seduced" by a man named Espey, he set about planning Espey's murder. But Sproule made a mistake in identifying his target and he killed an innocent man named Andrews instead. The community was outraged. As one journal reported: "It was a fearful tragedy, and the excitement was so great that the jail had to be guarded for a week to prevent the lynching of the prisoner. Mrs. Gordon undertook defence against the advice of the most distinguished lawyers in the State and obtained a verdict of 'Not Guilty,' amidst the most deafening cheers of men and hysterical cries of women, half-weeping jurymen joining in the general clamor of rejoicing."

Clara Foltz maintained a private law practice also primarily representing indigents in a variety of criminal and civil matters. When an adversary at trial suggested to the court that Mrs. Foltz might better be at home raising her children, Foltz coolly replied, "A woman had better be in almost any business than raising such men as you." While defending a criminal case, Foltz listened as the prosecutor mentioned her to the jury in his closing remarks:

She is a *woman;* she cannot be expected to reason; God Almighty decreed her limitations . . . this young woman will lead you by her sympathetic presentation of this case to violate your oaths and let a guilty man go free.

Foltz had heard that argument too many times before. She rose, asked for leave to address the court, and then, according to one source, "demolished both the legal and *ad hominem* arguments of the prosecutor and won her case."

Trial work was not Foltz's only interest. In 1893 she drafted and obtained passage of the statute that created California's prison parole system. She also helped to organize the Portia Law Club in San Francisco, and informally conducted a law school for women out of her Los Angeles office. After years of watching indigent defendants having to fend for themselves in criminal court, Foltz drafted a model statute that came to be known as the Foltz Defender Bill, providing for the creation of government-funded public defender systems to ensure adequate legal representation for poor criminals. Her bill was introduced in thirty-three states and became law in California in 1921.

Late in life when Clara Foltz was asked to describe her thoughts about practicing law, she said she had found it "hard, unpoetic and relentless." When they had to be, so were these early women lawyers.

3

WOMEN IN
THE URBAN LAW
SCHOOLS

Urban women in the late 1800s were restricted by a rigid class system that defined who they were and what they could accomplish. In contrast with the more egalitarian style of the West, eastern cities strictly enforced Victorian notions of femininity. Education for women was acceptable so long as it was a pastime, not preparation for a professional career. Deprived of opportunity and ambition, middle- and upper-class women in the cities had little chance to grow beyond the ladies seminary and the social club. Immigrant and working-class women were limited by traditional sex roles and economic demands that made professional training unthinkable.

Yet with industrialization and immigration bringing about dramatic changes in the cities, there was an explosion of opportunities and new ideas in the 1880s and 1890s that fanned the aspirations of women of every social class. The availability of free public school education enabled thousands of working-class children—girls and boys—to take advantage of professional opportunities that their parents never could have imagined for themselves. In doing so, they changed the character and composition of the urban bar.

For women seeking a legal education in the East, this period was a turning point. Unwilling to travel great distances to study law as Lemma Barkaloo and Lavinia Goodell had, these women were determined to overcome the resistance at home. Little more than twenty years later hundreds of urban women were graduating from law school because of these efforts.

In Philadelphia the battle for legal education for women began with Carrie Burnham Kilgore, said to have been "one of the first women in the country to ask for admission to the bar, and one of the last to gain it." Kilgore, who already held a degree in medicine, was refused admission to the University of Pennsylvania Law School in 1870. "My application was considered by the Board and laid upon the table—which of course was a refusal. . . . At that time tickets were purchased of each individual lecturer and when I made application to E. Spencer Miller for the opportunity to attend his lectures and to study law in the University as a student, he replied as follows: 'I do not know what the Board of Trustees will do, but as for me, if they admit a woman I will resign for I will neither lecture to niggers nor women.' "

In 1872, Carrie Burnham Kilgore sought admission to the state bar but was refused because she was a woman. She brought on a writ of mandamus to force the Pennsylvania State Board of Examiners to accept her and petitioned the Pennsylvania legislature for redress. It was 1883 before Kilgore gained admission to the Orphan's Court, 1884 before she was admitted to the courts of common pleas, and 1886 before she was at last admitted to the Pennsylvania Supreme Court.

During this period Kilgore decided to go one more round with the University of Pennsylvania Law School. She remembered, "In 1881, I, or rather my husband, purchased of E. Coppee Mitchell, who was then Dean of the Law Department, a ticket for me to attend the lectures of the University. I attended the first lecture which was a public lecture, accompanied by my husband and on the following day I commenced attending the lectures regularly, going alone of course, and on the second day, just as I left the building, I was handed a letter from the Board of Trustees who had convened meanwhile, saying that they thought it proper to inform me that if I attended the entire course and passed all the examinations, it was not at all sure that the University would graduate me or confer upon a woman its diploma. I replied that I should at least get the knowledge, and the matter of the diploma could be determined later. . . . It is impossible to appreciate the intense opposition to my admission to the University and the work for and to women. Now people wonder that there ever was opposition and, it seems, wonder if there really was opposition. The necessity for police protection was quite seriously discussed at the University."

Kilgore admitted she was treated courteously by many of the professors and students but said, "When I had graduated and was finally admitted to the Bar it was familiarly said to be 'the greatest victory since the civil war.'"

Kilgore remained for at least a decade more the only woman lawyer in Philadelphia. In 1890 she advertised for a woman law student to work in her office and promised that the successful applicant would have a good chance of working with her after admission to the bar, but at the time Alice McGee, a young girl clerking in a Warren, Pennsylvania, law office, was the only available candidate and she was too young and inexperienced to be considered.

In Boston only one school—Boston University—permitted women students in all its departments. As early as 1874, Elizabeth G. Daniels was registered for the law course; however, she did not complete it. In 1877, Mary Dinan Sturgess, a woman from Mansfield, Ohio, enrolled at the law school, but she too failed to get her degree. She later said the legal education she did receive was helpful to her in administering her family's estate. Lelia J. Robinson entered the law school in 1878. Completing the regular three-year course with honors, Robinson ranked fourth in a class of more than thirty students. Immediately after graduation Robinson applied for admission to the Massachusetts bar. Chief Justice Horace Gray blocked her application, claiming he could not act until formal briefs had been submitted and oral argument had been held to decide the issue. Gray then called on the Massachusetts Bar Association to appoint two representatives to contest the Robinson application. Unable to argue the matter on her own behalf, Lelia Robinson obtained the assistance of former Attorney General C. R. Train, a respected member of the bar. Her application, not unexpectedly, was denied. Robinson spent the following year campaigning to remove the state's restrictions for admission to the bar. Eventually she was successful, becoming the first woman lawyer in the state of Massachusetts, but Robinson never forgot her ordeal. She spent the next nine years compiling information about women law students and lawyers throughout the United States, which she developed into a comprehensive twenty-two-page article for *The Green Bag*, a popular lawyer's magazine at the turn of the century.

Following Robinson at the Boston University Law School were Jesse Wright, who after graduation practiced law in Topeka, Kansas, and Mary A. Greene, who in 1888 ranked second in a large class of men. Greene became an expert in matrimonial law, lobbied for legislation to uphold the validity of contracts between husband and wife and developed a series of lectures on the law for students at the Lasell Seminary. Anna Christy Fall was another distinguished graduate of the Boston University Law School who became known for her reform efforts on behalf of Boston's poor.

Hoping to increase educational opportunities for women in the Boston area, in 1915 a group of Radcliffe seniors tried to persuade the Harvard Law School administration to accept women. Their efforts were unsuccessful. One of the seniors, Elizabeth Chadwick Beale, the daughter of Harvard law professor Joseph H. Beale, persuaded her father to create a special female law school, which they called the Cambridge Law School for Women. That year they received applications from twenty-five graduates of Radcliffe, Bryn Mawr and Smith. Professor Beale was able to get the support of a number of other law professors including Harvard's Jens Iverson Westengard, Missouri's Manley Ottmer Hudson and George Washington University's Ernst Otto Schreiber, Jr. Unlike most other law schools during this period in the United States, Cambridge had a strict requirement that applicants be graduates of accredited four-year colleges. Cambridge's bulletin for the 1916–1917 semester states that "the purpose of the school is to give to women who are graduates of colleges a legal education substantially like that given to men in the best American law schools." This elitist strain can be discerned throughout the history of women's legal education in the northeast. When upper-class women found themselves having to mingle with lower-class women or men of other races in order to get a professional degree they often sought to establish new law schools rather than to adjust to established ones.

The Cambridge Law School boasted that its "programme of instruction is based upon that of the Harvard Law School" and that "the teachers are with few exceptions either teachers in the Harvard Law School, or teachers in other schools who are in residence at the Harvard Law School during the year as candidates for the advanced degree." Eleven women, including Elizabeth Beale, successfully completed the first year. But by the end of the second year, the Cambridge Law School experiment was over. According to Ronald Chester, a professor at the New England School of Law, Cambridge Law School was closed when Elizabeth Beale married and lost interest in her legal education. Others have suggested that the requirement of the college degree, at a time when most schools did not require one, made the law school so exclusive it was impossible to recruit applicants in numbers large enough for it to continue. Further, Joseph Beale's interest ended with his daughter's, since "he doubted that women of his generation would succeed in trying cases, but thought they would excel in office practice."

A more successful experiment was the creation of the Portia Law School in Boston in 1908. Whereas Cambridge was created with an especially restrictive admissions policy and failed, Portia Law School was open to all and survived. Portia began as an evening bar-review course for two women who were being prepared for the examination by Boston University law graduate Arthur W. MacLean. The size of the evening classes increased each year so that in 1919 Governor Calvin Coolidge signed into law a bill that empowered the school to grant the bachelor of laws degree to women. During this same period a "companion school," the Calvin Coolidge Law School for men, was created. Like Portia, it later became coeducational and continued to grow, eventually changing its name to the Suffolk Law School. In 1922 a day division of Portia was formed.

In 1935, in order to keep up with state bar requirements, Portia Law School obtained special legislation permitting it to establish Portia College, a liberal arts institution with power to confer college credits in preparation for the bachelor of laws degree. By 1948 the law school had a faculty of thirty and a student enrollment of four hundred and fifty. It would be 1950 before women were able to obtain a law degree at every institution in the Boston area, but Portia Law School thrived and in 1969 became the New England School of Law.

Opportunities for women had been no greater in the nation's capital.

Several years before Belva Lockwood began her campaign to gain admission to the federal courts, she actively fought for the right to attend law school. Lockwood, in 1869, had been refused admission to the Georgetown University and Howard Law Schools and to the Law Department of Columbian College in Washington, D.C. She received the following letter from Columbian College's president:

October 7, 1869

Mrs. Belva A. Lockwood

Madam, the Faculty of Columbian College have considered your request to be admitted to the Law Department of this institution and after due consultation, have considered that such admission would not be expedient as it would be likely to distract the attention of the young men.

Respectfully,

Geo. W. Samson,
President

Lockwood, who at the time she received Samson's letter was nearly forty years old, said his excuse was "ridiculous" and enrolled in the new National University Law School, which later became part of the George Washington University National Law Center. Fourteen other women began classes with Lockwood, but by the end of the semester only one other woman—Lydia Hall—remained. Shortly before commencement the men students warned they would boycott any graduation exercises that required them to share a stage with a woman and they threatened to walk out if the women students were recognized in any way. Bowing to the pressure, the administration withheld the women's diplomas and removed their names from the commencement program. Lockwood and Hall were outraged, but they assumed once the ceremonies were over, they would get their law degrees. They were wrong, for then the professors balked. Some wanted to give the women their diplomas but others thought the degrees should be withheld in order to save the school's reputation. Professor William Wedgewood, the man who had encouraged the women to study law, warned that even if the faculty could agree, there was still one more obstacle to be overcome. Lockwood and Hall would need the approval and the signature of Ulysses S. Grant, who was serving as president of the law school at the same time he was President of the United States. If the faculty could not agree, it was unlikely that Grant would want to involve himself in the controversy. Lockwood and Hall suspected it was a lost cause. Lydia Hall decided not to continue. Belva Lockwood applied for admission to the District of Columbia Supreme Court, but knew she would have little chance for success without her law degree. While waiting for the Supreme Court's decision, Lockwood campaigned in the South for President Grant's opponent, abolitionist Horace Greeley, and she practiced law in the only tribunals that would have her—police court, probate court and before justices of the peace. In 1873, Lockwood decided she could not wait any longer. With seemingly nothing to lose she wrote a stinging letter to President Grant:

> *No. 432 Ninth St., N.W.*
> *Washington, D.C.*
> *September 3, 1873*

> *To His Excellency, U. S. Grant, President U.S.A.*

> *Sir—*

> *You are, or you are not, President of the National University Law School. If you are its president, I desire to say to you that I have passed through the curriculum of study in this school, and am entitled to and demand my diploma. If you are not its president, then I ask that you take your name from its papers, and not hold out to the world to be what you are not.*

> *Very respectfully,*
> *Belva A. Lockwood*

There was no written reply from the President, but two weeks later Lockwood received her signed diploma.

Ten years later the dean of the National University Law School wrote in response to an inquiry that the school "as it now exists" was "not admitting women." Only Howard Law School had changed, giving "colored men and women" the opportunity of obtaining a law degree. In 1895 four out of the five law schools in Washington, D.C. —National, Columbian, Georgetown and Catholic University—were refusing applications from women. One of those rejected was Delia Sheldon Jackson, a Wellesley graduate whose father was superintendent of education for Alaska. At the suggestion of General John Eaton, a former commissioner of education for the district, Jackson visited Ellen Spencer Mussey, a woman attorney who three years earlier had graduated from Howard Law School. Delia Jackson asked for permission to apprentice in Mussey's law office, but Mussey, whose clients included Clara Barton and the American Red Cross, thought the added responsibility of supervising a law student would be too great. Mussey nevertheless understood the difficulty women had in gaining admission to District of Columbia law schools, so she promised Jackson that if two more women were interested, Mussey would ask her friend Emma Gillett, also a Washington attorney, to assist her in putting together a woman's law class. Gillett had been a law apprentice and then a law student. Unable to gain admission to any law school in the capital, she studied in the law offices of Belva Lockwood and finally was admitted to Howard, graduating in 1883.

Within a few months Nanett B. Paul and Helen Malcolm joined Delia Jackson at Mussey's law office on Louisiana Avenue, and Mussey and Gillett began holding a series of part-time courses. While the classes were informal, full instruction in the law was provided. Mussey taught constitutional law, Gillett lectured on Blackstone's *Commentaries,* and fellow attorneys Watson J. Newton, Gillett's law partner; Seth Shepard, associate justice of the court of appeals; and William C. Robinson, dean of Catholic University's law school, supplemented the instruction.

In 1898, when the women students were ready for their senior year, Mussey and Gillett assumed that their students' advanced training would qualify them for Columbian College, even though they were females. But Columbian's board of trustees was adamant—no women at the school. Mussey and Gillett realized their makeshift experiment was over. If women who were as well prepared as these could not get a formal legal education simply because of their sex, a new law school —for women—would have to be formed. That year Mussey and Gillett's Washington College of Law was incorporated and four of the seven trustees were women. Edward F. Bingham, chief justice of the District of Columbia Supreme Court, served as president. Tuition was set at $50 yearly and advertisements were printed calling the Washington College of Law "the only school south of Philadelphia admitting women." (In reality WCL was the only all-white school south of Philadelphia admitting women, since Howard had been accepting all races and both sexes for a number of years.) It was agreed that Mrs. Mussey would continue as dean of the law school and this earned her recognition for being the only woman in the world to hold such a prestigious position. The College of Law itself was the subject of articles here and abroad because it was the only such school "in the world which has women in its faculty and board of management."

At the end of May 1899, the College of Law held its first commencement exercises. Six women were seated on stage to receive their bachelor of laws degrees. Between orchestral selections that included "Hearts and Flowers," there were invocations and speeches to mark this "educational epoch in the history of the District." The Washington *Post* sent a reporter to cover the event who noted that "six young ladies became 'bachelors' yesterday evening and the event therefore was particularly interesting." John Hemphill, the featured speaker, was optimistic about the women's chances for survival in the legal profession. He suggested that opportunities for women would be available, then added, "But woman must realize that her attitude toward men is somewhat changed when she assumes the role of a lawyer. She now appears as a competitor, as one contending with men, and those in the profession will look upon her in the same light in which they do upon other members of the profession so far as business matters may be concerned."

As the Washington College of Law developed, the curriculum became more formal, students selected school colors (green and gold), a WCL flag was designed and exhibited and the school began taking men students. The first of these was Paul Sperry, who, in an address to his classmates in 1901, said that he hoped women in men's classes might meet with "the courtesy and cordiality he had received."

When Dean Mussey was called upon to talk about educational opportunities for women in the capital, she said:

Not enough is done to help girls become self-supporting. Women are admitted to less than 50 percent of the state universities although their taxes help to support these institutions. In Washington city there are no professional schools for white women except the Washington College of Law which I founded. Starting in 1896 with three students it now has an enrollment of 116. . . . Why must women knock at the doors of men's universities and plead to fit themselves for public service in law, medicine and the ministry?

Mussey continued as dean until 1913 when ill health forced her to step down. At her retirement Mussey observed:

Religious Intolerance has said to woman, "You cannot be trusted with your own soul and therefore I will take charge of that and tell you what you should believe and how you should feel toward God and man." Scientific Intolerance says, "You cannot be trusted with your own mind so I will do your thinking for you and then tell you as much as I think you ought to know." Social Tyranny says, "You cannot be trusted with your own person so I will regulate your conduct." The Lawmakers say, "You can bear sons and daughters, you can go down into the valley of death with each birth pang—but unless you are a soldier in battle you have no courage, you are not doing anything for your country and therefore you cannot have the ballot . . ."

She continued to actively fight for suffragist causes and was as much known for her successful drafting of the "Mussey Act," which gave increased rights to married women, as she was for her tenure as dean of the Washington College of Law.

Emma Gillett took over as dean for ten more years, then continued the tradition of keeping women in leadership positions by turning the post over to Laura H. Halsey. Through the years the law school continued to grow, so that by 1914 there were more men students than women—a result of women finally gaining admission to other District of Columbia law schools. In 1949 the Washington College of Law merged with American University, and today still retains its original name.

It was not until 1886, when Kate Stoneman became New York's first woman attorney, that women were able to study and practice law in New York. Lemma Barkaloo, Lavinia Goodell and Belva Lockwood had all been native New Yorkers forced to leave the state in order to further their professional ambitions. When Barkaloo and two others applied to the Columbia University Law School for admission they were immediately rejected. Columbia's George Templeton Strong made the following entry into his personal diary: "Application from three infatuated young women to the [Columbia] Law School. No woman shall degrade herself by practicing law in New York especially if I can save her. . . . 'Women's Rights Women' are uncommonly loud and offensive of late. I loathe the lot."

But by the turn of the century the demand for legal education for women was dramatically growing in New York. A combination of increased technology and cheap immigrant labor freed middle- and upper-class women from many of the household duties that had occupied them. With newfound leisure time on their hands, these women turned to education and projects sponsored by women's organizations for fulfillment outside the home. Eleanor Flexner in her history of the women's suffrage movement notes that club women in large cities were pioneering in such concerns as child care, community health and immigrant assistance, and their efforts were instrumental in "laying the basis for the social reform movement and the development of settlement houses."

One such woman was Mrs. Leonard Weber, a doctor's wife and prominent club leader who became interested in helping immigrants survive tenement living in New York City. She noted: "I was engaged in teaching a few poor women the first principles of hygiene and invalid cooking. To my amazement I found that most mental suffering resulted from wrongs which needed legal advice. My sympathy was aroused; I became painfully conscious of my own helplessness and I propounded a question to my friend Dr. E. Kempin, Doctor of Laws, whether it would not be possible to establish, with her at the head, a legal dispensary. Like an inspiration, we hailed this idea. When it was set to work

we secured the necessary funds and opened our Arbitration Society."
But regrettably the experiment lasted only one year. Weber explained
that "too many came, hundreds of women and men so that we could
not find a sufficient number of charitable women to help—such women
as could give the necessary assistance with that authority which comes
from legal knowledge." Dr. Emily Kempin Spyri, Weber's friend, was
a woman law professor from Switzerland, an expert in Roman law who
earned her Doctor Juris Utriusque from the School of Jurisprudence in
Zurich. At a time when there were no women lawyers in the city of
New York and only one in the state, Dr. Kempin was invited to conduct
a course on Roman law at the Law School of the University of New
York (now New York University), "the first modern instance of a
woman lecturing on law to classes of young men."

Weber and Kempin's Arbitration Society had no shortage of immigrant clients and no shortage of volunteers to help them; but without
the most basic knowledge of the law the women volunteers were of
little practical assistance. After closing the society, Weber and Kempin
decided to form another—the Women's Legal Education Society.
They started with a series of "parlor lectures" held in the homes of
various members. For an annual fee of $5, women could attend one or
all of the circuit seminars. Encouraged by the enormous interest
women were showing for law lessons, Weber and Kempin began con-
tacting the city's educational institutions seeking a sponsor for their
program. Only the University of New York responded favorably to
their request.

Vice-Chancellor Henry MacCracken offered the women a classroom
at 32 Waverly Place in Greenwich Village, and assisted them in the
printing of a bulletin that assured applicants the lecture hall for the new
woman's law class would be "on the upper floor of the building above
the noise and dust of the city." Students had a choice of morning or
evening sessions. Once the fall schedule was formally announced, New
York newspapers could not resist comment. Typical was this item from
the New York *Herald:*

The first woman lawyer we hear of bargained for a heart. New York's women
law students are bargaining for heads. Shylock was to get a pound as his part
if he lawfully carried out Portia's argument of his case. The University of New

York just gets a bit over a pound ($5) for furnishing these modern Portias with the inspiration for arguments, namely twelve lectures or one course of legal study.

While the lectures amounted to nothing more than an adult education class and by 1934 were officially absorbed by NYU's Division of General Education as an extension course, the instruction was vigorous. Kempin managed to cover elementary jurisprudence, contracts, sales, wills, negotiable paper, personal property, real property, mortgages, trusts, equity, corporations and constitutional law. Most important for the development of women's legal education, the woman's law class served as a training ground for those pioneers who wanted to go on for their LL.B. degrees. Isabella Pettus, a student at the woman's law class, saw an important purpose beyond that:

> . . . those who study here are not lawyers. But in the 20th Century, when almost as many women as men are self-supporting, a knowledge of the rudiments of law has become a necessity to them. The woman's law class aims to give to the average woman a glance at law. The knowledge of the leading principles of law, such as the force of custom, hardening into common law, the difference between the laws of personal and real property, and distinction between a contract and a tort, the obligations of the individual to the community, the importance of any paper issuing out of a court, the fact that when you invoke the law on any given point you have set in motion machinery you cannot yourself control, the operation of Surrogate's Courts—these are some of the subjects which are new to the average woman, while to the exceptional woman, who has a legal mind and intends to take up the study of law as a profession, the course is invaluable . . . it is a "trial spin," a birdseye view, a blazed path in the legal wilderness.

Like many others, Pettus went on to get her LL.B. from the New York University Law School and later took over the presidency of the Women's Legal Education Society.

The aim of the society was to become known to New York City women, particularly those who might be interested in attending the woman's law class. The society's first annual report stressed: "It was by no means desired that [their] work should be done in a corner, but on the contrary that it should become as widely known, appreciated and imitated as possible." In order to honor those who had completed the course and to encourage those who were considering enrolling, public graduation ceremonies were scheduled for the completion of the first semester. At the ceremonies, Dr. Kempin examined her students in the presence of Vice-Chancellor MacCracken, and completion certificates were formally awarded. A number of speeches were delivered and three members of the class gave scholarly readings of papers they had pre-pared: "Origin of Our Law," by Melle Stanleyetta Titus; "Considerations," by Cornelia Kelley Hood; and "Why I Study Law," by Mrs. Theodore Sutro, the valedictorian. The reporters who attended the commencement exercises ignored these aspects of the program, choosing instead to write about the physical appearances of selected members of the class. The New York *Times*, in its article headlined THESE WOMEN KNOW LAW BUT DON'T LOOK AT ALL LIKE TYPICAL LAWYERS, wrote that the graduates "did not wear gowns suggestive of any desire to look like learned women lawyers. On the contrary they were attired in pretty white dresses and looked as charming as the proverbial sweet girl graduate." The New York *Continental* added:

The valedictorian is pretty, piquant and lovable, rich in all the feminine graces and lives in the most artistic surroundings.

The word "lawyer" in itself suggests musty books and barren rooms when applied to a man and when associated with a woman, a vision with hair parted in the middle and "slicked" back over each ear, a half-worn out black dress, common-sense shoes, a pin at the throat containing the hair of some deceased relative, etc. Yet the woman selected to represent the little band of lawyers just graduated from the University of the City of New York is the embodiment of all that is deemed sweet femininity and is essentially apart from anything suggesting the dreariness of dull, dry law.

The 1891 ceremonies marked the end of Dr. Kempin's tenure with the Women's Legal Education Society. After only a year of heading the woman's law class, Kempin accepted an appointment at the University of Berne. She said she made the decision in order to be able to spend more time with her husband and children. But Mrs. Theodore Sutro believed there was another reason—the less-than-cordial reception Kempin received from the male students at the regular law school. Sutro told *Continental* reporter Margery Daw:

All winter Mrs. Kempin has lectured to the men students on Roman Law and they treated her ungallantly to say the least. Although they attended her lectures regularly, and with the greatest interest, they made no acknowledgment of gratitude and Mrs. Kempin is one of the best authorities in the world on the subject of Roman Law.

Near the close of the last term the men started a paper saying, "We the undersigned students of the Roman Law Class hereby subscribe . . ." and brought it to us to finish. It was a subscription for a watch. But we didn't see why we should help the Roman Law Class when we had no part in it. So we refused and bought the watch ourselves and the men made no recognition whatever of Mrs. Kempin's work.

She has been honored by being admitted a regular member of the University and the Empress of Germany has summoned her to appear at court immediately upon her arrival there to make public recognition of her work. Some day people will realize what she has done.

Fortunately for the woman's law class the administration at the University of New York did not share the view of its male students. Men such as Chancellor Henry MacCracken, Professor Isaac Franklin Russell and Dean Clarence Ashley not only accepted women at the law school but actively recruited them. Alice Dillingham, who died in 1985 at the age of 102, remembered the dean coming to Bryn Mawr in 1902 when she was a senior to "challenge" the women to study law. Dillingham, the only student in the class to take him up on the offer, went on to become valedictorian of the law school's Class of '05. The administration's attitude was in sharp contrast to most other law schools in the United States, where women were routinely excluded from classes or when they were seated were treated to ridicule or ostracism.

The press generally disliked the University of New York's policy of encouraging women to study law. In 1893 the Brooklyn *Chronicle* profiled the eight Brooklyn women who had graduated from the woman's law class. Under the headline LAW HAS CHARMS, the *Chronicle* noted:

The *fin de siècle* woman stops at nothing in the way of advancement, and it is scarcely surprising that the study of law, that would have shocked the sensibilities of the woman of 30 years ago, is today taken up with an independence born of the age.

Miss Hope Christiansen . . . is the handsome young daughter of Mr. William Christiansen, president of the Brooklyn Trust Company. . . . To look at this young lady and hear her laugh no one would believe that the deep subjects in life interested her, but a good deal of unusual cleverness is contained in her pretty little head with its wealth of dark braids . . .

Mrs. Ruth Ferriss Russell (wife of Professor Russell) is very pretty and exceedingly girlish, notwithstanding her legal knowledge . . .

Writers for the New York *Journal* were equally suspicious of the motives of women studying law, claiming it was "the latest fad now . . . to study law, and all the fair maids and matrons who can afford to are whiling away their time over the musty old law volumes at the University of New York! There is a woman preacher among the new students, two ex-soubrettes, a French milliner, a woman dentist, five employment agency proprietors and a bevy of society misses. . . ."

After Kempin left the faculty, Chancellor MacCracken appointed a new professor to take over the woman's law class and to consult with members of the Women's Legal Education Society. Christopher G. Tiedeman, who had been on the faculty of the University of Missouri Law School for more than ten years before coming to NYU, presided over a greatly expanded class in the second year. There were thirty-one women enrolled in this 1891–92 course.

The following year and for several years thereafter, Professor Isaac Franklin Russell, chief justice of New York's Court of Special Sessions, taught the woman's law class. The number of women students increased to fifty-seven in the third year, and Dr. Russell, in a speech before male members of the law school faculty, was quoted as saying, "As justice and equity know no distinction of sex, so the commonwealth of intellect cannot deny to women the freedom of the city."

There was a prevailing misconception that the woman's law class was providing an LL.B. degree. As numbers of women students and graduates increased, newspapers such as the Albany *Express* worried that the University of New York was producing too many women lawyers: "Married women could better serve themselves and humanity than by becoming lawyers . . . the increasing newness of the 'new woman' may justly be viewed with alarm." In reality, only a fraction of the women who studied in the woman's law class went on to become members of the bar but virtually every young woman in New York City who did obtain her law degree during this period also was a graduate of the woman's law class.

The University of New York Law School was officially opened to women in 1890. Its first three women graduates were Melle Stanleyetta Titus, Cornelia Kelley Hood and Katherine Hogan. Melle Titus, New York City's first woman lawyer, enrolled in the University of New York Law School in 1891. Despite an eight-week illness that incapacitated her in her senior year, she graduated from the law school with highest honors. She was one of the top four students in a class of over a hundred and was awarded a $100 prize by the faculty for her outstanding work as a law student. In March 1895, Titus became the first woman admitted to the United States District Court for the Southern District of New York and the first woman admitted to the Second Circuit Court of Appeals. Melle Titus never forgot the education she received from the Women's Legal Education Society. Shortly after earning her LL.B. she returned to the woman's law class to serve on the faculty and to encourage other young women to make application to the law school.

Cornelia Kelley Hood, another of the University of New York's first woman law graduates, was an ardent suffragist who strongly advocated legal education for women. After earning her law degree, Hood represented clients through the Legal Aid Society and the Consumers League. She set up a lecture series in Brooklyn that was modeled after the woman's law class and served on the faculties of both schools for a time.

Katherine ("Kate") Hogan, also one of the university's first women law graduates, founded and served as first president of the Interborough Association of Women Teachers in the City of New York. She was noted for her work in labor law, and at her death in 1906 it was said that "whatever claims may be made as to the exact brain in which the idea of equal pay was born, it is indisputed that Kate Hogan brought before the people of the state sex discrimination in the salary schedules of the Board of Education and sent the slogan 'Equal Pay for Equal Work' thundering round the world."

In 1895 these women and a number of other graduates of the woman's law class were instrumental in forming an Alumnae Association of the Women's Legal Education Society. Dues were $1 per year, and an advisory board was created consisting of distinguished male and female members of the bar. Among them was Phoebe Couzins, the pioneer woman lawyer from St. Louis. In a stirring address to the alumnae association, Couzins said:

Law has been said to be "the perfection of reason" but how absurd that statement is when only one-half of the human mind is engaged in the reasoning. What would art, literature, and poetry have been had the development been confined to the male mind alone?

And I tell you young ladies that when you get into the realm of the law you will discover . . . that man has been trying to do the housekeeping in the Temple of Justice for years all by himself, with the result of cobwebs all over the place. . . . Legal fiction is piled upon legal fiction and precedent on precedent until the whole storehouse of law is in a helpless confused condition. It needs women's wit, women's fairness and women's sense of right and righteousness to put the legal fabric in order and repair.

Couzins's speech was in keeping with the society's aims of using the law to improve conditions for women and for the poor. A scholarship fund was created so that each year the highest ranking member of the woman's law class would receive free tuition at the University of New York Law School. A look at the titles of the prize-winning essays submitted indicates the interest these women had in social reform: "The Legal Status of Defective Children," "Workmen's Compensation," "The Child and the Law," "Prison Education and Convict Labor," "The Application of the Writ of Injunction in Labor Disturbances," "Federal Control of Child Labor in Industry."

New York University's leadership role in the field of legal education continued up until the 1920s. By this time other law schools in the New York area were open to women as well. But the middle- and upper-class women who were studying law out of a sense of commitment or interest in advancing social reform were being replaced by working-class women who were seeking a law degree as a better means of supporting themselves. For these women the law school experience was particularly difficult. Libby Sachar, who was to become one of the first woman judges in the state of New Jersey, entered New York University Law School in 1921. "The boys in the class were poor like we were. If one of them asked you for a date you knew it would be flapjacks at Child's for thirty-five cents and a ride around Manhattan for a nickel." Sachar recalled having no problems with the administration but angrily remembered the professor "who suggested in front of the whole class that the only reason I was there was to get myself a husband. I snapped back, 'This is the last place I would come to look for a man' and then as soon as I said it I was sorry because I saw the expressions on the boys' faces and I knew I had insulted them. I was just so upset by the professor I didn't know what to do." Sachar remembers wanting to practice law from the time she was six years old when, as the only eyewitness to a stabbing, she was called to court to testify. "The judge asked me some questions about whether I knew right from wrong and I told him I did. Then he asked me about the knifing and I told him what I remembered. As I was leaving the courtroom, the judge said, 'You ought to be a lawyer.' I didn't know what a lawyer was but somehow I knew that was what I was going to be. When I got home I told my mother what the judge said but she didn't know what a lawyer was either." Sachar believes the best advice she got in law school was not to learn how to type. "For those of us who needed to earn a living, being a legal secretary was always a possibility. I didn't want to resort to that. I wanted to practice law." Sachar found a New Jersey firm that agreed to hire her, and although she is no longer on the bench, she continues to practice law today.

Lili Axinn Reinis fondly remembers her classes at NYU Law School. "The faculty was wonderful. They treated us better than the men students did." A 1926 graduate, Reinis likes to recall her Saturday morning classes with the now-famous Judge Joseph F. Crater, a man with entertainment and underworld connections who disappeared one evening in 1930 and never was seen again. "Judge Crater taught a ten A.M. class and almost always walked in wearing a tuxedo, having been out on the town the night before. He would come to NYU straight from whatever after-hours club he was last in. The judge was an excellent law professor and between the criminal or constitutional law he would tell us wonderful stories about show girls and celebrities."

By the 1930s when Helen L. Buttenwieser was a law student, New York University had become a more conservative place. Buttenwieser, who became chairman of the board of directors of New York's Legal

Aid Society and was part of the defense team on the celebrated Alger Hiss case, remembers: "There were lots of women in my class when I started in 1933. People thought there had to be something terribly mannish and aggressive about you if you planned to study law." While the faculty outwardly seemed to accept women students, Buttenwieser remembers attitudes were different where pregnant law students were concerned. "I had my third child during the period between Thanksgiving and Christmas in law school. The professors had fits that whole semester whenever they saw me. They actually went so far as to hold a vote as to whether it was improper for a young man to be in contact with a pregnant woman and from what I understand, they agreed that it was. I can't imagine why they thought so but they never did tell me about their vote. I'm not sure if it was out of embarrassment or if they feared what my reaction would be. It was only later, after I graduated, that I learned they planned to throw me out."

The Buttenwieser incident served as an indicator that attitudes about women's involvement at New York University Law School definitely had changed. In the post–World War II years and throughout the 1950s, women's enrollments remained at a low but consistent level as they did at other urban law schools throughout the United States. But an administration that once actively recruited women law students told applicant Susan Powers a half-century later, "What do you want a law degree for? You have children." Powers, a Phi Beta Kappa graduate of Smith College, persisted, only to be told, "Well, with your academic record I guess we can't keep you out." She recalls that in the 1960s when she attended NYU professors could, and did, make disparaging remarks to women students. "My moot court professor assured me that the only reason I won the competition was that my pregnancy impressed the judges and made them feel sorry for me." As late as 1967, NYU was tolerating "Ladies Day," the once-a-semester ritual made famous at Harvard Law School, where women students were called on to recite for the entertainment of the professor and the class. Powers recalled, "My civil procedure teacher had not called on me all year but here it was 'Ladies Day' and I was being asked to stand up and perform. I told the professor I would be glad to brief the case any other day but on this one I refused to recite. The younger women in the class were horrified. But I thought, Here were all these very bright young women who were falling apart in law school because professors like this were making them too nervous to really succeed. I didn't want to see that happen to them or me."

The late 1960s saw a change in New York University, one that helped to bring back the law school's reputation as "the first important law school to increase substantially the proportion of women law students" and to actively promote the abilities of women in the law.

In 1968 women law students formed the Women's Rights Committee and began looking at issues that affected women both at the school and in the marketplace. Its first target was the Root-Tilden Scholarship Program, which was restricted to men. One former student explained, "Ironically, it was rumored that the scholarship money had been bequeathed by a woman who wanted it used for the training of future leaders of America. Since it didn't occur to NYU that women fit into that category, the scholarship bias was never challenged." The Women's Rights Committee was successful in removing the restriction and by the 1969–70 semester, women were eligible for the program. In 1969 the committee formed a National Conference of Law Women, holding yearly meetings and influencing the American Association of Law Schools to establish the Committee on Equality of Opportunity for Women in Legal Education, which later amended the articles of the AALS so that sex discrimination by member schools was prohibited in admissions, placement and hiring.

Also in 1969 the first Woman in Law course was introduced into the curriculum, taught first by Diane Schulder and then by Eleanor Holmes Norton, then the New York City commissioner on human rights. Two years later the school established a clinical program on women's rights, and together with women from Columbia Law School charged a number of Wall Street law firms with discrimination in hiring.

By 1980 New York University had an unprecedented enrollment of women law students estimated at 40 percent. Lana S. Flame, who graduated from the school that year, recalls that "the atmosphere for women probably was better at NYU than it was at many other law schools. Most professors by this time knew enough not to make disparaging jokes or pointed remarks. Placement officers knew women expected and would fight for equal treatment from recruiters. But in retrospect only a fraction of the law professors were women and few women served important roles in the administration. It was obvious to us then as it is now that even at NYU a great deal more needs to be done."

4

LAST BASTIONS: THE IVY LEAGUE LAW SCHOOLS

Although women had been discouraged from seeking a professional education well into the beginning of the twentieth century, it was estimated that by the 1870s more than 11,000 women were enrolled in some 582 institutions of higher learning. While most of these women were earning degrees in education, the opening of law schools in the Midwest and West and in the major cities in the East permitted women to study law even though their opportunities for practice were severely limited.

Because law degrees during this period were rare for men and for women, the accepted route to passing the bar was through apprenticeships with established law firms. Women found it particularly difficult to obtain placements in these law offices.

Since success in the law at the turn of the century and the years immediately preceding did not depend on the law school attended, even the elite law schools such as Harvard, Yale and Columbia were not steeped in the traditions of excellence that characterized their undergraduate colleges. Consider this description of Yale Law School of 1870 that appeared in the *College Courant:*

Graduates of the Law School will remember the single room in the Leffingwell building which served at once for library, recitations, moot courts, debating societies, and lounging-place. They will not need to be reminded that any apartment more unsuited to what Milton calls the "still air of delightful studies" could hardly be imagined. Indeed, one cannot recall its dingy walls, its ill-furnished shelves, and its inadequate accommodations, without wondering that any professional school could maintain even a nominal existence, under such unfavorable conditions.

Frank L. Ellsworth notes that in the late 1800s "attempts at university law schools had been notably unsuccessful, and proprietary schools, which were merely offshoots of law offices, arose to fill the void the academic institutions failed to satisfy." Nevertheless, "as the law schools within colleges and universities became stronger, several models, notably at Harvard and Columbia, were held up for emulation."

In order to upgrade their standards, Ivy League law schools started making a number of changes in their style and curriculum and began requiring that their students take more than one year of courses. By 1876 Harvard was requiring the traditional three-year course of study. These law schools also ruled that a bachelor's degree was needed for admission (Harvard in 1885; Yale in 1896; and Columbia in 1903). They saw to it that the case method of legal study was adopted so that students learned legal theory and analysis by studying the development of actual cases rather than simply memorizing set principles of law. Most important, they began allying themselves with prestigious law firms and bar leaders, maintaining rolls of ". . . young men of wealth, of whom there is an increasing number, who wish to cultivate themselves and take their appropriate place of influence in society."

The notion that a special class of men required a special and better education in the law provides the basis for much of what separates the Ivy League law schools from the proprietary and urban law schools that developed throughout the nation. Today, as sociologist Cynthia Fuchs Epstein points out, "aspiring lawyers must attend law school. Where they go to school and how well they do there usually is of interest long after the lawyer is an established practitioner. The most efficient way to make a start in law is to attend a good law school, become an editor of the school's law review, and win a reputation for brilliance while still a student." So long as women were not part of the educational elite their chances of becoming Brahmins of the legal profession were that much diminished: "Restrictions or quotas on their entrance meant that channels to the larger firms served by Columbia, Yale, and Harvard were cut off, and channels to the other large firms that comprised the country's principal legal community and to posts in government and leading corporations were also severely limited." One New York lawyer described it this way: "I knew it would be difficult being a woman attorney. But I thought if I'm going to do it, I want the degree from Harvard. I didn't want to start out with two strikes against me—being a woman and not having the right credentials."

For most women these credentials were difficult if not impossible to obtain. Ivy League law schools, like the eastern legal establishment they served, were among the last to accept women.

In turning down Lemma Barkaloo's request for admission in 1868, Columbia appears to have been the first of the Ivy League law schools to reject an application from a woman. Three years later Harvard had its first opportunity to consider the issue. Helen M. Sawyer, in academic year 1871, applied for "admittance to the law school as a regular member." The records of the Harvard Law School indicate that "as there was no statute or regulation applying specifically to this situation, the Corporation after a full discussion September 29, and again October 13, 1871, refused the application."

The first request to Yale Law School for admission of a woman came not from the woman herself but from Yale graduate George G. Sill, who later served as lieutenant governor of Connecticut. His letter to the faculty was turned over to the University Corporation for consideration.

> Hartford, Conn.
> March 9th, 1872

Dr. Sir,

A young lady has applied to me for permission to become a student of law in my office. I advised her to seek admission into Yale Law School for one year and then enter my office. Are you far advanced enough to admit young women to your school? In theory I am in favor of their *studying & practising law, provided they are ugly, but I should fear a handsome woman before a jury. Please let me know whether she could be admitted if she should desire to do so, also send me your circular or catalogue.*

/s/ George G. Sill

The corporation, at its March 13, 1872, meeting tabled the "informal application" and no further mention of Sill or his candidate is made.

In 1885 the Yale Corporation suffered a stinging blow in what was less than affectionately called "the Jordan incident." Alice Rufie Jordan came to New Haven from her home in Coldwater, Michigan. Her academic and professional background was formidable. She had a bachelor of science degree from the University of Michigan, had spent one year studying at its law school, and the previous June had been admitted to the Michigan bar. Her first day at the law school was related to a reporter for the New Haven *Register:*

In the fall of 1885, there was a long snake-line of students which wound into the registrar's office. At the very end of the line stood a lone woman. She had a firm jaw and clear, cool eyes that stared straight ahead. The craning necks, the inquisitive eyes, the audible "who is she" left her passive and uninterested. The wild call of "fire" with which the presence of a woman on the campus has ever been hailed would have failed to ruffle the calm exterior of this well-poised woman. At last her turn came. With that instrument mightier than the sword, she wrote, "Alice Rufie Jordan, B.S. University of Michigan, 1885—Registered in Department of Law, Yale University."

The startled registrar cleared his throat. "I'm sorry, but women are not admitted."

"Why not?" the cool eyes rested upon him.

"Why—er—they never have been."

"You'll have to admit me," the young woman put in grimly, "there isn't a thing in your catalogue that bars women."

Alice Jordan was right. The men who drafted Yale's catalogue had never contemplated a woman applicant. Jordan was allowed to pay her preliminary fee and she began attending classes. Dean Francis Wayland and President Noah Porter could not agree on what the acceptable solution to the "Jordan problem" should be so they brought the matter before the University Corporation. Wayland's suggestion was that Alice Jordan be enrolled in the Annual Catalogue of the college, either as a candidate for a degree or as a special student. But the corporation had other ideas and on October 29, 1885, it "resolved, that the name of the young woman in whose behalf the Dean of the Law Department has addressed the Corporation, is not to appear in the Annual Catalogue." The corporation further authorized the treasurer of the school to "repay the fee which she has already paid, if she desires to cease her attendance on the exercises of the School." But Alice Jordan had not come this far only to back down without argument—she continued to attend classes with the consent of the law faculty and she received full credit for every examination she took.*

The following year, in June 1886, Dean Wayland and Professor William C. Robinson, representing a committee of the law faculty, presented their list of candidates for law degrees to the corporation. After much discussion it was agreed that degrees would be conferred on everyone on their list including Miss Jordan, but "in order to avoid any misunderstanding in future, the Corporation hereby direct the following to be inserted as a note in future annual Catalogues or Statements of the Course of Instruction in this college, viz.—It is to be understood that the courses of instruction are open to persons of the male sex only, except where both sexes are specifically included."

In 1890, when Massachusetts's first woman attorney, Lelia J. Robinson, was writing an article about women lawyers in the United States, she wrote to Yale Law School for information about its admissions policies. Dean Wayland sent Robinson a copy of the amended catalogue with a notation that "the marked paragraph on page 25 is intended to prevent a repetition of the Jordan incident."

Yale's restrictive policy continued until 1918 when Isabelle Bridge,

*The New York *Herald*, reporting on Jordan's success at oral argument for her moot court project at Yale Law School, paid far greater attention to her appearance than to her legal skills. In its May 2, 1886, edition it noted: "She is a very prepossessing brunette of about 24 years. She was attired in a rich black silk that glittered with bead work. A band of trailing arbitus nestled at the corsage and a bar of gold glistened at her neck . . ."

despite the stated limitation in the catalogue, submitted her application to the law school. Frederick C. Hicks's four-part history of the Yale Law School is curiously vague about the events that took place following the Bridge application. Without identifying him by name, Hicks mentions that a Yale law professor lectured at the western university Miss Bridge attended. After meeting Isabelle Bridge, the unnamed professor encouraged her to apply to the law school and promised to exert whatever influence he had to get a change in the existing rules. The professor's efforts were remarkably effective. On September 25, 1918, the law faculty voted to recommend Isabelle Bridge's admission. On October 21, 1918, the corporation approved the recommendation and asked the governing board of the school to draft a statement of the conditions under which women could be admitted to the law school. Three weeks later the corporation voted to admit as candidates for law degrees women who had graduated from recognized colleges. Bridge was accepted but she became too ill to attend, so the distinction of being the first woman law student at Yale under the new rules went to Josephine H. Powers, a teacher in the New Haven school system. Because it was necessary for her to work while attending law school, Powers did not receive her law degree until 1923. Five other women were accepted for admission in 1919, including Shirley M. Moore, the first woman to graduate after the "Jordan incident" (in 1920), and Matilda Fenberg, an Ohio schoolteacher who had always dreamed of becoming a lawyer.

In 1963, Fenberg looked back at her first day at Yale Law School: " 'Fellows, I am one of your sisters-in-law,' I said to the six men in the corridor of the Yale Law School. It was registration day in 1919, and no woman had in this century registered in the Law School. A sudden quiet seized the young men and they glanced down at me, for each of them was taller than I. A few seconds passed. Then smiles lighted up their faces and they began to laugh as they realized the significance of my introduction.

"When I arrived on campus at 9 o'clock that morning, I got into a line of men who were waiting to register. I could not help hearing the remarks that were being made, softly at first, then louder and louder and soon they were shouting 'Fire, fire.' A campus policeman came along and said to me, 'Women do not attend Yale College.' 'I know that,' I replied, 'but I am going to register in the Yale Law School.' It looked as if the campus policeman at Yale might keep me from registering. I stubbornly held on to my overnight bag and moved up whenever the man ahead of me moved up. I was becoming tired and only the excitement of the position in which I found myself kept me standing there, first on one foot and then on the other." Fenberg graduated from Yale in 1922 and went on to become a prominent Chicago attorney.

The situation was much the same at Columbia Law School, although events there occurred several years later.

In the fall of 1927, Helen Robinson, an honors graduate of Barnard, the women's college of Columbia University, walked up to a clerk at Columbia Law School and said she was ready to register for her first semester of classes. The clerk looked her over, said "Oh, no, you're a woman" and refused to process her papers. It was not until Robinson returned with her admission letter and a note from the dean that she was permitted to be seated with the first-year class.

Joining Helen Robinson in breaking the seventy-year all-male tradition at Columbia were Elizabeth Butler and Margaret Spahr. Butler entered Kent Hall with a master's degree in social economy from Columbia. Margaret Spahr had received her doctorate in public law from Columbia; the title of her dissertation was "The Supreme Court on Incidence and Effects of Taxation—An Analysis of Economic Theory Embedded in the Constitutional Law Derived from the Explicit Tax Clauses." Yet despite their obvious academic achievements, these women, and those in subsequent years, automatically were placed on probation their first semester while men students were not.

No official records of the law school explain why women were treated differently (or, until 1927, not at all), but Julius Goebel, Jr., author of Columbia's *A History of the School of Law*, pointedly mentions the "policy of deliberate anti-feminism that continued since the re-establishment of the Law School by Theodore Dwight." The only indication of faculty thinking on women at Columbia is reported in the minutes of its October 23, 1917, meeting. There, after little discussion, it was unanimously recommended that women be kept out on the grounds that to do otherwise would be "inexpedient and contrary to the best interests of the Law School."

After World War I, pressures increased for Columbia Law School to admit women. It was argued that excluding them was an "insult" to Barnard graduates, and if women were being admitted to the New York State Bar, they ought to have the best education possible. Others pointed out that women were allowed in all other Columbia graduate programs and there was no restriction on their taking summer law courses.

In 1920, Barnard College formally asked Columbia's law faculty to change its stand on admission. The request was denied, but this time three members of the faculty, Professors William Underhill Moore, Walter Wheeler Cook and Thomas Reed Powell, voted with Barnard. The remaining seven, including Dean Harlan Fiske Stone, held the line. Neither side gave any reason for its action.

Meanwhile, editors at Columbia's "Law Student Monthly" worried about the changing signs:

A question involving Columbia Law School tradition and unity is the increasing demand for the admittance of women. It is argued that the law school is the only graduate school at Columbia not admitting women, and that women are already admitted to the summer law classes. In fact the President of the university recently advised women seeking legal education here to see if they themselves could not convince the "powers that be" at Kent Hall.

One of our New York newspapers, in commenting on this question, pointed out what a blow to Columbia Law School tradition the admittance of women would be. But entirely aside from this, there is a very practical reason against such admittance, namely that the school is already crowded with the number of men students and that the enrollment next year will be even larger than this.

Not a bad argument considering that earlier editorial writers for the *New York Daily Register* (now the *New York Law Journal*) warned that if women were admitted to the bar, they would treat the law much the way they treat changing fashion: "One season all wills will be cut short, another all wills will be drawn long."

As greater numbers of women joined the New York bar, pressures increased to change the restrictive policies at all law schools and particularly those of the Ivy League. By 1925, Dean Harlan Fiske Stone had left Columbia and had joined the United States Supreme Court. Professor Thomas I. Parkinson, who was serving as acting dean, presented the faculty with a request from a new source: the National League of Women Voters and other women's groups had delivered stacks of petitions demanding that the gender restrictions be removed. They were not.

Finally in 1926, Professor Moore, who six years earlier had broken with the majority in favor of women, introduced a motion to consider women applicants for the fall 1927 semester. This time Moore had the votes. The resolution carried nine to one with no explanation as to how Moore got the faculty to change its position so drastically.

Lucy Somerville Howorth, a 1920 casualty of Columbia's all-male admissions policy who later got her law degree at the University of Mississippi and went on to become the first woman general counsel of a federal agency, the War Claims Commission, insists there is only one reason why they so abruptly changed their minds: Harlan Fiske Stone. "I was a graduate student at Columbia and I wanted to go to the law school, but everyone knew Harlan Stone promised women would be admitted to Columbia over his dead body. I wasn't surprised things changed soon after he left, but by then it was too late for me." Howorth recalls with delight the day Columbia's first women took their seats in class. "A group of us never forgot the Chief Justice's 'promise.' So when the breakthrough was announced, we sent a telegram to him at the United States Supreme Court saying something to the effect of 'We suppose you are lying prone on the steps of the Court today.' We never got an answer." Nor did Frances Marlatt, who applied to Columbia Law School for admission in 1922. In an interview with Cynthia Fuchs Epstein, Marlatt recalled: "At the time I was ready to enter law school, women were looked upon as people who should not be in law schools. . . . I went over to see Harlan Stone, Dean Stone, who was later Chief Justice [of the United States], and asked him to admit women. He said no. And I asked why he couldn't open the law school to women, and he said, 'We don't because we don't.' That was final and I didn't get in."

By 1927, Columbia had admitted women, but had they accepted

them? For pioneers like Ida Klaus, who entered the law school the following year, being one of the first meant "being in a hostile atmosphere. There were days I raised my hand until it dropped, but professors who didn't like the idea of women at the law school pretended we didn't exist and wouldn't call on us."

For Helen Robinson it meant sitting in class without anyone sitting next to her. "Those first days were so isolated. I can still remember the name of the first person to talk to me—Dan McGlinchey. Everyone else stayed away until they got to know us or stopped worrying what other students would think."

Words of encouragement were passed along with the hand towels in the law school's only women's bathroom—a men's room on the second floor that was converted by adding wo to the sign on the door. Though it was barely bigger than a closet, the women counted on it to be a lounge, a smoker, a study hall and a refuge. "There were days when resentment seemed to be everywhere," Ida Klaus recalls. "Siena Delahunt was one of my classmates. She was absolutely brilliant. She was also pretty and delicate, an Irish girl with big blue eyes and a pointed chin. She drank straight gin, smoked cigars, coughed her way through law school and had the foulest mouth around. We adored her and when the men got to know her they did too. But at the beginning she was treated terribly. I remember being in class when the professor called on her. The men stamped their feet so that her answer couldn't be heard. It didn't seem to faze Siena, but I was devastated."

Helen Robinson confirms that stamping was a sometime occurrence, but it never happened to her. "I did see William O. Douglas, who was teaching my course in sales, turn beet-red and run out of the class when it was done to him but that was over something else he said, not over treatment of women at the school."

By the end of the first semester, coping with stares and remarks was just one more subject women law students mastered. As time went on, they found a number of unexpected friends along the way. Helen Robinson recalls the encouragement she received from Professor Richard R. B. Powell, who taught estates and trusts, and from Professor Roswell Foster Magill, who invited her to assist him in writing a textbook on taxation. Ida Klaus remembers, "Professor Karl Llewellyn encouraged me to take a number of courses and Professor Herman

Oliphant, our version of 'Mr. Chips,' was supportive of Siena Delahunt and me. He offered Siena a job as his research assistant when she graduated, but she was ill and unable to accept. I got the job and found Professor Oliphant remarkably kind, a man who respected the work women could do."

The law school experience was as unique for each woman as were the women themselves. Elizabeth Butler, who attended the London School of Economics, received a fellowship from the New York School of Social Work. She decided social work was her first love and dropped out of law school after only one year. An Iowa resident, she devoted much of her time to New York's jails, including the workhouse on Welfare Island and the Harlem and Jefferson Market prisons. Butler directed social work programs at foster care institutions, finally retiring to join the board of overseers of Grinnell College.

Margaret Spahr, who had already earned her doctorate before entering Columbia Law School, was the first woman to graduate (in 1929) and was the first woman on the editorial board of the *Columbia Law Review*. After graduation she became an assistant professor of political science at Hunter College and wrote extensively on such subjects as the legal rights and disabilities of married women, the constitutional law of tax immunities, and the growth of political ideals and institutions. She died in 1973.

Helen Robinson began practicing law as a $15-a-week law clerk. An admiralty partner was outraged when at an important meeting she called a vessel an "it," not a "she." Robinson had tried to get a job through Columbia's Clerkship Committee, which placed students who ranked high enough in class, but she was rejected by all the firms that interviewed her. "What would I do with a woman here after five P.M.?" one partner asked her. After working for a firm that gave her "nothing to do," she went back to the Clerkship Committee and this time, through them, was hired by a firm in the financial district. When the firm moved from Rector Street to Exchange Place, Robinson by chance was given an office next to one of the partners. "He was very upset and insisted I be moved. He didn't want any of his clients to walk past my office and see a woman sitting behind a lawyer's desk." Robinson's next and final move was to Lord Day & Lord, where she worked in the estates field and became a partner. In 1969, after more than twenty years with the firm, she retired to Sharon, Connecticut.

Because Ida Klaus got her first job working for Professor Oliphant, she did not have the same problems other women had in finding a law job after graduation. Her family was poor so Klaus worked as a Hebrew teacher while attending classes. "That was against the rules. We were supposed to devote ourselves entirely to the study of law. But I needed to work to survive." Recalling the long subway rides from Brooklyn to Columbia each day, Klaus remembers always being "in perpetual motion. Some of the men in the class would imitate the walk-run that was my style." Her family was proud of her ambition but worried "what it was taking out of me. My mother was sure I was doomed to be an old maid if I insisted on becoming a lawyer." Klaus was interested in the law from childhood, believing at an early age that it ought to be used to bring about social justice and reform in places like Brownsville, her neighborhood, where poverty and labor problems were all too common.

Oliphant brought Klaus with him to Washington when he went to work for President Franklin D. Roosevelt in 1933. Soon Ida Klaus was working as a review attorney with the National Labor Relations Board. In 1948 she was appointed solicitor for the NLRB. Six years later, New York City Mayor Robert F. Wagner hired her as counsel to his new Department of Labor. Once there she drafted the "Little Wagner Act," the legislation that gave New York City employees the right to bargain collectively. In 1961 she was appointed chief adviser to President John F. Kennedy's task force created to design the program for collective bargaining among federal employees. From 1962 until her retirement in 1975, Klaus served as chief labor negotiator for New York City's Board of Education under the official title of Director of Staff Relations.

Despite the problems they had during their schooling, Columbia's women law graduates are enthusiastic about the education they received and are encouraged by the increasing numbers of women attending Ivy League law schools each year. Ida Klaus, who continues to be active in alumni affairs, recalls that "Columbia Law School taught me legal theory, philosophy and how to think. We who came from Columbia Law School were in a favored position because we could take novel issues and work with them to design new approaches to the law. When I was in Washington during the New Deal days, a lawyer in the Justice Department told me he could always tell a Columbia Law School graduate—by far they were the most imaginative and creative lawyers anywhere. Male or female, I think that's still true today."*

Klaus is supported in her view by Charles Rembar, whose book *Law of the Land* traces the evolution of the legal system in the United States. Rembar notes that "while jurisprudential rebellion started at Harvard, by the 1930s when real changes in the law occurred, there was more creative legal thought at Columbia and Yale. Not unusual. Batons pass. The avant-garde tends to rest at the place it has advanced to." So while Harvard continued to maintain its reputation for excellence, restrictive admissions policies and an overemphasis on tradition had their effect on the institution. Rembar believes that Columbia, in particular, "admitted the remarkable minds that came out of New York City's ghetto. They were kids too poor to live away from home and they came to Kent Hall carrying lunches in brown paper bags and marvelous learning in their heads." Some of them, like Ida Klaus, were women.

Harvard resisted women for at least another generation and when, in 1950, it finally admitted them, all but a few of the country's law schools had already done so. Even Arthur Sutherland's superbly complimentary history of Harvard Law School cannot explain the school's intransigence.

For nearly eighty years Harvard had stubbornly kept them out. In 1871 the Corporation had denied admission of one Helen M. Sawyer as a member of the Law School; in 1878 it barred another woman, not named in its minutes. In 1899 Frances A. Keay, a graduate of Bryn Mawr, was refused as a regular student of the Law School but was cautiously told that if Radcliffe would admit her as a graduate student with a view to attending the Harvard Law School, she could take the courses and examinations but not be eligible for the Harvard LL.B.†

---

*In February 1986, Barbara Aronstein Black was named dean of Columbia Law School.
†Beatrice Doerschuk in "Women in the Law: An Analysis of Training, Practice, and Salaried Position," a 1920 document for New York's Bureau of Vocational Information, claims that "in the Spring of 1899 a woman student was granted admission to the Law School at Harvard but this action was rescinded some months later." The woman is not identified.

Kenneth Weinberg, a graduate of the all-male Harvard Law School Class of 1948, is convinced that Roscoe Pound, who served as dean from 1916 to 1936 and who continued on after that time as a professor, greatly influenced attitudes at the law school. Weinberg vividly recalls the morning in 1945 when legal reformer Pound presided over his first-year property class. "Pound was quite old by then, a big husky man who in fifty years of New England weather never wore an overcoat, but always had on green eyeshades. His eyesight and hearing were failing but his mind was as sharp as ever. It was customary for students to invite friends to sit in on classes, and this day one of the guys brought a girlfriend with him. They sat all the way in the back and probably would have gone unnoticed but her broad-brimmed hat gave her away. Pound stopped the class, squinted, then asked, 'Is that a woman back there?' The student answered, 'Yes sir, this is my fiancée.' With that Pound thundered back, 'I don't permit women in my classes, get out.' "

Weinberg, who says he was brought up in that generation of men whose consciousness about women's issues was raised the day before yesterday, remembers being shocked when he actually saw the all-male policy being put into practice. "It wasn't something any of us really thought about then, but when that couple was forced to leave the classroom I remember thinking, this can't go on for too much longer."

It didn't. Four years later, on October 9, 1949, Dean Erwin Griswold announced that women applicants would be accepted for classes beginning in September. Griswold noted: "Women have made a place for themselves in the law, and now we have many women serving with distinction on the bench and at the bar." Now a restricted nonrestrictive policy was about to begin. Griswold's announcement came with the following qualification: "Opportunities for women in the law still are limited, however, and the Faculty is well aware that many able men are turned away from our doors every year. It is our expectation that we will admit only a small number of unusually qualified women students, for the present, at least."*

---

*Soia Mentschikoff, however, was a visiting professor of law at Harvard from 1947 to 1949. Mentschikoff, an expert in commercial law, later became dean of the University of Miami Law School.

The argument that there wasn't enough room for all the able men had been used many times before. Burnita Shelton Matthews, who at the time of the Griswold announcement recently had been appointed to the United States District Court for the District of Columbia, wrote an article about women and the law for the October 11, 1950, *Harvard Law School Record*. Matthews mentioned that when she was nominated to the federal court a number of newspapers suggested she had taken a seat that rightfully should go to a qualified man. "As Congress had created more than 20 new federal judgeships and only one had gone to a woman, the story was recalled of the little boy and little girl who were in a swing that was large enough for only one. The little boy said to the little girl, 'If one of us would get out of this swing there would be room enough for me.'"

Griswold's announcement was cheered by the editorial board of the *Harvard Law School Record*. "The admittance of women to the Harvard Law School marks another progressive policy change adopted by the faculty. While this will not be epoch-making in the advancement of women's rights, it is significant here since the denial to women of this opportunity to study at the Harvard Law School solely because of their sex could not be rationalized. It is not surprising that logic has won out as it is the spearhead of our legal training, it is surprising that it has taken so long."

Not to be outdone, "Omar," an unidentified poet for the *Record*, described what was soon to be the "New Look" at Harvard:

They got the job, and then the vote,
Invaded bars, and then the bar;
There seems a matriarchal note,
So strong appears their rising star;

We'll mourn the harried profs' morale,
As classes just are not the same,
For no one questions like a gal,
And no one reasons like a dame;
Despite the drawbacks to this dare,
Two years of staring at these walls,

(With sour judges pictured there)
Of trudging through depressing halls,
Of reading law, dull legal books,
Have made me sigh for long blonde curls,
For sweet young things with lots of looks;
And so I say "Bring on the girls!"

The "girls"—twelve of them—arrived in September 1950, making it obvious to all that women at Harvard were there to stay. One of the twelve, Beverly Sitrin Coleman, remembers her first day at the law school. "Dean Griswold was there to address the first-year class. I can no longer recall his exact words but they were something to the effect of 'Enjoy your stay at Harvard Law School, and as for the women in the class, personally, I didn't favor your admission, but since you are here, welcome.' "

Whether it was because they were specially selected or because the 1950s in general were quiet times on the nation's campuses, none of the first-year graduates came anywhere close to being a firebrand. Louise Florencourt recalls that "we were very careful how we conducted ourselves, it was very important for us not to be a spectacle." Charlotte Horwood Armstrong remembers that "it was so much a male world then that when they told us we were privileged to be attending Harvard Law School, we believed them. It never occurred to us that we had a right to be there."

The reception from faculty and students was mixed. "Men students in the first year didn't know what it was like without women," Armstrong recalls, "so I think they accepted us more readily than the upperclassmen did. The professors? Well, let's just say they were somewhat less than enthusiastic, although only a few would actively show it." One of those who did was W. Barton Leach, a brigadier general in the Air Force Reserve, who became a legend among women law students for his infamous "Ladies Day." On one special day set aside for women students only, "Leach sat in the audience and asked questions in a 'humorous' tone of the women, who were exhibited on the podium rather like performing bears." Charlotte Horwood Armstrong remembers Leach well. "I was flattened by him. He took sadistic delight in hounding women, but for men and women his style was teaching by humiliation, making fun of men students as well who brought their girlfriends to a Saturday class."

Finally, by 1968, "Ladies Day" came to an end:

> . . . we dressed in black, all wore glasses and carried black briefcases. We totally devastated Leach—knew all the answers, and, at the end, when he asked, "What was the *chose* in question?" (his big punch line—the answer was "underwear" and was supposed to embarrass us), we replied, "we've replevied a few samples," opened our brief cases, and threw fancy lingerie at the "boys." Leach almost had a stroke on the spot, and never had a ladies day again!

Ten years later Elise B. Heinz, a graduate of the Harvard class of '61, wrote a surprising defense of Leach and "Ladies Day," claiming it was done "tongue in cheek" and was rigged purely to provide classroom entertainment:

> I got a mysterious anonymous note requesting that I present myself in Dean Livingston Hall's office at a specified hour. When I got there, I learned that Dean Hall was out of town. . . . There was Bart Leach, grinning like the Cheshire cat, and my roommate, who was in his other property section. He handed out scripts which called for us to turn the tables on him, ask him questions, and take him to task for less than perfect answers in classic One-L fashion. He demanded (and got) sworn secrecy except for one male stooge, to be selected by us for whom there were a few lines in the script.

> On this occasion he did seat us at the front of the classroom. The charade went beautifully, to the amusement of most of the class (and the discomfort of a few of my friends who expected to see him take my head off at the knees). It went so well in fact, that many class members didn't realize it had been staged by Leach himself, so I came out of it with an unearned reputation for unparalleled chutzpah.

But while Heinz portrays a somewhat less than villainous view of Leach, she remembers that for women students at Harvard Law School, "quite possibly half the faculty and student body resented our presence—but the place was big enough that they didn't really matter. So we gritted our teeth each time someone told us the 'talking dog' joke (Why is a woman lawyer like a talking dog? It doesn't talk very well, but it's remarkable that it can do it at all) and went about our business."

All twelve of the first-year students, like those first women at Yale and Columbia, were more than qualified for admission to the law school. All had honors degrees, some had graduate degrees, and one, Miriam Clippinger, entered the law school with a doctorate.

Rosemary Masters, who was a first-year student in 1957, was a graduate of Mount Holyoke. "I went to school at a time where even a college with a feminist tradition like mine gave instruction in 'gracious living,' teaching us how to be perfect hostesses."

Just before entering Harvard Law School, Masters had an interview with Professor Arthur Sutherland. "He assured me that if I went to secretarial school, that, in addition to my law degree, would guarantee my landing a job with a prestige law firm as personal secretary to a senior partner. My first reaction was 'He's kidding.' My second reaction was 'Oh, my God, he's not kidding.' When my mother, who was a professor at Bryn Mawr, heard about my interview she was outraged."

Once she began classes at Harvard, Masters was not surprised at the reaction of the professors, but the attitudes of some of the men students bothered her. "After the first year I married one of my classmates. There was endless speculation by some of the men about what would happen if I got a higher grade than he did. They couldn't imagine that any man would live with a woman who did better on her final exams. Two years later they were still asking us about our marks. And I still couldn't think of a good enough answer."

Nowhere was the link between Ivy League law schools and the prestige law firms more apparent than during the third year of classes at Harvard Law School. Interviews with the established law firms were discussed over and over again with one goal in mind—being hired as an associate and moving on up to partner.

Roberta Good Brundage, one of the original twelve women, recalls being interviewed by four or five firms that were recruiting on campus. "I was turned down by all of them. One recruiter thought he would give me some friendly advice: 'Get yourself a good pair of walking shoes, you're going to be pounding quite a few pavements.'"

Charlotte Horwood Armstrong remembers that "the placement office didn't go out of its way to find jobs for women, but that could have been a measure of the response in the marketplace—firms thought we were oddities and weren't receptive to the idea of having us work for them." Armstrong decided to interview for the Central Intelligence Agency, but was told that since she was a woman, she would have to sign an agreement promising not to marry for seven years. "I never came back for a second interview."

Louise Florencourt fought feelings of rejection by rejecting the interviewers ahead of time. "I told myself I probably would not have enjoyed working for them in the first place." The Boston firm of Morgan, Brown & Kearns decided to take a chance on her even though they had never had a woman associate. It turned out to be a successful arrangement for both. From there Florencourt joined the antitrust division of the Department of Justice, where she found a number of other women attorneys who had been recently hired. "This was a complete change. When Thurman Arnold headed the division (he went on to become Solicitor General of the United States) he swore that so long as he was head of antitrust, no woman would ever be allowed to do that kind of work."

For those who did land jobs on Wall Street, it was clear that making partner was not part of the deal. "They would tell you clients didn't want to be represented by women lawyers and that contacts made at all-male clubs were part of the routine. But without client contact your chances of making partner evaporated. If you were willing to do Blue Sky* cases or trusts and estates work, fine. Otherwise everything else was out," Armstrong remembers.

No matter when the change took place, whether at Yale in the 1880s or Harvard in the 1950s, women who were determined to get an Ivy League education inevitably faced long periods of resistance, resentment and grudging accommodation. Biased professors and jeering students may have hoped that the atmosphere would make it impossible for these women to continue, but not surprisingly, their behavior had the opposite effect—it toughened women students and taught them how to survive the hostile environments they would find in government

*Blue Sky work involves the updating of securities laws and requires no client contact. More often than not it now is done by paralegals.

and industry. Armed with a prestigious law degree and training in handling themselves under extraordinary pressure, these women law graduates developed into legal trailblazers. Their efforts took the battle for equality out of the law school classroom and brought it into the prestige law firms and the highest levels of government. None of these institutions would ever be the same.

5

REBELS AND
REFORMERS

After making significant inroads in the struggle to practice and to study law, women in the late nineteenth century focused their attention on other social and legislative reforms. Not only were they active in the suffrage movement but they also spearheaded campaigns for equal rights, temperance, fair labor practices, birth control and world peace. Their law practices often centered on helping indigent women, whether these women were recent immigrants in urban settlement houses or farmers and laborers in rural areas. As historian Eleanor Flexner points out: "In seeking those who most needed their services they inevitably found . . . women at the bottom of the heap."*

For many of these early women attorneys, particularly those in the Midwest and West, temperance was a vital feminist issue that captured their immediate attention. While a hostile male press may have portrayed temperance activists as hatchet-wielding eccentrics, in reality they were women who well understood the helplessness of a family

*Similarly when Theresa Labriola, Italy's first woman lawyer, was asked about her career plans, she replied, "I shall throw myself heart and soul into every case where the proverbial woman is at the bottom of it."

dependent on an alcoholic husband for its survival. With the law of coverture placing married women under the absolute custody and control of their husbands, so that neither their children nor their earnings belonged to them, and with no welfare system to provide family assistance, the economic and emotional consequences of living with alcoholism were devastating. Coverture was perhaps best explained by the *Women Lawyers Journal* when it reprinted this popular feminist rhyme from England:

> Thus altho when you're a spinster
> You your own affairs may rule,
> Yet with vows pronounced at 'Minster
> You've become a helpless fool.

Early on, there was recognition that legal skills would be needed to further the goals of the temperance movement. In 1873 renowned temperance leader Frances Willard was urging her workers to familiarize themselves with the law and to consider the legal implications of their mission. In a document she titled "Hints and Helps in Our Temperance Work," Willard suggested: "A committee on Law should be appointed, members of which may address the Union from time to time until all are thoroughly familiar with the temperance law of the State. Then if some poor wife has the courage or the desperation to appear against the man who is destroying her home, go with her to court and help her all you can . . . petitions, appeals to voters, memorials and all similar documents should proceed from the Committee on Law."

Following Willard's lead, the first woman to practice before the Iowa Supreme Court, J. Ellen Foster, attained national prominence as a temperance speaker. Foster, who began practicing law in 1872, liked to tell audiences that she "read Blackstone while she was rocking her babies." For more than twenty years she traveled throughout the United States fulfilling "platform engagements" on the subject of prohibition.

Ada H. Kepley, the first woman law graduate in the United States, was active in the suffrage and temperance movements and published a temperance newspaper in Effingham, Illinois, called *The Friend of Home*. The title was particularly misleading, since the purpose of the newspaper was to print the names of local men who were frequenting saloons in the area. It was said she compiled her lists "while sitting near the front window of her Banker Street apartment, which overlooked a saloon." In Peggy Pulliam's historical account of Kepley, "Effingham's Fighting Female," she notes that "Ada's paper was eagerly awaited by her loyal temperance friends, and also by the people who wanted to know the names of the latest drunks and sinners. Naturally the paper caused much trouble in the County. Family fights, neighborhood quarrels and church squabbles resulted. Ada and her family were ridiculed and a saloonkeeper's son tried to shoot her. But nothing stopped her."

Lavinia Goodell, Wisconsin's first woman lawyer, was reported to have been "among the foremost workers in the cause of temperance and was associated with the leaders of the suffrage movement" before her untimely death at the age of forty-one. In tribute, one writer noted that "in all this work she manipulated a quiet and gentle spirit and was never obtrusive or overbold."

Nebraska's first woman lawyer, Ada Bittenbinder, was similarly involved in suffrage and temperance work. After her admission to the Nebraska bar in 1882, she became active in the Women's Christian Temperance Union and for six years served as its superintendent of temperance legislation. In 1888 she was named attorney for the national organization, "answering legal questions arising from the war on liquor traffic," and appearing ". . . repeatedly before Congressional committees to advocate bills backed by her organization." Bittenbinder tried unsuccessfully to prohibit the sale of liquor in the nation's capital and in federal territories and lobbied for national prohibition. She wrote the National Prohibitory Amendment Guide in 1889, which was designed to give women guidelines for organizing and carrying out temperance petition campaigns.

Returning to Nebraska in 1891, Bittenbinder ran for supreme court judge on the Prohibition Party ticket and received nearly 5 percent of the vote. But by 1894 both the temperance movement and Ada Bittenbinder were beginning to show signs of strain. Nebraska's *State Journal* noted:

The prohibition party is becoming less and less a factor in politics. The vote has steadily fallen off until now in Kansas and Nebraska combined it is less than it used to be in this state alone. It is not that the sentiment in favor of temperance and virtue is dying out . . . so long as such grand old men as Ada Bittenbinder were nominated, the rank and file voted as they prayed, but when she refused longer to be a martyr to the cause and run for governor, the weak-kneed ones deserted . . .

Another Nebraska woman lawyer active in suffrage and temperance campaigns was Alice Minick. Minick was twelve years old when she and her family left rural New York in 1857 to settle two hundred acres of Nebraska farmland. Home was a log cabin in Brownville, which they had reached by covered wagon. Minick's father was a staunch abolitionist who encouraged the use of his home as a "station" on the Underground Railroad. At the age of nineteen Minick married a cavalry officer. When she was widowed in 1888, she entered the University of Nebraska Law School and graduated three years later with "fine grades." But Minick found few clients and told a reporter that "a chilly atmosphere was noticeable" whenever she entered a courtroom. Encounters with trial lawyers and judges were not particularly favorable. "Some judges are fair to women lawyers, and others are not. I had a case set for hearing before a certain Nebraska judge. He made remarks which showed that he did not believe in a woman appearing as attorney in a case. I did not say anything to him in court—that would not have been dignified. But I saw him outside and told him that I would have the case transferred because of his prejudice."

After years of seeking help in the courts for families devastated by alcohol, Minick became a strong advocate of Prohibition. She served as a delegate to the International Women's Christian Temperance Union and she wrote extensively about the "octopus" of intemperance. When she was ninety years old she completed a novel about her childhood experiences in Nebraska, *One Family Travels West*, that was filled with references to the problems caused by alcohol. When the main character, Martha, suspects that her teetotaling husband has returned to drinking, she grabs a hatchet and heads for a feed store that doubles as the town's liquor supplier. Once inside, Martha smashes the store's glass shelves and kegs of wine, and shouts:

I am persuaded I cannot or will not demur in the course I have pursued in the past or the one I am pursuing at the present time, in this exposure of the hideous traffic in alcoholic beverage with its demoralizing effects within the home. Alcohol burns out the light of love and cripples beyond human estimation the soul. It hides its hydra-head 'neath the drunkard's couch and kindles the flame of hatred on the cotter's hearth. Finally, it breaks every link of moral obligation of divine origin.

Early women lawyers active in the temperance movement, as Bittenbinder and Minick were, believed that great social reforms would be possible once Prohibition was achieved, and so popular was this view that the Women's Christian Temperance Union swelled its membership to more than 200,000. It is said that when Carry Nation went on one of her saloon-smashing expeditions in Chicago she was "hauled before a magistrate to answer the usual charges of destruction of property and disturbing the peace. The judge told Nation that she was a "madwoman." Nation replied, "Of course I am. One, because I am a woman. Two, because I am sober. Three, because I believe it is possible for a sober woman to change the face of the world." A good many of the early women attorneys shared this outlook.

The link between alcohol and the women's reform movements continued well into the twentieth century, with women increasing their efforts to get the vote and to get women appointed to top-level positions in government. Under President Woodrow Wilson's administration, Annette Abbott Adams was named the first woman Assistant Attorney General of the United States. When Warren G. Harding was elected President in 1920 he, too, felt compelled to give a prestige Justice Department appointment to a woman. The appointment went to Mabel Walker Willebrandt, a thirty-two-year-old attorney from Los Angeles who was born in a sod shanty in Kansas and first attended school at the age of thirteen. Willebrandt was admitted to the California bar in 1915, and in order to gain trial experience, "served without pay in more than 2,000 cases as the first public defender of women in Los Angeles."

Despite the fact that her views on alcohol were liberal and she did not fully support passage of the Volstead Act, in 1921 Willebrandt was appointed the chief Prohibition enforcer in the United States and placed in charge of the Justice Department's tax cases and the Bureau of Prisons as well. It was a prestigious but predictably unpopular job. Lucy Somerville Howorth, a Mississippi lawyer who knew Willebrandt well, believes that the prosecutor's position was given to Willebrandt precisely because she was a woman. "Nobody in the Justice Department wanted that job. It had no political advantages at all. So of course they gave it to Mabel. And even though she wasn't a prohibition supporter, she took it and did an excellent job."

In his history of Prohibition in America, *The Long Thirst,* Thomas Coffey notes the problems Willebrandt had from the outset of her Justice Department career. "Always troubled by the difficulty of finding qualified prosecutors to work under her, and keenly aware that even good men could be corrupted by the huge sums bootleggers were willing to pay for protection, she carefully supervised the prosecutors in her division and quickly dismissed anyone who lost her confidence." This led to a number of department controversies that when leaked to the press made it seem that Willebrandt was in trouble with her subordinates and with the Attorney General as well. "Despite the fact that Mabel Walker Willebrandt came to be known in the press as 'Prohibition Portia,' she regarded prohibition prosecution simply as part of her job and by no means the best part."

Willebrandt continued to stage raids in major cities and "argued more cases before the United States Supreme Court than any contemporary except former Solicitor General William D. Mitchell," but by the spring of 1925 she had "suffered so many setbacks in her difficult job that her friends wondered why she stayed with it." As Coffey points out, it was increasingly impossible to "delude herself about the constantly growing number of people who no longer respected the liquor law as it stood," and her efforts to enforce it.

Four years later Mabel Walker Willebrandt resigned from the Justice Department and established a lucrative private practice in Los Angeles.

After repeal of Prohibition, women lawyers changed their views drastically. Instead of working to close down drinking establishments, they centered their efforts on getting women into them. This was the specific aim of Anne Davidow, who in 1985 was the oldest living woman attorney in Michigan.

Davidow, who graduated from law school in 1920, was an ardent suffragist and union organizer who decided she would not take her husband's name after marriage and would not wear a wedding ring. "When I was about to give birth to my daughter, mother came rushing down to the hospital with a borrowed wedding ring. She was afraid I would disgrace myself—and her."

Davidow recalls standing outside factory gates in Detroit urging workers to support the suffragist cause. "I would be wearing my VOTE FOR WOMEN button and the men would come out and laugh and say, 'Oh, you don't want to be doing this.' My argument was that if they thought enough of women to have them raise their children, how could children respect their mothers if they didn't have the vote?"

After law school Davidow went into private practice, and with attorney Henrietta Rosenthal and others helped to form the Michigan Women Lawyers' Association. "Henrietta and I would sit in Recorder's Court [criminal court] hoping to get some appointments and sometimes we did, but the judges and the court officers always treated us like we were queer creatures."

In the 1940s Davidow was involved in a general practice with her lawyer brother. A group of women came to their office to see if Davidow could help them get jobs as bartenders. Under Michigan's liquor laws women could work as bartenders only if they were the wives or daughters of a licensed bar owner. "It was ridiculous because the reason for the law was so that a woman's morals would not be corrupted by working in a bar. But at the same time it was all right for women to work as barmaids and actually go out from behind the bar and serve drinks and mix with customers. Add to that the qualification that you had to be related to the bar owner and it made absolutely no sense at all. I thought we had a good case."

The United States District Court for the Eastern District of Michigan thought otherwise. With one dissent the three-judge panel denied an injunction to restrain the enforcement of the Michigan law. *Goesaert* v. *Cleary* went directly on appeal to the United States Supreme Court and Anne Davidow found herself in Washington wondering whether she could effectively handle an argument before the nation's highest court. "I was too worried and nervous to think of anything but getting through it. My husband was home in Michigan and he was ill so I was anxious to get back. But they kept putting off our oral argument, so that we had to come back to the Court every day for nearly two weeks. I had only one suit that was appropriate for an appearance before the Supreme Court and I kept worrying what I would do if these delays went on much longer."

Anne Davidow survived oral argument and questions from the Justices, most particularly Felix Frankfurter, who was to deliver the majority opinion of the Court. "I did not suspect the outcome. Judge Frankfurter's decision not only went against us but was disappointing in what it had to say about women." Frankfurter wrote:

The fact that women may now have achieved the virtues that men have long claimed as their prerogatives and now indulge in vices that men have long practiced, does not preclude the States from drawing a sharp line between the sexes, certainly, in such matters as the regulation of the liquor traffic. Since bartending by women may, in the allowable legislative judgment, give rise to moral and social problems against which it may devise preventive measures, the legislature need not go to the full length of prohibition if it believes that as to a defined group of females other factors are operating which either eliminate or reduce the moral and social problems otherwise calling for prohibition. Michigan evidently believes that the oversight assured through ownership of a bar by a barmaid's husband or father minimizes hazards that may confront a barmaid without such protecting oversight. . . . Nor is it unconstitutional for Michigan to withdraw from women the occupation of bartending because it allows women to serve as waitresses where liquor is dispensed.

Justices Rutledge, Douglas and Murphy dissented from the majority opinion, supporting Davidow's argument that the Michigan statute was invalid as a denial of equal protection.

Little more than twenty years later, attorneys Faith Seidenberg and Karen DeCrow, active in the National Organization for Women, challenged the right of public drinking establishments to bar women patrons. DeCrow, who had joined the Syracuse chapter of NOW after learning that she was being paid less than the men at the publishing house where she was employed, admits that she wasn't a feminist at the time, "I just wanted more money." But the pay differentials pointed up to her the many areas of law and society in which women were treated differently and were receiving less. In 1972, DeCrow graduated from Syracuse University Law School. She served as president of NOW from 1974 to 1976.

Faith Seidenberg long had a reputation of being a dedicated civil rights lawyer. A graduate of the Syracuse University Law School in 1954, she served as legal counsel for the Congress of Racial Equality in 1965–66, as vice-president of the National Organization for Women and as a director on the national board of the American Civil Liberties Union. Seidenberg was one of three lawyers who brought suit against the U.S. Equal Employment Opportunity Commission forcing them to outlaw separate "male" and "female" job descriptions in the classified advertisement sections of newspapers.

In January 1969, DeCrow and Seidenberg decided they would seek entry into McSorley's Old Ale House, a century-old saloon in New York City that prided itself on its men-only policy. While women sometimes "invaded" McSorley's by dressing like men, those who were discovered were treated to hoots and catcalls by owners and patrons alike. Not unexpectedly, the two women were barred at the door; they immediately filed suit in federal court. In June 1970, Judge Walter R. Mansfield ordered McSorley's to open its doors to women. The New York *Times* considered the decision worthy of front-page coverage, noting that "Mrs. Seidenberg and Mrs. DeCrow have succeeded where generations of women—bold, wheedling, disguised or defiant—have failed." It quoted Judge Mansfield: "McSorley's is a public place, not a private club, and the preference of certain of its patrons is not justification for discrimination under the equal protection clause of the United States Constitution."

Mansfield went on to note that "the feelings of McSorley's clientele about the sanctity of its masculine atmosphere bear no rational relation to the suitability of women as customers of McSorley's." And, as though answering the assertions of Justice Frankfurter in *Goesaert* v. *Cleary*, Mansfield noted that women no longer were considered "peculiarly delicate and impressionable creatures in need of protection."*

·   ·   ·

---

*A similar lawsuit was brought and won in Connecticut against Yale University's famous all-male bar, Mory's, by Katherine Emmett in 1974. See *Daly* v. *Liquor Control Commission* 35 Connecticut L.J. No. 35.

Beginning with Margaret Brent's demand for a voice and vote in the Maryland Assembly in the seventeenth century and extending more than three hundred years later to Geraldine Ferraro's unsuccessful vice-presidential bid, women have sought equal opportunities in government and equality of treatment in government institutions—and have achieved them only rarely.

Frequently frustrated by the limits they found in the law, a number of the early women attorneys took to soapboxes, the lecture circuit, campaign platforms and the streets to bring about social change. As a Washington, D.C., law student, federal judge Burnita Shelton Matthews picketed the White House in support of suffrage. When U.S. magistrate Marilla Ricker was a private attorney in New Hampshire, she insisted on paying her taxes under protest until her state supported equal rights for women. Tennessee lawyer and feminist Sue Shelton White was arrested in the nation's capital for chaining herself to government buildings in support of suffrage.

Katherine Robinson Everett, who in 1983 was ninety years old, tried her first case more than sixty-five years ago in North Carolina. She believed that women attorneys "always have been more interested in helping people and fighting for causes than in simply making money." Everett recalled that "what made me want to study law in the first place was seeing all these beautiful and talented women lawyers from New York marching for suffrage at President Woodrow Wilson's inauguration. They were so eloquent, so impressive, and they talked about using the law to deal with human rights and human problems. They made it clear that being a lawyer wasn't just a job, it was a way of bringing about important changes in society. I don't think I will ever forget the day I saw that suffrage march."

Ellen Martin was one of the earliest women attorneys in the United States who took to the streets rather than the courtroom in her effort to secure equal voting rights for women. Martin, who was admitted to the Illinois bar in 1876, is believed to have formed—with attorney Mary Frederika Perry—the first female law partnership in the nation. Both women spent much of their adult lives campaigning for suffrage and women's rights.

In 1891 Martin's astute reading of the Lombard, Illinois, city charter convinced her that although women could be barred from voting in state contests, legally they were entitled to vote in municipal elections. She discovered that under the articles of incorporation "all citizens of the state of Illinois above the age of 21, actually residents of the town of Lombard for 90 days before an election for municipal officers, shall have a right to vote at such election." Nowhere was the usual language that voters must be male, white and 21. So Martin, "wearing her hair severly [sic] pulled back from her face in a knot, her spectacles still perched on top of her head . . ." triumphantly organized and led a delegation of fourteen women through the main street of town to the polls to demand their right to vote.

Town officials unsuccessfully tried to keep secret the news of Ellen Martin's suffrage march and vote, but the news quickly traveled back to her native Jamestown, New York. When the First Political Equality Club of the city of Jamestown learned of her achievement it immediately sent its good wishes and congratulations by way of "resolutions of respect for Miss Ellen A. Martin for her recent voting in Lombard, Illinois, thus pioneering the effort for equal Political Liberty":

Knowing Miss Martin, as we do, it is not difficult for us to appreciate her earnestness and determination, when armed with the ballot and fortified by her law-brief, Ethan Allen-like, she demanded her right and compelled compliance. Confident in her legal premises and anticipating their mode of warfare, she disarmed her enemies by choosing her own challenger and, before the election Board could rally to other defence, she had her vote safely deposited in the sacred box. . . . Independence of this character, though slurred by the rabble and scoffed at by the unthinking and inconsiderate, will win applause and, in due time, rescue our country from threatened overthrow.

Historian Margot Fruhe, who uncovered newspaper accounts of the Martin vote, noted the town's reaction to the woman lawyer's interpretation of city law:

Completely taken by surprise, the three election judges, Reber, Vance and Marquardt, allowed the women to vote, thereby earning the disgust of the local male population. There was immediate talk of reorganizing under the state law which specified that every free white male citizen . . . shall have the right to vote. Since there is no legal record of women voting in Lombard after 1891, in municipal elections, it seems likely that this is what was done. In fact only diligent research of the newspapers of that year produced the above story. Even the town minutes record the election as ordinary and uneventful.

Far from ordinary were newspaper accounts of Kansas lawyer Mary Clynen Lease, one of the greatest orators of her time. Newspapermen, unaccustomed to a woman seizing the platform and commanding the attention of crowds of up to 20,000, called her everything from the "Wichita Cyclone" to the "Ironjawed Woman of Kansas" to the "Red Dragon." One publication, the Greenwood County *Republican,* found her to be enough of a political threat to warn its readers that Mary Lease was "political humbug in the shape of a brazen faced female commonly known as 'Old Mother Lease, the she-lawyer.' Woman full of venom and brass, of hard words and abuse of others. Beware of her. She advises you to defy the law of the land."

The woman who engendered such extreme reaction was the oldest child of an Irish political activist who came to America in the 1850s and who died in the Andersonville prison during the Civil War. As a child, Lease was sent out to work to help support the family, but she continued to attend school and earned her teaching certificate at the age of fifteen. After learning that wages out West were considerably higher, she applied for a teaching position at the Osage Mission in Kansas, which paid nearly double her Pennsylvania salary. A Kansas reporter noted that "she arrived at 18 to astonish much older folks with her positiveness and learning. A pretty girl with unusually piercing blue eyes, she had suitors in plenty." The man she chose to marry in 1873 was Charles Lease, a druggist who was about to give up his pharmacy to try homesteading. After their marriage he and Mary Lease filed a land claim in Kingman County and spent the next several years farming and raising a family of four children. But it was becoming increasingly evident that they could not survive at homesteading. Dorothy Levenson in her book *Women of the West* profiles Mary Lease's struggles and describes the problems that families such as the Leases encountered on the plains, among them erratic weather conditions, prairie fires and grasshoppers. Even when farmers survived these natural disasters and brought in a healthy crop they were so dependent on storage elevator operators and railroad companies to ship their wheat to the eastern markets that it was impossible for them to make a substantial profit. More often than not they had to borrow money from banks at exorbitant interest rates, and foreclosure on farms was a frequent occurrence. As a result, farmers began to organize to fight the railroads and the banks, and granges began to be formed throughout the West.

The Lease family moved to Wichita so that Charles could return to working in a pharmacy. According to Levenson, the family was still so poor that Mary Lease began washing clothes for other people, earning a meager fifty cents a day. In order to get through the drudgery of her days, she borrowed books for herself and her children, then copied out pages and tacked them on a wall for reading while she was washing clothes. A local attorney took an interest in her and suggested that if she was going to study while doing laundry, the subject might as well be law. In less than a year Mary Lease was on her way to Topeka to take the bar examination. She passed and immediately let it be known that she would never take a fee for her services, since she believed lawyers had a special duty to help the poor and work for social justice.

In 1888 Mary Lease gave her first public speech on a subject of special interest to her deceased father: Irish nationalism. Her talk was so well received it led to invitations for others on a variety of topics, such as women's suffrage, temperance and labor reform. Lease admitted that at first she was reticent about giving speeches but warned that now "my tongue is loose at both ends and hung on a swivel so I'm likely to have considerable notoriety in the near future." The Wichita *Eagle & Beacon Magazine* called this "a prophecy which turned out to be a masterpiece of understatement."

In the late nineteenth century the Populist movement was growing in Kansas, due in large part to the dissatisfaction of farmers and laborers who were being exploited by big business. Mary Lease was eager to join the cause. In a public square at Olathe, Kansas, she forcefully delivered an address that captured the angry mood of her farm audience:

You farmers were told two years ago to raise a big crop. Well, you did and what became of it? Six-cent corn, ten-cent oats, two-cent beef and no price at all for butter and eggs—that's what became of it. The politicians said we suffered from overproduction. Yet 10,000 children starve to death every year in the United States. The common people are robbed to enrich their masters.

What you farmers need to do is to raise less corn and more hell!

Instantly she was a force in Kansas politics, more in demand than any other speaker on the lecture circuit. Mary Lease took an active role in Populist politics, particularly in the 1890 campaign. Writer Leta Bright notes that while Lease made one hundred and sixty speeches that year, she still was so poor that she was "clad in a high-collared dress which was black so that it wouldn't show the dirt." By now Lease was thirty-seven years old and described as "a tall stately woman with dark hair, blue eyes, and having the face of the dreamer and the poet."

She continued to draw crowds eager to hear her brazenly take on the big-money interests. Lease told a cheering audience of several thousand Kansans:

For one hundred years the stock jobbers, land robbers, bondholders and pirates have knocked unceasingly on the doors of congress and congress has in every instance acceded to their robber demands. . . . You may call me an anarchist or a socialist. I care not, but I hold to the theory that if one man has not enough to eat three times a day and another man has 25 million dollars that last man has something that belongs to the first. Our laws are the output of a system which clothes rascals in robes and honesty in rags!

Senator John Ingalls of Kansas, worried about Mary Lease's increasing influence in the state, decided to attack her involvement in what he perceived to be an all-male domain. "Woman has no place in politics," he announced. "Mrs. Lease had better be home mending her children's stockings." Ingalls, whose political judgment up until then had been formidable, could not have picked a worse issue or opponent. From that point on, Mary Lease doggedly stumped the state of Kansas to campaign against him, and she successfully put an end to Ingalls's sixteen-year career in the Senate. Even after his political defeat Lease continued to attack him. Ingalls's response: "It seems the only creatures low enough to scalp the dead men are Indians and women." The following year Populist governor Lorenzo Dow Lewelling appointed Mary Lease president of the State Board of Charities, the first woman to hold such a high-level position, but he later tried to remove her when she became too outspoken about the needs for reform. Lease successfully sued to retain her position, but it was becoming apparent that with the passage of time both she and the Populist Party were having much less influence in Kansas politics.

In 1900 Mary Lease moved to New York City to work as a political reporter for Joseph Pulitzer's liberal New York *World*. Once in New York, Lease continued to be a popular speaker on her favorite issues: women's suffrage, birth control and labor organizing. Still convinced that lawyers had a duty to give free legal services to the poor, Lease opened a law office on the Lower East Side of Manhattan but refused to accept fees. The Kansas City *Star*, noting the observations of some, said that those who ridiculed the small and dingy office were the same people who "scoffed at the idea that a Kansas woman could have legal ability or sincere intelligence. They did not know that the rent was paid out of the woman's pocket and she would not accept a penny of remuneration for the cases, lost or won."

The move to New York did not temper Mary Lease's views of politics, the legal system or herself. Toward the end of her career she bitterly complained:

Of course you know how justice is carried on in New York. Perjury, jury fixing and bribery of magistrates has been the recipe for law practice in every world metropolis from Babylon down to the racketeering New York of today. When a New York corporation lawyer receives a $100,000 fee it does not all go into his pocket. It is split five to seven ways before he gets the verdict.

I had studied the law like an honest Abe Lincoln hoping, through the knowledge of corporation law, to fit myself to head the greatest corporation of all as President of the United States. In that position I could have been the advocate of the poor man politically and economically. . . . In battling for the rights of the common people I was not equipped to win. So I gave up the aim of being the advocate of the people from high political office and decided to devote my life to doing what good I could individually among the poor. I took their cases without pay. And I never lost a case that went before a jury.

Lease's view that governmental institutions were corrupt and that attorneys ought to devote themselves to bringing about social reforms was shared by an equally colorful Kansan—Lyda Burton Conley.

Conley, a native of Kansas City, was the first native American woman lawyer in the United States, and it was said of her that "trouble was her prerogative; she thrived on trouble." Conley was a descendant of the Wyandotte tribe, which settled in Kansas in the mid-nineteenth century and was nearly wiped out by a smallpox epidemic that killed Conley's mother and three hundred others in 1844. The victims were interred at Huron Park in separate Indian burial grounds.

In 1904 Lyda Conley and her sister, Lena, learned that Congress and the U.S. Secretary of the Interior had authorized the razing of the Indian cemetery to make way for a commercial development project. The Conleys were outraged that the sanctity of the burial grounds would be violated in such a cavalier manner and they decided to act quickly. As *Kansas* magazine reported:

And, so, in the stillness of the night, these two women, the "Conley sisters," as every one knows them in Kansas City, went into the cemetery, unloosed the iron gate, and with crude boards, painted with even more crude letters, they wound their way through the little place, and at every spot where slept a blood relative, these women planted a sign at the head of the graves: "Trespassers, Beware!"

They builded a hut within the grounds, close to the graves of their parents, with tiny windows overlooking the cemetery on all sides. They loaded their guns and took up their abode in that city of the dead, and the word went out that the first man to turn a sod over one of those graves would either turn another for the Conley sisters, or have some other person perform a like service for himself.

Onlookers called their six- by eight-foot shack Fort Conley. Lena, who preferred to use her Indian name, Floating Voice, maintained the cemetery grounds by "felling dead trees with an ax while awed bystanders admired the play of her muscles. . . ." When that didn't work she put curses on anyone who invaded the area and tried to disturb her peace. Realizing her sister's unorthodox methods would not be enough to prevent federal troops from tearing down Fort Conley, Lyda decided to use more conventional means. Her solution was to study law and to represent herself and the Wyandottes in a lawsuit against the United States government. Armed with a musket and standing watch in the

wood-frame shack, Lyda Burton Conley studied for the bar examination and prepared research for her upcoming litigation.

All the while the Conley sisters continued to erect barriers on the
cemetery grounds and to place TRESPASS AT YOUR PERIL signs along the
perimeters. Building contractors repeatedly tore down the fences only
to have Lyda and Lena put them up again. One reporter who came to
cover the siege found the assignment overwhelming: "The writer took
a pencil and tried to figure the number of times the fence was destroyed
and rebuilt during a fortnight in the winter of 1907, but gave it up."
On at least one occasion the sisters defended their barricades with
sticks and stones.

The legal situation was equally confusing. Newspaper reports indicated that for nearly six years "the rightful ownership of the cemetery
remained in doubt unless it could be said that the Conleys owned it
by the right of possession. There was a federal order to remove the
bodies to Quindaro cemetery, but it was qualified in such a way as to
leave grounds for suits in the federal courts and Lyda Conley took full
advantage of this opportunity, supported by women's clubs and others
with whom sentiment outweighed commercialism and twentieth-century progress."

Lyda Conley was not yet a member of the bar—she would gain
admission in 1910—but nonetheless she began proceedings in the U.S.
District Court in Topeka, seeking to enjoin the federal government
from removing the bodies from the cemetery and from selling the land
to speculators. When the Topeka justices refused to grant an injunction
Lyda Conley knew she was on her way to the U.S. Supreme Court.

Now she was the subject of even greater interest in the press. She
told an interviewer for *Kansas* magazine that she was determined to
win her lawsuit:

"I will go to Washington and personally defend it," she told me and when
I, in my ignorance, asked her whether she was admitted to practice in the
supreme court, this brave woman replied: "No, but I am willing to take the
examination, if I can find any one at the capital who will stand sponsor for
me. But," she continued, "you know one can plead his own case in any court
and this I intend to do. No lawyer could plead for the grave of my mother
as I could, no lawyer could have the heart interest in the case that I have."
"Shall I win?" she asked as a smile played over her features. "If I do not then

there is no cemetery in this land safe from sale, at the will of the government. The land was once deeded in perpetuity by the government, as a burial place for the Wyandotte tribe; by common consent it has been used as such all these years, and Congress overstepped its authority when it dared to pass a law to disturb those graves. If I lose, then I will admit that the constitution of the United States is as Greek to me."

Conley submitted a sixty-nine-page legal brief to the U.S. Supreme Court in *Conley* v. *Garfield et al.* and went to Washington, D.C., to argue the case. Not unexpectedly, the Supreme Court refused to interfere with the decision of Congress and the U.S. Department of the Interior. But while the Conley sisters may have lost the case, in effect they won the battle. Their actions brought so much attention to the proposed land deal that in 1912 the House Indian Affairs committee reported a bill prohibiting removal of the cemetery. For the next forty years the cemetery remained virtually untouched while Lyda Conley continued to watch over it and to take on a few small cases. A friend remembered Conley as being intellectually capable for the practice of law but "as a lawyer, she almost starved to death. She wouldn't prosecute anybody and she wouldn't defend anybody guilty except an Indian. So she didn't have many cases."

For women lawyers like Lyda Conley success was hardly ever measured in financial terms. She studied law to further a cause she believed in and the depth of her commitment made the struggle possible. A reporter once asked her what she would have done if federal troops actually had been sent in to take over the cemetery. Conley insisted such an event never would have happened, but when pressed for an answer, passionately said, "We had two large American flags in the shack, and in the event of the troops putting in an appearance, we had decided to wrap the folds of the flag around us, and tell the boys in blue to shoot—for they would have to do that before they could disturb those graves . . . we were fighting for the grave of our mother, and what could any one do in such a case like that, but die rather than surrender?"

The notion that commitment to a cause was more important than financial success inspired many of these women to study law and to practice under difficult conditions. Prior to World War I, attorney Mary Lilly bitterly complained: "Men have accused the woman lawyer of being a failure. A failure, forsooth, because she has not grown rich in the practice of law, and that in the short space of twenty years. The man's standards again—the acquisition of wealth and power. I would say to these accusers the aim of the woman lawyer is not so much the acquisition of money as to make an impression in the laws of this country as will benefit the whole race . . ."

Women such as Illinois's Catherine Waugh McCulloch and Sophonisba Preston Breckinridge were prominent among a number of women activists who were volunteering their services to settlement houses in Boston, Chicago and New York during this period. McCulloch had been warned by a senior member of the Evanston bar, Albert Early, that her work on behalf of women's causes and the poor was jeopardizing her career. He told her, "If you want to make a success in your profession, stop spending so much time on church and temperance and suffrage. The people who ask you to speak at churches and clubs for the love of the cause will bring all their valuable business to me and other men who concentrate on business." McCulloch remembered being stung by those remarks but grudgingly admitted, "He was not very far wrong." Still she refused to give up her commitment to social and legislative reform and to giving legal assistance to the poor.

Sophonisba Breckinridge, who in 1904 became the first woman graduate of the University of Chicago Law School, earned her doctorate at the university as well. She was considered a pioneer in social services administration and was named president of the American Association of Schools of Social Work. Breckinridge also helped to found the Social Service Review.

California's first woman lawyer, Clara Shortridge Foltz, who with Laura De Force Gordon successfully sued the Hastings College of the Law for admission, spent ten years in New York City running a law practice to help immigrant women. Her office was aptly described as "a rendezvous for the poor, the sick and the despairing."

In 1901 Rosalie Loew became attorney in chief of the Legal Aid Society of New York. Two years earlier she helped to found and served as first president of the Women Lawyers' Association (now the National Association of Women Lawyers). At a time when Legal Aid was offering the following advice to immigrant men to help them avoid marital difficulties—"Do not interfere with a woman in the management of purely domestic affairs—and do not keep a lodger"—it was considered "something of an event" that a woman should hold such a high position. Loew never doubted her ability to handle the job. She had shown remarkable self-assurance at her admission to the federal district court in Trenton. When her sponsor, attorney James S. Wight, moved Loew's admission to the U.S. District Court he told the presiding justice that he supposed it would be more gallant if he paid Loew's admission fee. Loew flatly rejected the offer. "My first legal advice after being admitted to practice in this court shall be to you—and it is this: never allow your sentiment to run away with your pocketbook."

Annie Savery, an 1874 law graduate of the University of Iowa, devoted her career to promoting women's suffrage. She said she studied law without any real intention of practicing but never refused to handle the case of "some poor woman who should be without money." Oregon's Olive Stott Gabriel, a noted suffragist and later president of the National Association of Women Lawyers, also had a reputation of "never having refused a woman's case." Detroit's Martha Strickland, who maintained a practice assisting poor women and who wrote extensively on the status of women in the law, urged female attorneys to work vigorously on behalf of equality: "Women's legal rights have been brought to the bar of masculine knowledge and manly chivalry. The result is that women have suffered and through women all humanity have suffered . . ."

The heyday of the suffragist and equal rights movements coincided with those of the progressive, populist and socialist movements in the United States in the period surrounding World War I—and it was not surprising to find women lawyers active in several camps.

Montana's first woman lawyer, Ella Knowles Haskell, was admitted to the bar in 1889 and began handling charity cases and becoming active in state politics. Observers claimed her interest was in bringing about social change and that "she was a vigorous opponent of anything which she regarded as an injustice."

In Wisconsin, Belle Case La Follette, who was born in a log cabin and went on to become the first woman law graduate of the state university in 1885, was an outspoken supporter of the rights of women and workers despite the fact that she was married to the governor of the state. When asked if her political views needed to be tempered in view of her husband's position, she insisted they didn't and proudly said, "I am more radical than Mr. La Follette," implying she would have more to say on issues in the future. The New York *Times* in describing La Follette said that "for her the question before the people always was—'which shall rule—wealth or man; which shall lead—money or intellect; who shall fill public station—educated free men or the feudal serfs of corporate capital?' "

While socialist and radical activity may, at times, have been considered a predominantly urban pursuit, by 1912 there were 118,000 members of the Socialist Party living in all areas of the United States. During this period the Socialist Party's voting strength was even higher, consisting of almost 6 percent of the total electorate in 1912 and being responsible for the election of approximately 1,200 public officials.

Two women attorneys from the Southwest during this era were proving just how effectively they could organize farmers and laborers in rural America. Ida Hayman Callery, daughter of an Oklahoma socialist, was a teacher in the federal school for Creek Indians in the early 1900s when she was recruited into the Oklahoma Socialist Party. She became secretary of the statewide organization, then four years later took over as secretary in Arkansas, holding that position for three consecutive terms. Callery achieved remarkable results in a very short period of time and quickly came to the attention of national organizers. A. W. Ricker of the New York *Call,* a socialist newspaper, noted in 1912 that

teaching and training mountaineers and cotton pickers to pay dues and keep locals alive has not been easy. It was not until Ida Callery, a native Arkansas girl, but who was raised and schooled in Oklahoma, was brought into the State by the Executive Committee and made its State Secretary, that the organization has been made self-sustaining. She is a typical woman of the Southwest prairies, to whose native independence and courage have been added the culture and enlightenment of education. She is small and wiry, and can pound the typewriter all the day and into the night without nervous prostration. She has literally reached out into the mountains and valleys and led the people into organizing and maintaining locals . . .

Within six months Callery increased membership in the Arkansas Socialist Party from 400 to 2,376. Her next priority was greater participation for women within the party:

It has been my plan from the first to develop local workers. I believe that if we are to take over the government we must first learn to conduct our own organization. . . . My special work for women is to make the comrades understand that women are to be brought into the locals and suggest plans for the comrades by which they might be brought in.

At the expiration of her term of office in 1916, Ida Callery joined her husband's law firm in Pittsburg, Kansas. She said her purpose was "to help and brighten the lives of the poor and distressed who crossed her path . . . in the practice of law the same ideal was ahead of her that had always been, the emancipation of the working class." But within a year, Ida Hayman Callery was dead of cancer at the age of thirty.

The woman who virtually picked up where Callery left off was Caroline Lowe, who also had been a teacher and an effective organizer for the Socialist Party in Kansas. Mari Jo Buhle, author of *Women and American Socialism,* points out the difficulties Lowe faced in her organizing efforts in southeast Kansas:

Unlike the Kansas towns where a mystical, Christian Socialism had flourished, this region was dotted with coal towns where class-conscious miners filled the party's ranks, although their wives played a more marginal role. Lowe sought to recruit these women through schoolhouse meetings in towns like Pleasanton, Fort Scott, and Englevale. She sold subscriptions to party publications and distributed thousands of membership applications. During the summer of 1909 she toured the encampments of Oklahoma and achieved regional fame as a popular speaker.

By 1912 Caroline Lowe was secretary of the Socialist Party's women's national committee, then went on to head the women's department at national headquarters in Chicago. It was during this period that she began studying law and in 1916 was admitted to the Kansas bar.

Lowe immediately joined the defense team that was representing seventy-four members of the Industrial Workers of the World, or

"Wobblies," as they popularly were called, radical unionists who were being tried in the state of Washington for murder. The *Illinois Miner,* a pro-labor journal, noted Caroline Lowe's involvement in the case and added that "so successful were the lawyers for the defense that the jury found a verdict of not guilty despite the fact that newspapers all over the country were calling for convictions."

The *Miner* felt Lowe's commitment to the socialist and labor movements was significant:

Headquarters of the I.W.W. from coast to coast were raided on September 5, 1917, and a whole sale arrest of officials followed. The Great Red Scare was at its height. More than one hundred workers were herded into Chicago for trial and again Miss Lowe took the side of the defense. The trial which followed lasted for five months. This was the famous case of the U.S. vs. William D. Haywood, et al. Despite all the efforts of the workers' lawyers, however, public opinion had become so inflamed against the I.W.W. that the jury verdict of guilty was practically a foregone conclusion.

Miss Lowe did not abandon her labor clients. For six months in the winter of 1918 and 1919, while workers were being hounded by all the forces of organized wealth, she put up a courageous battle on the behalf of defenseless men and women persecuted for holding unorthodox opinions. She aided in the defense of the deportees brought to Ellis Island in New York in the infamous "Red Special" and was finally rewarded by the unconditional release of the defendants. Then came the trial of twenty-five I.W.W.'s at Wichita, Kansas, on charges identical with those brought at Chicago. Once more Miss Lowe was found on the side of the defense.

Historian Thomas Braker notes that between trials Lowe traveled to Connecticut to assist Kate Richards O'Hare in her fight for prison reform. And when she wasn't involved in criminal defense work, Lowe was helping immigrants and championing suffragist causes.

In 1923 Lowe became a partner in the firm of Callery & Callery in Pittsburg, Kansas. Its largest client was the United Mine Workers of America, and it handled a substantial amount of workmen's compensation cases filed on behalf of injured miners. But Lowe never lost her passion for labor organizing and socialism:

In my opinion the one vital problem facing the labor movement is the achieving of working-class solidarity. If a woman be employed, her immediate problem should be to organize her fellow-workers into the union if there is one. If not, she should do all in her power to educate her fellow-workers to the realization of the need of a union. If she is not employed in industry she should do all within her power to aid in the organization of those who are. The most effective weapon in the hands of a constructive labor movement is a strong industrial organization and women as part of the working class must aid in constructing and wielding this weapon.

In New York City in and around the World War I period, women lawyers were championing a variety of reform and radical causes. Most of them had graduated from the New York University Law School and continued to be active in the social and political life of Greenwich Village after earning their degrees. Perhaps the best known of these "new women" was Crystal Eastman, who with her brother Max edited the magazine *Liberator,* the radical journal that first printed John Reed's eyewitness account of the Bolshevik Revolution, "Ten Days That Shook the World." After graduating with honors from Vassar and earning her law degree at New York University in 1907, Eastman was appointed to the New York State Employers' Liability Commission. During the next two years she drafted the New York State Workmen's Compensation Law and wrote extensively about the need to correct unsafe working conditions. Her book *Work Accidents and the Law* is believed to have been responsible for major reform of factory conditions in New York and in cities throughout the United States. Eastman wrote that "when healthy women and men die because of preventable disasters we do not want to hear about relief funds—what we want is to start a revolution."

Crystal Eastman was equally committed to the causes of suffrage, birth-control reform and world peace. With pacifist Roger Baldwin she founded the American Civil Liberties Union (called the American Union Against Militarism) and helped to defend conscientious objectors and war resisters during World War I. With pacifist Alice Paul and others she formed the Women's Peace Party. Eastman's friends included a number of radical women attorneys who also had received their law degrees at New York University. These included the wealthy Ida Rauh, who "had renounced so hotly all the frills and luxuries of bourgeois life that she lived almost like a pauper. She would bring one informal garment and would lie . . . reading or sleeping all day long." Unlike Crystal Eastman, who seemed to do everything well, Rauh dabbled in a lot of things but managed to accomplish very little. Shortly after earning her law degree, Rauh joined the Legal Aid Society. She handled one case that required her to represent a client in surrogate's court, then quit. That one experience, she claimed, convinced her that "practicing law meant fraternizing with Tammany Hall politicians," something she did not care to do. Rauh then went on to try acting, sculpting, painting and radical politics. Later she was arrested for her involvement in a birth-control march and demonstration. Arrested with her was Jessie Ashley, sister of New York University Law School dean Clarence Ashley, the strong supporter of NYU's woman's law class and of women's enrollment in the regular law school. After graduating from NYU Law School, Jessie Ashley went on to obtain her master of law degree. She then joined the faculty of the woman's law class. In 1913 Ashley served as defense counsel for Elizabeth Gurley Flynn, the labor organizer for the International Workers of the World who was prosecuted by the government for her participation in "subversive activities." Ashley helped to found the Women Lawyers' Association in New York and ran on the Socialist ticket for chief justice of New York's highest court, the court of appeals. Ashley strongly believed women could make a difference in the law and often encouraged her students to join the profession and then change it. Her view was that women lawyers were too often accepting of the laws men had made and not outspoken enough about needed reforms:

Many of our unjust and vicious laws regarding women have been painfully changed by the efforts of women. When women really understand the legal conditions and complications our country faces their first impulse (if they are not lawyers) is to change things "somehow" and they succeed, too, after a bitter struggle. But unless "retained" to draw a particular bill, or to investigate a particular situation, our women attorneys are not found in the ranks of those seeking changes. They are found reverencing the law, particularly the Constitution and the Supreme Court. To point out to them the abominable "not guilty" decision in the Triangle Fire case is to hear merely, "Well, that is the law." To ask them why it takes years to get rid of the use of a poison in the manufacture of matches that causes the horrible disease "phossy-jaw" is to hear an exposition on the property rights of the manufacturer. If asked why it is a worse crime to steal a diamond than to steal a girl we hear that it is almost impossible to "do" anything about the girl and easy to handle the theft of property.

Also in the group of radical women lawyers from New York was Inez Milholland Boissevain, who had applied for admission to Columbia Law School but was rejected because of her sex. Boissevain went to NYU Law School instead, and after graduation represented a number of poor clients for no fee. She joined Jessie Ashley in becoming an active member of the Women Lawyers' Association and in fighting for social causes, but may have been more dedicated to the bohemian lifestyle than to the causes that captured the attention of the radicals in Greenwich Village. Max Eastman caustically observed, "Inez, for all her radical opinions, lived a high-geared metropolitan function-attending, opera-going, rich-girl's life. Her time was full of meaningless appointments and her house was always full of male guests—a kaleidoscopic succession of men about town, millionaires, bounders, authors, opera singers, labor fakes, and now and then an earnest socialist or a real celebrity."

Considerably more dedicated to the cause was Carol Weiss King, a wealthy young socialist who was an authority in immigration law. She also obtained her law degree at NYU and it was said that "from the first her interest was in defending the victims of anti-radical hysteria whose civil rights had in one way or another been violated." King joined the law firm of Hale Neels & Schorr and wrote a number of the important briefs in deportation cases that reached the United States Supreme Court. Most of these were centered on allegations that her clients knowingly had in their possession for the purpose of distribution printed matter that advocated the overthrow of the government of the United States by force.

King went on to participate in the landmark Supreme Court case *Herndon v. Lowry,* involving the convictions of Georgia and Oregon radicals in which the "clear and present danger" test was applied; the first of the "Scottsboro Boys" cases; defense of the president of the

International Longshoreman's and Warehouseman's Union, who was facing deportation; and defense of clients being prosecuted under the McCarran Act.

Sharing King's views on civil liberties was Dorothy Kenyon, an attorney who also had had a privileged background. Kenyon described herself as having been a "social butterfly" until a trip to Mexico "awakened her to social injustice." From that point on, she devoted herself to assisting liberal and radical causes. After she passed the bar in 1917, Kenyon did research for the government on wartime labor and prepared studies for the 1919 peace conferences. Still maintaining her influential contacts, she was among the first women attorneys to gain admission to the prestigious Association of the Bar of the City of New York while at the same time chairing commissions on welfare, public housing, minimum wages and revising procedures for New York City's women's courts. Kenyon made no secret of her view that women were being unfairly prosecuted in prostitution cases and urged that there be stronger enforcement of "exploiter" pimps and johns.

In 1936 Mayor Fiorello La Guardia named Dorothy Kenyon his First Deputy Commissioner of Licenses. Three years later he appointed her to the city's municipal court. But it was in her capacity as commissioner that Kenyon received the greatest notice. The public was intrigued with the notion of a woman being in charge of licensing the city's burlesque houses and strip clubs, particularly at a time when women's groups actively were urging that these establishments be raided and closed down. To the delight of many, Kenyon refused to ban burlesque in New York, claiming that she would not participate in a process that removed "the only beauty in the lives of icemen and messenger boys."

Kenyon was an active supporter of the American Civil Liberties Union, as were Eastman and King, and she served on its board of directors. In 1950 Wisconsin senator Joseph McCarthy accused her of being "affiliated with at least twenty-eight Communist front organizations." Although friends advised her to remain silent to the attack, Kenyon refused, calling McCarthy "an unmitigated liar, a coward to take shelter in the cloak of congressional immunity." Dorothy Kenyon died in 1972. She perhaps best described her life and her career when she told a reporter for the New York *Times*, "I always pick the losing cause. I guess I'm crazy about the underdog. But I think I'm helping women by my way of life."

Dorothy Kenyon's decision to keep open the burlesque houses was reversed a year later, and when it was, a number of women lawyers were responsible for that change. Edith Spivack, one of the first women graduates of Columbia Law School and currently New York City's executive assistant corporation counsel, recalls that when she joined city government in the 1930s, Mayor La Guardia, at his wife's urging, was hiring a number of women attorneys to key positions, among them Rosalie Loew Whitney and Dorothy Kenyon. There were enough women to form an association that met monthly and was called the Women of the Administration. Its purpose was to discuss the operations of their respective agencies and to give mutual support. Spivack remembers, "Mayor La Guardia was leaning towards closing down the notorious Minsky's burlesque house, but Minsky's attorneys were insisting that the dance performances were not obscene and in fact were works of art." La Guardia decided to let the Women of the Administration see the show for themselves and give him their opinion. Spivack recalls, "There were about ten of us and the most memorable had to have been Rosalie Loew Whitney. By then she was a sedate older woman, with a huge bosom, and she always wore old-fashioned dresses, the kind with high collars and stays. We walked into Minsky's to our reserved seats in the fourth and fifth rows and the first thing I noticed was how crowded with sailors the audience was. We were absolutely shocked by the striptease show, but after a while I got used to it and it just seemed so doggone tasteless and boring and the humor was so low." Spivack's delegation informed the mayor that the dancing it had witnessed definitely could not be considered a work of art. Shortly thereafter Minsky's was closed and moved across the river to New Jersey.

The burlesque-house incidents serve as a reminder that well within this century women still were being viewed as the keepers of society's moral and spiritual values, better able to exercise judgment in these areas and to offer advice to men in power than to wield that power themselves. When the advice was consistent with male views of respectability and family life, it was accepted—when it suggested more extensive rights and decision-making power for women, it was questioned or ignored. In the fight for reform of birth-control and abortion laws, women found themselves almost entirely alone.

In 1914 attorney Isabel Giles pointed out that "it has taken until the twentieth century for women to realize that men and women 'sin two by two, and that they are punished one by one, and the woman is the one.' " In the 1920s Crystal Eastman, who by then had an international reputation in labor law, was speaking out about the need to connect family planning with the economic independence of women. It was an unpopular issue. Still she insisted that "the immediate feminist program must include voluntary motherhood. Freedom of any kind for women is hardly worth considering unless it is assumed that they will know how to control the size of their families. 'Birth control' is just as elementary an essential in our propaganda as is 'equal pay.' Women are to have children when they want . . ."

Yet it would not be until the 1930s that the United States Supreme Court invalidated the Comstock Law prohibiting the mailing of obscene material—which was how contraceptive devices were defined.

The attorney most associated with changes in the birth-control and censorship laws and with the development of the reproductive rights movement is Harriet F. Pilpel. After graduating with honors from Vassar College, Pilpel went to Columbia Law School and graduated in 1935, ranking second in her class. Currently she is counsel to the New York law firm Weil, Gotshal & Manges and general counsel of the Planned Parenthood Federation of America.

Pilpel remembers that her interest in birth-control issues began early in life. "I grew up hearing my mother and her sister lamenting the fact that women can't have lives of their own because they're prey to a biological event." Her grandfather, she insists, was "either oversexed or his wives were particularly stupid because he had nine children by his first wife and seven children by his second." Pilpel's mother was the thirteenth of those sixteen children, and Pilpel remembers her as being "a very dependent person," whose example she was not eager to follow.

Despite her brilliant academic record, she received few job offers. "What a shame," one Wall Street lawyer told her, "with your record we would hire you on the spot—if you were a man." One hiring partner for a large firm offered to give her a position in the estates department, where two other women attorneys held jobs, but one look at the surroundings convinced Pilpel to look elsewhere. "We went up a staircase and there, like in a Dickens novel, were these two unfortunates bent over a stack of law books. I knew I couldn't spend my life doing that."

She decided to attempt an interview with Morris Ernst, senior partner of Greenbaum, Wolff & Ernst, an attorney known for his supportive views of women in the legal profession and for his expertise in civil liberties litigation. Ernst told Pilpel he would give her only five minutes to convince him to hire her, and "in even less time I did." It was the beginning of an association that was to last forty years, bringing Pilpel well-known clients with such diverse interests and backgrounds as Margaret Sanger, Jerome Kern, Alfred Kinsey and Edna Ferber.

Pilpel participated in a number of important reproductive rights cases, including *United States* v. *One Package,* a federal lawsuit that affirmed the right of a gynecologist to receive "a package containing 120 vaginal pessaries more or less, alleged to be imported contrary to section 305(a) of the Tariff Act of 1930 . . ." and *United States of America* v. *31 Photographs* in which a foundation for later developments in obscenity law was established when "obscene" materials were released to sex researcher Dr. Alfred Kinsey for scientific use at Indiana University. Pilpel recalled that before Dr. Kinsey accepted her as his attorney, she and her husband had to travel to the Midwest to give a detailed "case history" on their sex life that covered more than five hundred items. "People like to think sex research is interesting but frankly I found most of it quite boring," she later said.

Pilpel continued to work in the field of reproductive rights, participating in the landmark cases *Griswold* v. *Connecticut,* in which the U.S. Supreme Court struck down a state law banning the distribution of contraceptives, and *Roe* v. *Wade,* the 1973 case in which the Supreme Court ruled that a woman's right of privacy included the right to decide whether or not to have an abortion. She still is convinced that the struggle women have had in the area of reproductive rights is indicative of the larger problems they face in achieving equality in all areas of their lives.

Sharing Pilpel's view are a number of women attorneys who sought positions in government with the hope of reforming almost entirely male-dominated Cabinets and legislatures. Three-term congresswoman Bella Abzug, who was as much known for her sharp intelligence and outspokenness as she was for her wide-brimmed hats, insists that "whoever conducts our government will have to recognize this is not a 'for-men-only' nation. . . . I can recall house discussions on abortion in which it was clear that some of my male colleagues knew less about the uterus than about a U-Haul, but that did not stop them from deciding the fate of women." Similarly, when Democratic vice-presidential candidate Geraldine Ferraro was in Congress she recalled the debate she had with a prominent supporter of a bill that would limit the right of women to have abortions. "We were talking about victims of rape, a subject I was particularly familiar with, since I had been chief of the bureau in the District Attorney's office that handled rape prosecutions. And here was this congressman telling me that if rape victims were so concerned about possible pregnancy, why couldn't they be mandated to have a D & C procedure immediately following the rape? That way an abortion wouldn't be necessary. His lack of understanding, let alone his lack of compassion, made me wonder why women were so trusting of men to make laws that so greatly affected their lives."

The link between fighting for the rights of women and fighting for the rights of the poor has always been obvious to women lawyers, since so many of their female clients have been at the poverty level. Several studies have indicated that more women than men are poor and it is harder for them to escape poverty. Of all Americans living in poverty, 75 percent are women and children. By the year 2000 it is predicted that figure will rise to almost 100 percent.

Up until the 1960s women lawyers who were fighting for causes or defending the poor found they had little or no support from their male counterparts. In many counties women's bar associations provided the only legal assistance available to the poor. Lillian Rinenberg, an attorney who worked in the Queens Women's Bar Association Legal Aid Bureau in the 1940s, remembered that "representing the indigent, we saw so much misery—children who were abused and later became criminals, people who were desperate in one way or another. On the one hand, men would be protective of us and say these kinds of cases were too rough for women to handle, but we were really the only ones who were willing to take on free cases. So we were the ones who visited prisoners in jail and went out and talked to gang members and did the work we believed lawyers had a responsibility to do."

Seeking to examine the motivations of women practicing law and to explain the affinity they seemed to have for helping the underdog, James J. White, a professor at the University of Michigan Law School, sent questionnaires in the mid-1960s to several thousand attorneys— male and female—requesting information about their career aspirations and their attitudes toward the law. As the responses poured in, White was startled to find that not only were there pronounced differences in income between male and female attorneys but many male attorneys believed the disparities were justified: "Women lawyers are just bleeding hearts who do not understand the usual business motives" was a typical response. Intrigued by these attitudes and by the high concentration of women in public-interest areas of the law, White began looking for explanations:

It is sometimes suggested that differences between male and female status in the bar are attributable to the different motives which men and women have for entering the profession. The argument is as follows: Women are really social workers who wish to become lawyers for the unselfish reason of helping the poor and oppressed; although these motives are laudable, they render the woman a less able representative of the profit-motivated business client than is a standard male lawyer who, like the businessman, is strongly influenced by monetary motives.

He concluded that there was overwhelming evidence of "nonfunctional discrimination" against women in the legal profession and that prejudice was at least as significant a factor as the woman's own personal work preferences in making career choices.

But whether it was choice or discrimination that placed heavy concentrations of women attorneys in public-interest law, in the tumultuous late 1960s and 1970s defending the poor and the disadvantaged began to have an appeal all its own to the young law graduates—male and female—who were reluctant to join the corporations and Wall Street and who sought instead to join the growing ranks of "movement lawyers." Regrettably, it did not take long for the women lawyers to realize that the liberal political views espoused by their male counterparts did not extend to the advancement of women within the profession.

In her revealing book *Lawyering,* Helene Schwartz details her frustrations as attorney for some of the most well-known radicals of the day —Abbie Hoffman, Rennie Davis, Dave Dellinger, Tom Hayden and Jerry Rubin—who as part of the "Chicago Eight" were prosecuted as a result of events surrounding the Democratic National Convention in Chicago in 1968. Schwartz had graduated from Columbia Law School in 1965. The placement bureau cautioned her not to bother applying for a job on Wall Street even though her academic record had been excellent. When a prestigious law firm specializing in libel law found itself overburdened by scientist Linus Pauling's lawsuit against the *National Review* and its editor William F. Buckley, Jr., Schwartz was hired to work on this assignment only. She recalled being told to snub any secretaries she might meet in the ladies' room and to understand that she was being paid less than the men lawyers because "success is more important to a man than to a woman."

Because her work with the firm was highly satisfactory, Schwartz was offered full-time employment and handled a variety of commercial cases involving contracts litigation, admiralty law and "battles over corporate profits." Despite the intellectual challenge and the variety of the cases, she remembered feeling as though something was missing. It was at this time that the Chicago Eight were convicted of crossing state lines with intent to incite a riot and their lawyers, Leonard Weinglass and William Kunstler, were summarily convicted of contempt of court. Weinglass, whom Schwartz knew through a mutual friend, asked her to work on the appeal, and although her sympathies clearly were with the defendants, she could not help being put off by what she perceived as sexist attitudes on the part of her clients and co-workers—something she had not expected to find among movement radicals. In fact, Schwartz was to learn that she was invited to join the defense team because as one lawyer told her, "the women's movement has been on my back because we never had a woman in a decision-making position on this case." Later she was told that a number of women were calling the Chicago defendants and their lawyers "unmitigated chauvinists."

Schwartz was joined in the appellate work by constitutional lawyer

Doris Peterson. After completing the tedious job of reading the 22,000-page trial transcript, Schwartz claimed her favorite part of the case was when Abbie Hoffman, having been asked whether he and the others had conspired to come to Chicago to disrupt the Democratic convention, convincingly answered, "We couldn't even agree where to have lunch."

Schwartz brought and won a motion in the U.S. Court of Appeals seeking a post-trial hearing to determine if there had been any improper communications between the judge and the jury during jury deliberations. She assumed she would be handling the actual hearing, since she was most familiar with jury issues and had drafted the successful papers. But several male lawyers opposed her taking the lead in court. "The clients have no confidence in Helene," one said. Schwartz interpreted this as an indication they would not permit a woman to make an important court appearance. Finally, Arthur Kinoy, one of the defense team lawyers, said, "This has gone far enough. Why don't we just put the truth on the table. This is a women's lib question pure and simple. Admit it. You would never be saying this if Helene wasn't a woman." Kinoy's tactic worked. Helene Schwartz appeared before the court and in the end the convictions were reversed.

Throughout their careers these women attorneys who fought so hard on so many fronts too often were characterized as "dreamers" who did not understand the importance of making money and gaining power and who were wasting their legal knowledge on a personal dream of what law and society should be. Women lawyers themselves would disagree and would add that whether they were carrying forth a crusade or helping the less fortunate, they did so out of a sense of responsibility, never once minimizing the very real toll such work was taking on their careers and on their personal lives.

Shortly after Colorado attorney Mary Lathrop opened her office in Denver in 1896, she commented that "the woman who seeks an easy and healthful occupation should select washing and scrubbing instead of the law." More recently that view was shared by Nancy Walseth, an Oregon attorney who one evening in 1979 found herself evaluating the choices she had made in her legal career:

So I go to college, four years. Learn to think. I go to law school right away. Three years. Learn the law. So I graduate from law school, pass the bar. . . . I set up practice. I do all the things I'm supposed to. I get on the appointment lists. I help the downtrodden. I get restraining orders. I have a messy desk. I do a good job for my clients. They do not pay me. They do not *pay* me. I am not compensated for my work. . . . I must borrow money to keep up my charitable existence—I do so. I go on for another few months. I do not charge poor clients as much as I need to. Sometimes someone will sound poor on the phone and I will quote her a half rate. Then she roars up in a $10,000 jeep. I am a sucker. What happened to college? What happened to intellectual camaraderie? Law is cigarette smoke and greasy hair and being poor.

Walseth was expressing all of the concerns and the frustrations of women who practice public-interest law. But while she could readily list the drawbacks, the benefits of such a career seemed harder to describe. Walseth thought about it, threw the evening's work into an old briefcase and as she walked out the door at the end of a very long day, she reflected, as countless other women lawyers before her undoubtedly had, "I have a good brain and I am not going to give up. I hereby rechristen this endeavor."

6

DOUBLE IMPAIRMENT: BLACK WOMEN LAWYERS

Feminists have long seen parallels between the treatment of blacks in American society and the treatment of women. It is not surprising that activist women in the nineteenth century turned their attention first to the emancipation of blacks and then to equal rights for women. Writer Angelina Grimke, prior to the Civil War, wrote that "women ought to feel a peculiar sympathy in the colored man's wrong for like him she has been accused of mental inferiority and denied the privileges of a liberal education." But while their goals often were similar, blacks and feminists were unable to work together to achieve them. Susan B. Anthony is reported to have said that she would cut off her right arm before she would ever work for or demand the ballot for the Negro and not the woman. Frederick Douglass opposed all suggestions after the Civil War that the right of black men to vote be tied to the right of women to vote, claiming that this was "the black man's hour."

The result was that blacks and women went their separate ways. What seemed to be lost on both factions was that their insistence on working apart ignored the black woman in the first instance and forced her to divide her loyalties in the second. Sojourner Truth, the former slave and feminist, was one of only a few people who noticed the devastating consequence on black women. At an equal rights convention in 1867 she forcefully stated her opposition to ratification of the Fourteenth Amendment because it excluded black women: "There is a great stir about colored men getting their rights, but not a word about the colored women; and if colored men get their rights, and not colored women theirs, you see the colored men will be masters over the women, and it will be just as bad as it was before."

While their circumstances may not have been entirely as bad as they were before, freedom for black women accounted for a great deal less than it did for their husbands and brothers. One important difference was the treatment of black women in the area of education. As historian Eleanor Flexner points out: "Inevitably, the Negro girl suffered more deprivation than her brothers. If a white woman was supposed to be mentally incapable of receiving the same education as a man, and Negroes were inferior to whites, it followed that the Negro girl had the least possible potential for mental growth."

Despite the educational gains made by blacks in the period of Reconstruction, by 1890 only thirty black women had college degrees, while there was a substantially better showing among black men. Jacqueline E. Jackson, in a study she did of black professionals, concluded that "black females have had less access to the more prestigious institutions of higher education and have been most disadvantaged with respect to graduate and professional education."

After the Civil War, Phoebe Couzins, one of the first woman lawyers and herself white, was an outspoken advocate of equal rights for blacks and women: "I have had opportunities of seeing and knowing the condition of both sexes and will bear my testimony, that the black women are, and always have been, in far worse condition than the men."

Couzins's view was supported by Anna J. Cooper, a teacher in the Washington, D.C., colored schools at the turn of the century, who complained that black women were not being encouraged to seek a professional education: "I fear the majority of colored men do not yet think it worthwhile that women aspire to higher education . . ."

The admissions practices of Howard University's School of Law in the late 1800s give weight to both Couzins's and Cooper's positions. While priding itself as being an institution offering professional educa-

Belle A. Mansfield

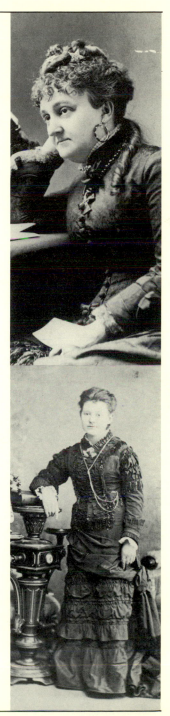

ABOVE: Belle A. Mansfield, the first woman formally admitted to the bar in the United States in 1869 (STATE HISTORICAL SOCIETY OF IOWA— SPECIAL COLLECTION) *ABOVE RIGHT:* Myra Bradwell, founder and editor of the *Chicago Legal News*, in 1868. Her newspaper for the Midwest bar was a lively mix of legal news, stinging editorials and columns on women's rights. Bradwell passed the Illinois bar but was denied admission on the grounds she was a woman. She took her fight to the U.S. Supreme Court, but the Justices refused to intervene. (CHICAGO HISTORICAL SOCIETY) *BELOW RIGHT:* Alta M. Hulett, the first woman lawyer in Illinois, in 1873. (CHICAGO HISTORICAL SOCIETY) *BELOW:* Esther McQuigg Morris, the first woman judge in America. In 1870 she held court in a log cabin in South Pass City, a frontier mining town. Judge Morris insisted litigants leave their shooting irons at the door. Not one of her seventy opinions was ever reversed on appeal. (WYOMING STATE ARCHIVES, MUSEUMS AND HISTORICAL DEPARTMENT)

ABOVE: Ada H. Kepley, who in 1870 was the first woman law graduate in the United States, organizing a children's temperance march in Effingham, Illinois. An ardent suffragist, she urged women to seize political power: "I work as hard as a man. I earn money like a man. I bear the burdens of community like a man. I am robbed as a woman." (WILLIAM L. BROOM, JR., EFFINGHAM COUNTY HISTORICAL SOCIETY)

BELOW: Carey May Carrol and the graduating class of the University of Missouri-Columbia School of Law in 1896. (TRANSCRIPT, UNIVERSITY OF MISSOURI-COLUMBIA SCHOOL OF LAW)

LEFT: Clara Shortridge Foltz, who in 1878 became the first woman lawyer in California. Foltz and suffragist Laura De Force Gordon forced Hastings College of the Law to admit women. Noting the struggles she had to gain acceptance, Foltz called the law "hard, unpoetic and relentless." (COURTESY, THE BANCROFT LIBRARY)

"The lords of creation men we call,
And they think they rule the whole;
But they're much mistaken, after all,
For they're under woman's control!"

Women of Stonington, Arouse!

THROW OFF THE YOKE
OF THE OPPRESSOR MAN.

ON MONDAY EVENING, NOVEMBER 5, 1888,
AT 8 P. M.,

Miss HANNAH LEE,
THE LONG TONGUED ORATOR
Will emit Impassioned Yawps at

BOROUGH HALL!

In advocacy of the election of

BELVA A. LOCKWOOD

TO THE PRESIDENTESSCY OF THE U. S.

BELVA A. LOCKWOOD WILL BE PRESENT.

THE BELVA A. LOCKWOOD QUARTETTE WILL FURNISH DISCORD

BELVA A. LOCKWOOD Club will make a Triumphal Parade that will
THE BELVA A. LOCKWOOD Club will include the principal streets of the Borough.

At 7 o'clock, preceding the address, the Belva A. Lockwood Club
Be Just Too Lovely For Anything.
After the Address a Grand Banquet will be tendered to the Club at MUSIC HALL.

Come One, Come All, and Bring Your Chewing Gum.

ABOVE: Portrait of Belva A. Lockwood, the first woman lawyer to argue a case before the U.S. Supreme Court and to open up the federal courts to women. She ran for President in 1888 on the Equal Rights Ticket. (NATIONAL PORTRAIT GALLERY)

LEFT: Alice G. McGee, a lawyer and actress who starred in *The Queen of Sheba.* An attorney of considerable ability, she was nonetheless remembered for her extraordinary beauty. In 1890 one reporter described her as "a strikingly handsome blonde, tall, well formed and graceful, with a creamy white complexion, pink-tinged cheeks, ripe red lips, two rows of even pearly teeth, a tangle of light brown curls that fall over a well-shaped forehead, and a pair of large, earnest, honest blue eyes, shaded with long lashes that add the crowning beauty to a well-nigh perfect face." (WARREN COUNTY HISTORICAL SOCIETY)

ABOVE MIDDLE: Lyda Burton Conley, the first native American woman lawyer. She studied law while camped out on her ancestral burial grounds in order to prevent the land from being used for commercial development, and she argued her own case before the Supreme Court. (WYANDOTTE COUNTY MUSEUM)

ABOVE RIGHT: Julia Radle Kline at her graduation from the Dickinson School of Law in 1899. (DICKINSON SCHOOL OF LAW)

BELOW LEFT: "Yellin' Mary Ellen" Lease, one of the greatest orators of the Populist period, who rallied farmers into political action with the words, "What you farmers need is to raise less corn and more hell!" (KANSAS STATE HISTORICAL SOCIETY)

BELOW RIGHT: Tiera Farrow at her graduation from the Kansas City School of Law in 1903. She went on to become a successful criminal defense lawyer but complained that her male colleagues viewed her as "just another woman freak." (WYANDOTTE COUNTY MUSEUM)

ABOVE: Chief Justice, and former President, William Howard Taft, attending the first annual session of the Women Lawyers Association in 1923. (NATIONAL ASSOCIATION OF WOMEN LAWYERS)

BELOW: "Suitcase Mary" Margaret Bartelme, a juvenile court judge in Chicago, who insisted that young girls leaving detention homes be given a satchel filled with

new clothes to help them make a fresh start. Bartelme was an outspoken advocate for the rights of adolescents and children, and was an 1894 graduate of Northwestern University Law School. (NEWS GROUP CHICAGO, INC., 1986, WITH PERMISSION OF THE *CHICAGO SUN-TIMES*)

BOTTOM: The specially convened Texas Supreme Court in 1925, which consisted of Texas's first woman lawyer, Hortense Ward, as chief justice and Ruth Brazzil and Hattie L. Henenberg as associates. When a case involving a men's club came before the court the all-male panel was forced to step aside due to a potential conflict of interest.

The female panel was sworn in for the purpose of hearing *Johnson* v. *Darr* only. (AUSTIN HISTORY CENTER)

ABOVE: Lucy Somerville Howorth, who graduated with first honors from the University of Mississippi Law School in 1922. She was a successful private practitioner, served in the state legislature, and went on to become the first woman general counsel of a federal agency. (ROBERT JORDAN)

LEFT: Florence Ellinwood Allen, the first woman to serve on a federal appeals court and the first to be considered for appointment to the Supreme Court. In 1949 she received word that despite President Truman's interest in nominating her for the Court, he declined to do so because "the Justices don't want a woman. They say they couldn't sit around with their robes off and their feet up and discuss the problems." (WESTERN RESERVE HISTORICAL SOCIETY)

BELOW: Cecelia Goetz delivering the opening argument for the prosecution in the Krupp trial at Nuremberg. In order for Goetz to join the prosecution team, Telford Taylor had to sign a waiver of disability—the disability was that she was a woman.

Queen of the Lady Lawyers

Fortune Vecchiarelli of 21-16 42nd street, Long Island City, is crowned queen and the most glamorous woman lawyer by Appellate Court Justice Henry Wenzel of Richmond Hill at the Queens Women's Bar Association dinner at the Hotel Pierre, Manhattan. Looking on is Mrs. Marie Beary of Forest Hills, chairman of the dinner committee.

ABOVE RIGHT: Florynce Kennedy at a college lecture in Boulder in 1973. Her direct style led to her being called "Foul Mouth Flo." Kennedy frequently told students, "If you want to know where the apathy is, you're probably sitting on it." *(COLORADO DAILY)*

BELOW: The first women at Harvard Law School in 1950 as seen by the readers of the *Harvard Law School Record. (HARVARD LAW SCHOOL RECORD)*

" ... Some Facts and A Few Figures."

Left to right, front row: Ruth Marshal, Roberta Good, Ann Pfohl, Louise Florencourt, Carolyn McTear; rear row: Edith Henderson, Mary O'Connell, Beverly Coleman, Miriam Clippinger, Charlotte Horwood.

ABOVE: Constance Baker Motley and NAACP Legal Defense Fund director Jack Greenberg on the steps of the Supreme Court in 1964. Motley's clients included Martin Luther King and James Meredith. At the time the photograph was taken she had argued and won six cases before the Supreme Court. (NAACP LEGAL DEFENSE AND EDUCATIONAL FUND, INC.)

BELOW: Sandra Day O'Connor being sworn in as Associate Justice of the Supreme Court in 1981 by Chief Justice Warren Burger. (WIDE WORLD PHOTOS)

tion to victims of racial discrimination, Howard seems initially to have resisted the admission of black women to its law classes. In 1890 Lelia J. Robinson, the Massachusetts attorney and writer, reporting on the barriers that existed at Howard Law School, claimed that its first woman law student, Charlotte E. Ray, gained entry "by a clever ruse, her name being sent in with those of her classmates as C. E. Ray, and that she was thus admitted, although there was some commotion when it was discovered that one of the applicants was a woman." Robinson went on to report: "In 1880 the names of four women were enrolled as students of this school, all of whom graduated in due time. One of these, Mrs. Louise V. Bryant, of Washington, I have not heard from; Mrs. M.A.S. Carey, a widow, colored, graduated in 1883, took her diploma as attorney at law, and has been practising four years in Washington. This lady writes me that she took a course in this same school at an earlier date, being enrolled as student in September 1869 —the first woman to enter the school—but that she was then refused graduation on account of her sex."

Moreover, in the case of Eliza A. Chambers, who entered Howard Law School in 1885, Robinson noted that Chambers "completed the full three years' course, took both diplomas which are earned thereby, and was then admitted to the Bar. She writes me however that the Law School faculty refused to hand in her name to the examiners, for admission to practice, omitting her from the list of her male classmates whom they recommended, simply because she was a woman. She has been in practice since her admission giving special attention to matters in equity, with patents, pensions and land claims."

Charlotte E. Ray, who used her ingenuity to become the first woman law graduate of Howard University, is reported to have been a member of Phi Beta Kappa. She was born in 1850, the year the dreaded Fugitive Slave Act was passed, and Ray's family played key roles in the Underground Railroad. In the 1860s Ray was sent to study in Washington, D.C., at the Institution for the Education of Colored Youth founded by Myrtilla Miner, a white woman who devoted her life to the unpopular cause of educating black children. The school was constantly under attack from people who did not believe in instruction for the "colored" and eventually it was burned to the ground.

After Charlotte Ray graduated from the Miner School she was taken on as an instructor in the Normal and Preparatory Department of Howard University. While teaching at Howard, she registered for evening classes at the law school. J. C. Napier, an 1869 classmate of Ray's, described her as "a Negro girl about the complexion of Frederick Douglass, with long straight hair. There was never the least doubt that she was what we term a Negro. She was an apt scholar."

Ray's ability in the law surprised visitors to the law school who expected little, if anything, from a woman, and a black woman at that. General O. O. Howard, president of the university, revealed in his third annual report dated July 1870, that a trustee of the law school was amazed to find "there was a colored woman who read us a thesis on corporations, not copied from the books but from her brain, a clear incisive analysis of one of the most delicate legal questions."

After graduation from Howard Law School, Charlotte Ray took and passed the District of Columbia bar. She was admitted to practice in April 1872—the first woman lawyer in the District of Columbia and the first black woman lawyer in the United States.

Phoebe A. Hannaford, writing for the journal *Daughters of America*, noted that "in the city of Washington, where a few years ago colored women were bought and sold under sanction of law, a woman of African descent has been admitted to practice at the Bar of the Supreme Court of the District of Columbia. Miss Charlotte E. Ray, who has the honor of being the first lady lawyer in Washington, is a graduate of the Law College of Howard University and is said to be a dusky mulatto, possessing quite an intelligent countenance. She doubtless has also a fine mind and deserves success." M. A. Majors, author of an 1893 study of prominent black women, said of Ray: "Her special endowments make her one of the best lawyers on corporations in the country; her eloquence is commendable for her sex in the court-room, and her legal advice is authoritative."

Clearly there was every expectation that Charlotte Ray would have a future in the law. While jobs for blacks in Washington, D.C., were difficult to obtain, historian Richard Kluger estimated that in the late 1800s "more than 10% of the nearly 25,000 federal employees in the District were Negroes and there were perhaps 25 other black lawyers making a living in town. In the whole country in the 1890s no more than 600 to 700 black lawyers were members of the bar, and though the ones in Washington were not hired by the government, a distinct black upper class and a broadening middle class existed in the city . . ."

But the double impairment of being both black and female prevented Charlotte Ray from joining this professional class. Much as she tried to develop her own law practice, the clients—black and white—simply would not retain her. Kate Kane Rossi, a white criminal lawyer from Wisconsin who was a friend of Ray's told a reporter for the *Chicago Legal News* that Charlotte, "although a lawyer of decided ability, on account of prejudice, was not able to obtain sufficient legal business and had to give up active practice. Ray returned to her native New York City and resumed teaching, this time in the Brooklyn public schools. Although she remained active in women's clubs, she lost touch with the legal community and died in obscurity in Woodside, Queens, in 1911.

Ray's failure to succeed at the bar coincided with the emerging view in the early part of this century that blacks were, on the whole, lazy, shiftless and subhuman. Not only were blacks freely referred to as "darkey," "mammy" and "nigger" by members of the legal profession and members of the press, but movies such as *Birth of a Nation* and songs such as "All Coons Look Alike to Me" were part of the popular American culture. Newspapers frequently depicted black conversation in demeaning dialect for the amusement of readers: "Well suh, boss, he split mah lips and knocked two of mah teef loose . . ."

In 1912 the American Bar Association confirmed it had admitted three Negro lawyers, but quickly assured its members that a resolution had been passed "that as it never has been contemplated that members of the colored race should become members of this association, the several local councils are directed, if at any time any of them shall recommend a person of the colored race for membership, to accompany the recommendation with a statement of the fact that he is of such race." As always, for black women the situation was even worse. Howard Washington Odum, in his doctoral dissertation "The Social and Mental Traits of the Negro" at Columbia University, asserted in 1910 that "the Negro has few ideals and perhaps no lasting adherence to an aspiration toward real worth. . . . He has little conception of the meaning of virtue, truth, honor. . . . The Negro woman constitutes a serious feature of the situation. She fails to assist the men in a better struggle, she is inefficient and indisposed to be faithful. She is a hindrance to the saving of money and the industrial development of the family."

In 1914 *Case and Comment,* a popular magazine for lawyers, devoted an entire issue to the accomplishments of "the new woman lawyer." Not only was no mention made of Charlotte E. Ray or of any other black woman lawyer but the only reference to black women at all was an anecdote about an ignorant "mammy" who mistakenly wanders into a Boston courtroom.

Black women who were willing to fight the battles against racism and sexism had few, if any, role models. In 1918 Iowa's Gertrude E. Rush was the only black woman lawyer west of the Mississippi. By the 1940s there were only fifty-seven black women lawyers in the entire United States.

One woman who was keenly interested in the lives of her sister attorneys was pioneer lawyer Sadie Tanner Mossell Alexander. She reported on black women attorneys for the *National Bar Journal* in 1941, and wrote: "In preparing this article I was astonished to find little assembled material on the entry of American women into the learned profession of the law and shocked to ascertain that no one could tell me when or who was the first Negro woman admitted to practice before an American court." Her research led her to confirm that Charlotte E. Ray was indeed the first black woman lawyer in the United States.

Sadie Tanner Mossell, born in 1898, was herself a woman of many "firsts." The daughter of the first black male graduate of the University of Pennsylvania Law School, she carried on the tradition by becoming the law school's first black woman graduate and Pennsylvania's first black woman lawyer. Before doing so, Alexander graduated from the University of Pennsylvania with honors in 1918 and obtained a master's degree in economics one year later. Her next achievement was to earn a doctorate in economics at Penn—the first black woman in the United States to obtain a Ph.D.

For Sadie Alexander, and for the black women who came before her, a career in the law meant practicing with a "double handicap." Alexander recalls the indignities she suffered both as a woman and as a black. "A woman friend and I signed up for a course at Penn that was being offered to the men only. When that professor came into class he saw us and chased us out. He told us he didn't care who said we could stay there—he wasn't about to teach a woman. Yes, those were rough times."

The racial issue came up most dramatically after Alexander graduated from college. "I had been accepted into Penn's Ph.D. program, but I was called down by the administration to answer for the 'trouble' I had caused in the library. I didn't know what they were talking about, but I knew if this wasn't straightened out, I would be out of the program. It turned out the librarian had confused me with another black girl who had removed all the books from one particular section, and as the saying goes, 'All Negroes look alike.' " She completed her didactic work and her dissertation within three years, but found that the hardest part of the doctoral program was getting the money to have "A Budget Study of 100 Negro Migrant Teachers" printed.

After obtaining her doctorate, Alexander could not find any college that would hire her. She moved South, and because she needed work, took a job with a black insurance company in North Carolina. In 1923 she married Raymond Alexander, the first black graduate of the Wharton School of Business, and moved to Philadelphia to occupy herself as a housewife. "I stayed home for one year and almost lost my mind —it was then I decided I had better go to law school."

Gaining admission to the University of Pennsylvania Law School was not a problem, but Alexander bitterly remembers her experiences there. "The dean of the law school during my years was Edward Mikell, a very prejudiced man. He directed that under no circumstances was I to be admitted to the club formed by the handful of women who attended the school at the time. It was after our admittance to the bar that the women told me of the dean's feelings. I was treated either with indifference or with disdain, so I would go home directly at twelve noon when classes were over and study alone until about six P.M. No one invited me to lunch—neither women nor men, so I just adapted myself to what was."

Sadie Alexander was invited to be a member of law review, indicating honors work at the law school, but neither her work on law review nor her doctorate in economics was sufficient for employment in any Philadelphia law firm except her husband's. She finally found a law job with the Office of the Philadelphia City Solicitor, representing the city in orphan's court. The product of a broken marriage ("my mother was a brilliant woman who would turn the pages of her book while stirring the stew, but she never got over my father's leaving her"), Alexander was especially concerned about orphaned and abandoned children and was a strong proponent of strict child support and custody laws.

She believed that at her city job, sex, not race, would be the issue. "No sooner was I assigned and situated than I became pregnant. I felt the burdens of the world on my shoulders and feared having to give up my job with people saying 'Isn't it just like a woman to go off and get pregnant.' My husband felt I should resign the post as soon as my pregnancy was in evidence but I refused and stood firm, both for myself and for all women."

After eight years with the city, Alexander joined her husband in private practice. "We experienced a great deal of discrimination in our time. Listen, anyone with any sensitivity is aware of the manipulation of people. Many of those who refused to acknowledge my presence at Penn Law School act just fine today. My husband and I were almost denied entrance to movie houses and hotels. Fortunately we were in a position to protest, to actively do something about it." But after more than fifty years at the bar, Alexander still believes black women need to enter the profession in greater numbers. "We have so much yet to do."

Two of her contemporaries, Violette Neatly Anderson and Eunice Hunton Carter, found as she did that jobs in government offered black women lawyers greater opportunities for their talents. Anderson became the first woman to serve as a prosecutor in Chicago and in 1926 is reported to have been the first black woman lawyer to argue a case before the United States Supreme Court.

Eunice Hunton Carter, a New Yorker who obtained both her bachelor's and master's degrees from Smith College, earned her LL.B. at Fordham Law School. Carter started out in private practice but soon was hired by New York County district attorney William C. Dodge to handle low-level prosecutions in the city's magistrate's (criminal) court. Hers was a job most other prosecutors disliked and avoided. Richard Hammer, a frequent writer on organized crime, points out that

Dodge's decision to hire Carter unwittingly resulted in the biggest organized crime prosecution in the nation's history:

Assistant District Attorney Eunice Carter had been given the thankless job . . . of prosecuting the endless parade of whores picked up in the brothels and on the streets of Manhattan. Though she won few convictions—the magistrate's courts, where such trials were held, were perhaps the most corrupt in the city—Mrs. Carter observed some rather striking coincidences. On the witness stand, most of the prostitutes told almost identical stories, how they were poor working girls from out of town who just happened to be visiting a friend when arrested; they were all represented by the same law firms; if they were fined, the same bondsmen appeared with the money; and hovering in the background was always the same disbarred lawyer, Abe Karp, who was known to have close contacts in the underworld. Soon Mrs. Carter decided she was dealing not with free-lance purveyors of joyless sex but with a huge and tightly controlled organization. She took her suspicions to Dodge, who ridiculed them.

But Carter didn't stop there. A new special prosecutor, Thomas E. Dewey, had been appointed to investigate corruption in New York and Eunice Carter decided to take her findings to his office. Dewey liked what he heard and hired Carter away from Dodge. The appointment made her one of Dewey's "twenty against the underworld," as he later would call his prosecution team. Her associates included such notables in rackets prosecutions as Frank ("Mr. District Attorney") Hogan and Stanley Fuld, Murray Gurfein and Charles Breitel, all of whom went on to distinguished careers in the judiciary.

In his autobiography, Thomas Dewey admits that while he was fascinated with Mrs. Carter's theory about organized crime's infiltration into prostitution, he still felt the best way to crack down on racketeers was to go after loan sharks, not prostitutes. But, Dewey recalls, Carter and Gurfein persisted:

So quite reluctantly I authorized them to commence a full-scale investigation . . . with the help of informers, skilled police work and discreet wiretapping, an astonishing picture emerged. . . . Until a few years before, and we did not know just how long before, prostitution had not been organized into a racket . . . then the bookers of women, "bookies" or "bookers," appeared on the scene. They were men who knew numbers of prostitutes and numbers of madams and made their living from a fast-growing business of sending girls from house to house. By 1933 there were at least four big bookers who ran large chains of houses of prostitution . . . the business was flourishing to the point that it attracted the attention of major racketeers.

Just as Carter suspected, the racketeers were moving in, providing bondsmen, lawyers and "protection" in exchange for 50 percent or more of the take. Dewey later estimated that in New York City the racket was grossing $12 million annually on prostitution alone during these Depression years.

By 1936 Dewey's staff was convinced that a single "combination" was pulling all the prostitution rackets together:

Our observant Eunice Carter learned that out of the 175 arrested girls, not one of whom had gone to jail, every single one of them had been "bonded." Our investigation knew that tremendous pressure had been brought to bear upon the four major bookers and they had been "taken over" by the same combination.

Among those involved were "Little Davie" Betillo, one of Al Capone's former bodyguards and "Tommy the Bull" Pennochio, a well-known gangster who made his living from narcotics. Investigators knew that if these men were involved, they were only scratching the surface. In order to get to the next level, Dewey ordered a major raid of eighty houses of prostitution in the hope of finding prostitutes or operators who were willing to talk. One hundred sixty policemen were handed sealed orders and sent out to make simultaneous arrests. The raid netted far fewer people than the investigators had hoped, but by the end of it, "We had a hundred prostitutes and madams jammed into our offices, including some of the best-known women in the business. Our madams included Polack Frances, Silver Tongued Elsie, Sadie the Chink, Nigger Ruth, Jennie the Factory, Cockeyed Florence, Max the Barber (a male madam), Fat Rae, and Jennie the Fox." Only three of the hundred were willing to talk, but little by little Carter was able to put together the full details of the prostitution racket. This time there was convincing evidence that Charles ("Lucky") Luciano was at the head of the operation. In the end, after an exhausting trial, Luciano, the top Mafia leader in New York, was convicted. The success of the Luciano trial led to Dewey's appointment as Dodge's successor for New York County district attorney. After he was sworn in, Eunice Hunton Carter was appointed chief of his Special Sessions Bureau, where she supervised more than fourteen thousand criminal cases each year.

During the period of Carter's success, black women lawyers were beginning to get appointments to the bench. Jane Mathilda Bolin, a former assistant corporation counsel in New York City, who was an honors graduate of Wellesley College and Yale Law School, became the first black woman judge in the United States when Mayor Fiorello La Guardia appointed her a justice of New York's domestic relations court. Similarly, Edith S. Sampson, the first woman to obtain a master of law degree at Loyola University in Chicago in 1927, was appointed a referee of the juvenile court of Cook County.

During the Depression years, however, black women lawyers who were not employed by the government found it especially difficult to get work. At a time when blacks and women were suffering the greatest economic losses, black women lawyers were facing enormous obstacles to their advancement in the legal profession. In the South, courts and law libraries were totally segregated. In the North, black women lawyers faced humiliating treatment based on racial and sexual bias.

Minneapolis lawyer Lena O. Smith, who was admitted to the Minnesota bar in 1921, may have been the earliest of the black women lawyers to devote herself almost entirely to civil rights law. Smith was an outspoken advocate for minorities in Minneapolis, serving first on the NAACP's Legal Redress Committee and later as president of the NAACP's Minneapolis chapter.

Bessie Geffner, who in the 1930s helped to found the Queens County Women's Bar Association in New York City, remembered the difficulty she had arranging an organization dinner because one of the members, Florence Lucas, was black. "Very few hotels in the thirties and forties would serve blacks and we didn't want Florence to be embarrassed. I went from place to place insisting that any hotel that wanted our business would have to agree ahead of time to seat Florence. A number of the hotels refused. I never told Florence about this but it taught me all I needed to know at the time about the treatment of black women in New York City."

The situation had not changed much by the early 1950s. Marian Sullivan, an expert in patent and trademark law, remembered, "I was fresh out of law school and pounding the pavements in search of a job. I'm not exaggerating when I say I went to one hundred firms. No one wanted a woman lawyer. Well, my ancestry is 'fighting Irish' and I wasn't about to give up. But I remember one day when I was feeling particularly awful, a receptionist called me over to deliver still one more rejection. She thought she would make me feel better by telling me how they had just rejected a colored girl who had the *nerve* to apply for the position. I remember thinking no matter how bad it was for me, it had to be worse for her. I never learned who she was but that night I went home and said a prayer for her."

The 1950s saw a number of black women lawyers actively becoming involved with the civil rights movement. Among them was Ruth Harvey Charity, a former president of the National Association of Black Women Attorneys, who gives her present age as "thirty-nine and holding." Born and raised in Danville, Virginia, Charity was the daughter of professionals. Her mother was a teacher and her father was a minister and school principal. Ruth Harvey Charity remembers two separate incidents in her childhood that shaped her interest in civil rights. The first occurred during a hot and humid summer in downtown Danville. "I was passing a drugstore with my mother when I noticed a young white girl, about my age, sitting at the counter eating an ice cream sundae. I told my mother I wanted to stop and have a sundae too, but she wouldn't listen. She dragged me away from there and told me I couldn't have one because we were Negroes. I was never so angry. As young as I was I remember saying to my mother, "Aren't we Americans too?"

That incident sharpened Charity's interest in the stories that some of the parishioners at her father's church were telling about life in Danville. "There was a social club for white women and it seems the members had all gotten together and agreed what they would pay their black domestics. The maids worked seven hours a day at least, seven days a week, and the wages they were getting were pitifully low. And then there was always the problem of where you could and couldn't go in town. After hearing all this, I resolved to myself that someday I would be a lawyer and do something about this, although I admit I didn't have the slightest idea what it was I was going to do."

Charity began studying at Bennett College, then transferred to Howard University, where she majored in political science. She entered Howard Law School the following semester and remembers that the first day in class one of the men students leaned over and said, "What are you doing in law school? Shouldn't you be in home economics?" Charity was relieved the professors did not express a similar view.

She quickly became interested in civil rights activities, as she predicted she would, and was elected president of the NAACP chapter at Howard.

"In 1944 we organized the first sit-in in the nation's capital. It was at a well-known restaurant and I was scared to death. The sit-ins were organized in shifts so that we always had coverage at the lunch counters. The restaurant staff glared and refused to serve us but they didn't do or say anything to us. When we got back to the campus one of the faculty members said, 'Your parents didn't send you to this university so you could get involved in sit-ins.' But the important thing to us was that we won—the restaurant was desegregated."

After law school Charity returned to Danville and went into private practice. She was outraged that her hometown had two libraries—a facility for whites with a fairly extensive collection of books, and "a cubbyhole" for blacks that was a quarter of a mile away. "If a black student wanted a book that was in the white library, an order would have to be put in and somebody from the white library would have to drop it by; you couldn't do it the other way around. It was a terrible practice." Still maintaining her membership with the NAACP, Charity filed suit against the city of Danville for its discriminatory practices. "We won it and after some more sit-ins we got the Danville city park desegregated, too."

Ruth Harvey Charity received little welcome from Virginia's legal profession. "White lawyers simply would not talk to you in or out of court. Today some of them still won't. They still think if they act friendly, they'll be called a 'nigger lover.' " She recalls an incident in the clerk's office when she was told she was not allowed to handle the record books. "I was furious. I insisted I had every right to examine them, I was a lawyer and I was going to bring all kinds of lawsuits. The clerk just stopped and stared at me like I was right out of the zoo." She got the books.

Charity developed a successful practice, taking on a number of criminal cases. "Sometimes I found there was an advantage to being a woman. You could argue a defense like you were the boy's mother and he was a good kid who just needed a little straightening out." The strategy often worked. But Charity is proudest of her defense of 1,300 civil rights marchers who were arrested in Danville in 1963 at the height of the civil rights movement. Martin Luther King was involved in the planning of the demonstrations and both he and the Reverend Ralph Abernathy took part. The lawsuits were successful and all 1,300 demonstrators were freed.

Ruth Harvey Charity next became active in Democratic Party politics, serving with the National Committee for eight years. As members of the National Bar Association, the organization for black attorneys, she and attorney Wilhelmina Jackson Rolark were disgusted with the "predominantly chauvinistic" attitudes of the association. Not much had changed in the century after Charlotte E. Ray sneaked her way into Howard Law School in order to study law with black men. Charity remembers, "In the National Bar Association women were only permitted to hold office as high as secretary—the men wouldn't allow us to become president, vice-president or treasurer. We formed a women's division of the National Bar Association and I later succeeded in being named the association's first woman vice-president," but Rolark believed black women lawyers needed an organization of their own and she founded the National Association of Black Women Attorneys. Charity soon joined her.

When asked if black women lawyers have a special duty to help black women enter the legal profession, Charity insists they do. "We're still living in a separate society. After all, if we don't bring them along, who will?"

Constance Baker Motley shared Ruth Charity's interest in civil rights, but unlike Charity, Motley had few, if any, childhood dreams about her future. She was the daughter of a cook and a housewife and was the ninth of twelve children. After high school she took a job varnishing chairs for a building reconstruction project.

Motley's parents wanted her to get an education but did not have the money for college. "My mother's aspirations for me were limited but realistic. She thought I might make a fine hairdresser."

In 1938, when Motley was a sophomore at Hillhouse High School in New Haven, she described some of her feelings in a poem:

> Someone told me that God made the World
> And everything from stone or wood;
> And when he had finished it,
> He said that it was good
> He worked on it six long days,
> On the seventh He rested content;
> But I have often wondered
> If this is the place He meant.
>
> Men made the slum where I live,
> With its mountains of sin;
> They jammed the houses together
> To keep beauty from entering in.
> I often think it is true
> That real things have never been seen.
> 'Cause I've lived here all my life
> And never seen grass that was green
>
> I don't think God made my world
> Cause it's misery, not fun.
> If he made a beautiful place
> This couldn't be the one . . .

That same year, Motley attended a lecture given by a lawyer in her community, George Crawford. His topic was *Gaines* v. *Canada*, a civil rights case that recently had been decided by the United States Supreme Court. In the *Gaines* case, Charles Houston, leading the NAACP legal defense team, argued successfully that if the state of Missouri was committed to the principle "separate but equal," it would have to either create a special law school for black applicant Lloyd Gaines or grant Gaines permission to attend the University of Missouri's law school. Chief Justice Hughes, delivering the majority opinion, held that Gaines's right was "a personal one. It was as an individual that he was entitled to the equal protection of the laws, and the State was bound to furnish him within its borders facilities for legal education" equal to those offered whites. The implications of the *Gaines* case were encouraging to blacks and Crawford's lecture convinced Constance Motley that she wanted to be part of the civil rights actions that were bound to come.

Two years later, Motley attended a neighborhood meeting George Crawford called at the Dixwell Community House. At the meeting was Clarence W. Blakeslee, a wealthy white Connecticut businessman who was known for his philanthropic works in the black community. Blakeslee had been instrumental in building "Q" House, a community center that contained a gym, a lounge and a reading room, but unexplainably was rarely used by black residents. Blakeslee had come to Dixwell to find out why.

After a number of community leaders spoke, Constance Motley asked if she could be heard. She bluntly told Blakeslee and the audience that the board operating community programs such as "Q" House was composed of "outsiders" who knew nothing about the wants or needs of neighborhood residents. Despite the strong message, Blakeslee was impressed with what he heard. He told George Crawford that "the Baker girl made more sense in two minutes than the entire meeting had." He wanted to know more about her.

Crawford arranged a meeting, and the first thing Blakeslee asked her was, "Why aren't you in college?" Motley quickly answered "Money." Blakeslee wanted to know what she would do if she had a college education, and she replied that she wanted to be a lawyer. He was surprised by the answer, but after giving it some thought, said, "Well, if I can send my grandson to law school, I guess I can send you too."

Blakeslee's generosity took Motley, the daughter of West Indian immigrant parents, to Fisk University in Nashville. In the winter of 1941, on her trip down to college, she got a firsthand look at how blacks were treated in the South. "My train stopped at Cincinnati on the way to Nashville, and I was told I had to change to a 'for colored only' car. I had never been in a Jim Crow car before and I don't think I will ever forget that experience."

Once in Nashville, Motley learned that being black prevented her from attending the theater, eating in restaurants, and trying on clothing and shoes in department stores. "Colored women were expected to give their size and buy without trying on, so the clothing never touched you. After a couple of times I decided if I needed clothes, I would wait until I was back in New Haven; I wasn't going shopping in Nashville anymore." Restricting herself almost exclusively to the Fisk campus and resenting it, Motley decided to transfer to a northern school. She signed up for courses at New York University and within two and a half years earned an honors degree in economics.

After receiving an acceptance from Columbia Law School, she again discussed her future with Clarence Blakeslee. Blakeslee insisted, "If you're going to be a lawyer, you're going to have to look and sound like one." He arranged for her to buy an appropriate wardrobe and saw to it that she spent the summer taking public-speaking courses.

Motley was the second black woman ever to attend Columbia Law School, the first being Elrita Alexander, now a North Carolina judge. She recalls the dean, Young B. Smith, as being "southern-gracious, while letting you know he believed a legal education was wasted on a woman. He thought there was only one reason why a woman would go to law school—to get herself a husband."

Between her second and third years of law school, she, like most other law students, tried to find summer employment in a law firm. "In the spring of 1945 I made an appointment over the telephone for an interview at a midtown law firm. I was sitting in the waiting room when I noticed an older, white-haired man peering out at me from behind one of the doors. He seemed surprised and appalled to see me, and when I looked his way he quickly slammed his door. The next thing I knew, the receptionist was telling me there was no appointment and there would be no interview. They weren't about to take a black woman law student, even for a summer."

In her third year at Columbia a friend mentioned that he was going to clerk for Thurgood Marshall, then director of the NAACP Legal

Defense Fund. He invited Motley to come along. "From that first day I knew this was where I wanted to be. I never bothered interviewing anywhere else."

Motley's first assignments put her on the team that brought the series of civil rights cases that eventually culminated in *Brown* v. *Board of Education,* the landmark Supreme Court case that struck down the concept of "separate but equal" in education.

In addition to *Brown* there were three cases Constance Baker Motley worked on that were particularly important to her. The first, *Sipuel* v. *Oklahoma State Board of Regents,* involved a young black girl who was seeking admission to the University of Oklahoma Law School. Sipuel had all the necessary qualifications, but the state of Oklahoma claimed it was planning to open a "substantially equal" law school for Negroes. The U.S. Supreme Court sidestepped the issue, permitting Oklahoma to designate a clearly inferior proposal as meeting the separate but equal test.

In *Sweatt* v. *Painter,* Motley was involved in the application of a black student who wanted to enter the University of Texas Law School at Austin. In order to avoid a court test, the Texas legislature appropriated $3 million for the creation of a separate university for blacks, one that would also contain a $100,000 law school. When the law school was completed it consisted of three basement rooms, a very limited library and a few second-rate instructors. This time the Supreme Court could not avoid this issue: the Court virtually declared segregation in education unconstitutional per se. The NAACP saw this as a signal to shift the emphasis in its strategy by attacking segregation head on instead of continuing to bring the separate but equal lawsuits, leading to the landmark *Brown* v. *Board of Education* case.

Constance Baker Motley found that the Legal Defense Fund provided her with enormous trial experience. In 1949 she represented a group of black teachers who were being paid substantially less than white teachers. "John Lynch and I were the first black lawyers since Reconstruction to go to federal court in Alabama, and the trial was the biggest event in town. The federal court wasn't segregated but none of the blacks knew that, so they all took seats upstairs. When the word got out that there was not only a 'nigra lawyer' but a 'nigra woman lawyer' as well, it seemed as though the whole town decided to see what was going on. They had to keep the huge oak doors open because of all the spectators."

Throughout this period Motley tried cases in eleven southern states and in the District of Columbia. "Often a southern judge would refer to the men attorneys as Mister, but would make a point of calling me 'Connie,' since traditionally black women in the South were called only by their first name." She remembers being more tired and discouraged than afraid, although her life was constantly in danger. "We were in a southern town for a long trial, and I knew it was going to be impossible to stay in a decent hotel. Usually in these situations a black family would agree to put you up. But there was so much publicity involved with civil rights cases that no black family dared have us—they were too afraid. A black doctor invited us to dinner, but that was about it. I wonder how many lawyers have had the experience of preparing for trial in a flophouse. That was the only room I could get."

While opportunities for black women seemed better in the North, Motley recalls indignities at home too. "Thurgood Marshall's favorite story about me happened in 1948. I was a member of the Association of the Bar of the City of New York. Two elderly white men who were at the door where you signed in totally ignored me and carried on a conversation about anything rather than acknowledge my presence. Finally one of them looked me over and said, 'You can't come in here. This is a private organization.' I told him I was a member and signed in. He looked at me, looked at the book, looked at me again and said, 'All right, come this way, *Constance.*'"

Motley became the NAACP Legal Defense Fund's principal trial attorney, arguing ten cases before the U.S. Supreme Court and winning nine of them. She helped to get James Meredith admitted to the University of Mississippi, served as counsel to the Reverend Martin Luther King, Jr., in Birmingham, and sought enforcement of the 1964 Civil Rights Act against Lester Maddox in Atlanta.

After leaving the NAACP, she moved on to politics—successfully running for the New York State Senate and in 1965 becoming borough president of Manhattan, the first black woman elected to either position.

President Lyndon Johnson, whom Motley believes was "the greatest friend blacks had since Lincoln," nominated her to the federal court of appeals, but Mississippi's Senator James O. Eastland blocked her appointment. Johnson persisted, and in 1966 Motley became the first black woman in history to sit on the U.S. District Court for the Southern District of New York, thus paving the way for the later appointments of Judge Mary Johnson Lowe and Second Circuit Court of Appeals judge Amalya Kearse. In 1980 Motley was elevated to chief judge of the district court.

When asked if blacks and women have common goals, Motley answered, "I don't think blacks are able to perceive white women as a disadvantaged group, so there can't be much of an alliance. But black women are aware of the joint problems of discrimination and exploitation and I think they definitely can see the parallels."

One lawyer particularly attuned to the combined problems of racism and sexism is Florynce Kennedy, known to several generations of college students for her outspoken views and her outrageous political activities.

In the 1960s and 1970s, "Foul Mouth Flo" was the colorful spokesman for nearly every movement to come along—antiwar, pro–black liberation, pro–equal rights. She organized a "Hollywood Toilet Bowl" festival to protest a California TV station's refusal to hire a woman media buyer and explained that "there are very few jobs that actually require a penis or a vagina. All other jobs should be open to everybody." She also put together a "Pee-in at Harvard Yard" to protest the lack of bathroom facilities for women at Lowell House. And when the New York Catholic Archdiocese became increasingly active in abortion issues, she showed up outside St. Patrick's Cathedral with a crowd of demonstrators who carried handfuls of wire coat hangers. Calling herself "a hustler," Kennedy is guided by the belief that "if you want to know where the apathy is, you're probably sitting on it."

Born nearly seventy years ago in Kansas City, Missouri, Florynce Kennedy graduated at the top of her class at Lincoln High School. She recalls her parents running a "laissez-faire household," in which she and her sisters were given a tremendous sense of security and worth. "By the time the bigots got around to telling us we were nobody, we already knew we were somebody."

In 1942 she moved to New York City, where she took a variety of jobs to help her pay for college. She decided she would go to Columbia University, although she heard the entrance requirements would be difficult. "I find that the higher you aim the better you shoot," says Kennedy, "and even if it seems you're way beyond yourself when you set up your goal and take your aim, it always turns out that you can do a lot more than you thought you could." Early on, she knew she was going to be a lawyer. "All I had to do was to look at lawyers and then look at mothers to know which I would rather be. Who with any taste and brains would want to be changing diapers all day?"

Gaining admission to Columbia Law School after her graduation from the university was nearly impossible—not because she was black, but because she was a woman.

The Associate Dean, Willis Reese, told me I had been rejected not because I was Black but because I was a woman. So I wrote him a letter saying that whatever the reason was, it felt the same to me, and that some of my more cynical friends thought I had been discriminated against because I was Black. That was a smart tactical move because just at that time Black people were beginning to sue the graduate and professional schools for their racist admission policies, and when I went to see the Dean I was so cocky I made him nervous—he didn't particularly want a lawsuit.

I said, "If you have admitted any white man with lower grades than mine, then I want to get in too." That was probably the first time I used what I call the "testicular approach." I've found that when you apply the right kind of pressure to the appropriate sensitive area, people become even more concerned than you are about your progress and happiness and contentment . . . the irony was that in the end he let me in and kept out my white friend from Barnard who had better grades than I did.

Kennedy soon became disgusted with Columbia's emphasis on establishment law. "Law school made me see clearly for the first time how the law was used to maintain the bullshit rather than to change things and that justice was really a crock of shit." She particularly remembers her Negligence Law class:

. . . We had a Dean [Young B.] Smith, a Southerner, who made a big point of not being able to pronounce the plaintiffs' names if they were foreigners. And there was the Palsgraff case against the Long Island Railroad, which established the principle that the plaintiff may not recover even if injured. I used to laugh and say that the kid couldn't recover because her feet were too big for her age—if her legs had been shorter, her foot wouldn't have been on the track and the train couldn't have run over it. Anything that could possibly be twisted into putting the blame on the victim was part of the accepted theory of negligence law as we were taught it at Columbia.

After graduation from law school in 1951, Kennedy joined a small New York firm, then later went into private practice for herself. "It was very tough at first, but I managed, barely. My clients always had a hard time paying legal fees and one Christmas I had to work at Bloomingdale's to pay the rent."

In the 1950s Kennedy began representing black musicians and artists in contract and royalty disputes. Among her clients were saxophonist Charlie Parker and singer Billie Holiday, who liked to call her "the hip kitty from Kansas City." Kennedy remembers:

The first time I ever saw her was up in Harlem, where she sang "Strange Fruit" at a benefit for Emmett Till, the young black who was lynched in the South for whistling at a white woman.

She was so exploited all her life by record companies, her agents and the unions that it was actually in the interest of any one of those groups to disgrace her in the final weeks of her life. . . . Billie Holiday never got her sickness and death benefits, which she had paid for probably twenty-five years; they all went down the drain or into some pig's pocket.

At the time of Holiday's death, Kennedy was already handling Charlie Parker's estate and seeing a pattern of exploitation by record companies and agents against black entertainers:

I elected to do something with the law that had not been done before because I could not see any way within the limits of my financial situation to sue all the companies that I knew owed royalties.

Kennedy began bringing petitions for orders of discovery, forcing the record companies and the agents to open up their books.

But by the late 1960s, Kennedy was completely disenchanted with the law. She cut down on her practice and stepped up her involvement in demonstrations instead. In 1966 she led a group of pickets outside the offices of the Benton & Bowles advertising agency to protest their hiring and programming practices. Carrying signs such as LEAVE BOLD UNSOLD and JIM CROW LIVES ON MADISON AVENUE, her protest was short-lived. The agency executives quickly invited her upstairs to talk. "Ever since, I've been able to say, 'When you want to get to the suites, start in the streets.' "

In 1970 Kennedy attended a symposium at Columbia Law School and gave a stunned audience her view of the legal system:

Ours is a prostitute society. The system of justice, and most especially the legal profession, is a whorehouse serving those best able to afford the luxuries of justice offered to preferred customers. The lawyer, in these terms, is analogous to a prostitute. The difference between the two is simple. The prostitute is honest—the buck is her aim. The lawyer is dishonest—he claims that justice, service to mankind, is his primary purpose . . . [but] he represents the client who puts the highest fee on the table. . . . The question arises in discussing the generic sense of the whorehouse as representative of the legal system, whether all lawyers are the same. This is like asking whether everything that gets into a sewer is garbage.

Since then she has been mostly on the college lecture circuit, stirring up audiences with her bad language and her controversial ideas. To women not committed to the equal rights movement, she says, "Women are dirt searchers. Their greatest worth is eradicating rings on collars and tables. Never mind real estate boards, corruption and racism—here's your soapsuds. Everything she is doing is peripheral, expendable . . . and nonnegotiable. Cleanliness is next to godliness." To community leaders who try to present themselves as resident members of the disadvantaged class, "I say, go to the ghetto, listen to the people there—but don't stay too long, and for Christ's sake, don't get into bed with the malaria patient. If you want to kill poverty, go to Wall Street and kick ass or disrupt." On the nation's criminal laws in the 1970s: "A very average prostitute in almost any part of this country can get $100 a night minimum, or if she is fairly well known she might make as much as five hundred dollars. A run-of-the-mill file clerk nets about $100 a week, and a run-of-the-mill housewife will get zero a week for filing, fucking, ironing, having the baby, nursing the baby, baby sitting, and the whole megillah. In my opinion, a government that cannot provide full employment for women who don't have degrees, and even those who do, has a pretty big nerve making the most lucrative occupation a crime. Remember, nobody ever died from a blow job."

The transformation of Florynce Kennedy from serious and committed lawyer to movement "character" may have had something to do with the isolation black women lawyers say they feel as they work in a mostly white professional society. At some point each one invariably talks about the loneliness and feeling of separateness that comes over her in a law school class, in court or at a large law firm. "You're a curiosity, a spectacle. You can never be inconspicuous so you either try to blend in, much as you know you never can, or you get used to being looked at," is the way one young attorney expressed it. If you have Florynce Kennedy's sense of bravado and fun, you even begin to enjoy it.

In the 1970s, as more black women entered the legal profession and government agencies began cracking down on employer discrimination, the black woman lawyer became a valuable commodity. Cynthia Fuchs Epstein, in studies she conducted in 1972 and again in 1978, found that, ironically, many black women attorneys got their chance because of their "double impairment." Epstein quoted one woman who knew she was hired to improve equal employment statistics in the early 1970s. "I'm a show woman and a show nigger, all for one salary."

Denise Carty-Bennia, a professor at the Northeastern School of Law, recalls her days at a well-known Wall Street law firm. "I was given an office that was situated so that absolutely everyone in the firm had to notice me at some point in their day. I was the caged monkey." The tokenism didn't end there. "Every Friday the firm had a late afternoon cocktail party. I'm not much of a drinker and I hate office social events so I always skipped them. Well one of the partners was getting more and more insistent about my going, telling me it was important for everyone in the firm to see me. I knew exactly what he meant and decided I would cooperate. But being a bit of a showman myself I decided I would add a prop. I wore a sign around my neck that said, "I am the new nigger," and watched as everyone pretended not to notice."

Active in black politics, Carty-Bennia represented the minority stu-

dents who boycotted Harvard for its failure to hire minority law professors, and served as co-chairman of the National Association of Black
Lawyers. Her law school education and her Wall Street work helped
to convince her that former congresswoman Shirley Chisholm was
right when she said that being a woman was tougher than being black.
"At the law firm, all kinds of outrageous practices were tolerated against
women. I was literally ordered not to speak to the secretaries when I
met them in the bathroom. I watched partners humiliate a woman
associate with a weight problem who had been first in her class at
Harvard Law School and was considerably smarter than they were, all
the while they ignored their own waistlines. I saw that it was fine for
women and blacks to drive themselves as associates but unrealistic for
them to expect to make partner."

Carty-Bennia's view is echoed by Deborah Jordon, a corporate lawyer who says she always felt she was "an outsider." Because of her mixed
black, white and American Indian ancestry, "there was a time when
I felt I didn't belong anywhere. White students would say insensitive
things, blacks would call me 'yellow nigger,' and often being a woman
meant you weren't taken too seriously in college or law school." Jordon,
a Phi Beta Kappa graduate of Brown University and an honors graduate
of Yale Law School, clerked for a federal judge, and then joined a Wall
Street firm. "It was a disastrous experience. You could sense the partners preferred that women stick with the paper work. Being tough in
representing a client seemed to create a tension that made men lawyers
very uncomfortable." Jordon decided the opportunities for black
women were greater in government.*

Yet despite Jordon's view, black women have not greatly succeeded
on the national political level. The civil rights and women's movements
raised expectations about what that electorate could deliver. And while
the careers of Congresswoman Yvonne Braithwaite, former U.S. Equal
Opportunity Commission chairman Eleanor Holmes Norton and Ambassador Patricia Roberts Harris broke a number of barriers in the early
1970s, black women lawyers say they are not keeping up with the gains
made by their male counterparts.

*After serving as counsel to New York City's deputy mayor and to the City College of New York,
Jordon joined the corporate law department of the National Broadcasting Company.

One woman who made a substantial difference in the way black women lawyers are viewed in politics was Barbara Jordan, the congresswoman from Texas who in serving on the House Judiciary Committee during Watergate captured the respect of the nation.

Born in 1936, Barbara Charline Jordan grew up in Houston's Fifth Ward—a poor black neighborhood. The greatest influence on her life was her grandfather, John Ed Patten, who years earlier was falsely accused of shooting a white policeman and spent seven years in a Texas penitentiary for his "crime." "The case and subsequent appeals reflected all the racial biases of the times," Jordan says, and when Patten was finally pardoned he was a broken man. Nevertheless, after his release he maintained high aspirations for his family and was disappointed when his daughter, Barbara's mother, did nothing more with her life than marry and have children.

Barbara Jordan recalls the "almost ritual" Sundays when she and her grandfather would go down to Matt Garner's Barbecue and at the back door get themselves a bag of "reg'lars"—the ends of beef that would be thrown away rather than served to paying customers. They would come home and spend the evening eating and talking. "In the early years it was certainly the case that he was the only one who talked to me—because mostly what adults do to children is to give them catechism in some form or another. But in terms of instructions about how to live, that is missing."

As a teenager, Barbara Jordan was an avid reader and a skilled debater. When she was asked to list her "favorite fashion fads" in her high-school yearbook she mentioned "the poodle cut and loud-colored shoes." In her senior year she was Wheatley High School's "Girl of the Year," and it was certain she was heading for college. But educational opportunities for blacks in the early 1950s were limited, so Barbara Jordan enrolled at Texas Southern University, the institution for blacks created by the Texas legislature in the hopes of avoiding a desegregation battle at the all-white University of Texas. Barbara qualified for TSU's debating team and traveled throughout the South to participate in competitions. She and her team would travel by car, staying in rooming houses and motels that were "for coloreds only," and eating sometimes at the back doors of restaurants. Her debating team won several medals and to her amazement and delight tied in a match with

Harvard. "But I realized, starkly, that the best training available in an all-black, instant university was not equal. Separate was not equal, no matter what face you put on it."

Jordan was a pre-law student at Texas Southern University and wanted to go to Harvard Law School, but decided her chances for admission would be better at Boston University Law School. It was a hardship for her family to get the tuition money together, and once they did, there was virtually nothing left for daily expenses or trips back home. "So I went to the law school and walked into a room with all freshman law students, about six hundred, because that was in the days when the attrition rate was awfully high—they would get in all that money from freshmen, and then half of them would punch out. There were six women and [of the six] two black women." Jordan remembers:

Everything was so different to me. "Contracts," "property," "torts" were strange words to me. Words I had not dealt with. And there I was. Can you understand how strange this was to my ears?

And the contracts professor, he started marching up and down talking about "promisor" and "promisee." And I said, "For crying out loud"—the only thing that sounded familiar to me was criminal law because you could read in the newspaper about murder and rape, and they didn't talk about lessor, lessee . . . I could understand a burglary.

Unlike the other students, many of whom had lawyer relatives and took their degrees for granted, Barbara Jordan left her law school graduation ceremonies and went back to her room to make sure her name was on the scroll. She remembers that when she saw it, she sat down and cried.

Jordan took and passed the Massachusetts bar exam, then returned to Houston to start a private practice, taking and passing the Texas bar as well. She quickly became interested in local politics but lost her first two campaigns for statewide office. A professor at Rice University came to her headquarters to offer some advice: "You know it's going to be hard for you to win a seat in the Texas legislature. You've got too much going against you: you're black, you're a woman and you're large. People don't really like that image."

In 1965 Barbara Jordan's district was reapportioned, creating a new Eleventh State Senatorial District composed mostly of blacks, Chicanos and whites who were union members. This time she felt she could win. She told her campaign audiences, "I ran a race in 1962. You endorsed me and I lost. I ran a race in 1964. You endorsed me and I lost. I want you to know I have no intention of being a three-time loser." Jordan was right. She beat her opponent by a two-to-one margin and became the first black woman in the Texas State legislature.

Seven years later, in 1972, she was elected to the United States Congress, again the first black woman in Texas to achieve such high office. She recalls the good-natured kidding she received from the members of the Texas delegation. "My fellow Texans said that they would stand around me for the swearing-in. [Someone] said, 'Well now, but that might take away from Barbara Jordan. People might not be able to tell which one she is.' "

Jordan, like Judge Motley, considered Lyndon Johnson a great friend of blacks and a personal friend as well. When word of his death reached the House, Jordan found herself making her first speech on the floor —an impromptu eulogy for the former President. "Old men straightened their stooped backs because Lyndon Johnson lived," she said. "Black Americans became excited about a future of opportunity, hope, justice, and dignity. Lyndon Johnson was my political mentor and my friend. I loved him and I shall miss him."

And then in 1974 came Watergate. Jordan was a member of the House Judiciary Committee as was another woman attorney, Elizabeth Holtzman from New York, now the Kings County district attorney. Peter Rodino, the chairman, announced that the committee would be going into the matter of the impeachment of Richard Nixon. The members of the Judiciary Committee decided it would benefit the public—and themselves—to have televised proceedings in which each member could make a fifteen-minute statement to a national audience. Jordan's turn came on July 25. Improvising from research notes, she began:

"We the people"—it is a very eloquent beginning. But when the Constitution of the United States was completed on the seventeenth of September in 1787, I was not included in that "We the people." I felt for many years that somehow George Washington and Alexander Hamilton just left me out by mistake. But through the process of amendment, interpretation, and court decision I have finally been included in "We the people."

Today I am an inquisitor. I believe hyperbole would not be fictional and would not overstate the solemness that I feel right now. My faith in the Constitution is whole. It is complete. It is total. I am not going to sit here and be an idle spectator to the diminution, the subversion, the destruction of the Constitution.

Jordan went on to give a forceful and informative talk on the history of the constitutional basis for impeachment of a President, explaining it so that the viewing audience could understand the issues. She concluded that "if the impeachment provision in the Constitution of the United States will not reach the offenses charged here, then perhaps the eighteenth-century Constitution should be abandoned to a twentieth-century paper shredder."

Overnight the congresswoman from Texas became a national political asset. At the 1976 Democratic National Convention, Jordan was asked to make the keynote speech and once again she captivated her audience. Convention chairman Robert Strauss, a fellow-Texan, is reported to have said, "I told those sons-of-bitches she'd be the hit of the show, I told them." The New York *Times* agreed, describing Jordan as "an American success story." After the election President Jimmy Carter offered her a position in his Administration that was said to be a Cabinet-level or United Nations post, but it wasn't the job she wanted, that of Attorney General, so she reportedly turned him down. Since 1979 Jordan has been a professor at the University of Texas at Austin.

The distinction of being the first black woman in a presidential Cabinet went instead to Patricia Roberts Harris, who was appointed Secretary of Housing and Urban Development and later served as Secretary of Health and Welfare in the same Administration. Harris, who also had the distinction of being the first black woman ambassador, was born and raised in Illinois and died in 1985. As a student at Howard University she, like Ruth Harvey Charity, participated in the 1943 sit-ins to desegregate Washington, D.C., restaurants. She graduated first in her class at George Washington University Law School and went on to serve as professor and dean of Howard Law School. Harris was a member of the 1968 National Commission on the Causes and Prevention of Violence and was a partner in a prestigious and political capital law firm.

After her nomination for Secretary of Housing and Urban Development, Patricia Roberts Harris appeared at confirmation hearings in the United States Senate. Senator William Proxmire asked her, "Will you really make an effort to get the views of those who are less articulate and less likely to be knocking on your door with outstanding credentials?" It was an innocuous question, one that deserved little more than a yes answer, but Proxmire appeared to have struck a chord. Patricia Roberts Harris gave a reply that aptly describes the feelings of black women lawyers—in and out of public life. "Senator, I am one of them," she answered. "You do not seem to understand who I am. I am a black woman, the daughter of a dining-car waiter. I am a black woman who even eight years ago could not buy a house in some parts of the District of Columbia. If my life has any meaning at all, it is that those who start as outcasts may end up being part of the system. I assure you that while there may be those who forget what it meant to be excluded from the dining room of this very building, I shall not forget."

7

WOMEN IN THE
COURTROOM

Early in 1881 Anne C. Southworth, a young Massachusetts law student, wrote an essay called "Why Should Not Women Be Lawyers?" Citing existing prejudice against women in the profession, Southworth listed the arguments she most frequently heard against a woman's practicing law:

She lacks strength of body;
She lacks strength of nerve;
The practice of law renders her unrefined by contact with baser natures;
It exposes her to insult;
It unfits her for a domestic life;
It is a source of domestic disagreement;
She is intellectually unfitted.

Southworth devoted the rest of her article to refuting these arguments, wondering what it was about trial work that was considered too demanding for women even though sweatshop labor in factories was not. Criticizing those who believed in female fragility, Southworth wrote that "for years they have watched [woman] grow thin and stoop-shouldered as she passes in the gray of early dawn and the shadow of the evening to and from the great factories. They have seen the hectic flush rising in her pale cheeks and have heard the hollow cough; perhaps they have even shaken their heads and solemnly predicted that such close confinement was killing or at least enervating her; but they have never seriously objected to allowing her to kill herself in that manner if she chose."

The notion that law, particularly trial work, requires a physical strength that women simply do not possess was demonstrated in a short story that lawyer Charles Moore wrote in 1886 for the Hartford *Daily Times.* Moore tried to imagine what might happen if a woman attorney turned up in his hometown, Old Litchfield, Connecticut. In "The Woman Lawyer," a delicate young Mary Padelford arrives on the Claremont stagecoach and is greeted by attorney Walter Perry, "a man vigorous in mind and body," who remarks that if Miss Padelford "possesses enough physical strength I wouldn't be surprised if she makes a success." In only a short time it becomes evident that while Miss Padelford is superbly qualified to draft legal documents, clearly she is no match for the rigors of the courtroom. In her first major case it is only with Walter Perry's help that she gets through a critical legal argument. During a particularly stormy trial in which she is pitted against two tough and unscrupulous adversaries, Miss Padelford falls from her chair in a faint and then whispers, "Oh take me away, take me away." By the story's end, Miss Padelford announces her decision to give up practicing law and to leave town. "I am loath to abandon the law practice," she says, "but my physician warns me against trying cases in court." Miss Padelford gives up a courtroom career, marries Walter Perry and spends the rest of her life helping him in a law partnership.

A century later women are still underrepresented in the courtroom and still find resistance to their participation in trial work. In 1983 it was estimated that fewer than 6 percent of all state trial judges in the United States were women and that only about 8 percent of all federal judges were women—despite significant gains made in recent years. The Association of Trial Lawyers of America reported that in 1978 only eight states had more than 4 percent of their women attorneys actively engaged in litigation practices. And although an exclusively female jury was convened in America as early as 1656, women were not even permitted to serve as jurors in every state of the union until well into this century.

Burnita Shelton Matthews, in a 1927 article for the *Women Lawyers Journal,* indicated that even seemingly progressive states like New York were regularly quashing women juror bills on the grounds that their citizens were not ready for such "experimental legislation." Matthews pointed out: "One picture which is often conjured up is that of a mother being dragged off for jury duty while hubby sings to the crying baby:

> Nice little baby, don't get
>   in a fury,
> Mama, it may be, must sit
>   on a jury.

Alice McClanahan, another lawyer from this period, supported Matthews's view, recalling that those who feared women's participation in the courtroom "seemed to be saying that the right to serve on juries was nothing more than a demand by neurotic women who had a yearning for importance . . . as though jury service would convert women into the kind of creature that eats its young."

While resistance to women jurors was widespread, adverse reaction to women lawyers practicing in the courtroom was even greater. McClanahan, who was a Legal Aid lawyer before joining her father in private practice, claimed: "You have all the difficulties which confront young men lawyers starting out and more than double their handicaps because of your sex. You will meet with rudeness, be patronized, swept aside and often have to fight for the merest right. You will find judges inclined to give the best of an argument to your male opponents. You will be condescended to, ignored, and you will have to fight every step of the way."

In 1914 a woman lawyer wrote a letter to the editor of the New York *Sun* to comment on her "chances" in the legal profession. Preferring to remain anonymous, she candidly noted:

When the girl lawyer tries her first case the jury will smile affably upon her and so perhaps will the Judge, but there is one person who will not smile and that is the opposing counsel who objects to a woman adversary. There are some lawyers who go so far as to say that given a woman plaintiff and a woman attorney and the defense might just as well lie down if the case be before a jury. Be this as it may, it is an ordeal for a woman at the outset of her practice to encounter in the person of the opposing counsel a courteous, well-bred gentleman whose antagonism is obvious. She knows that he is thinking that she has no place in the courtroom; if she is a good-looking girl she ought to be married; if she isn't good-looking she ought to be dead or else justifying her existence by serving in the capacity of overworked stenographer to some dignified member of the nobler sex.

Those who would suggest that these turn-of-the-century women were guided more by paranoia than by perception should compare these views with those of then contemporary bar leaders such as Theron G. Strong, author of *Landmarks of a Lawyer's Lifetime*. In his 1914 memoirs Strong wrote:

It is now more than thirty years since Mrs. Lockwood was admitted, and the right of women to practice was established, but I have never yet seen a woman plead a case of any kind in court, and I have never yet met with a woman lawyer except . . . concerning the settlement of some unimportant litigation, and I think it may be safely asserted that there is no prospect that women will be seen except as a *rara avis* in the ranks of the legal fraternity.

While Strong was mistaken about the numbers and accomplishments of women lawyers in the profession, his was a widely held belief: Women had no place in the courtroom.

Detroit attorney Martha Strickland disputed such views. Admitted to the Michigan bar in 1883, she became a county prosecutor and had extensive trial experience. In 1891 Strickland wrote an article "Women and the Forum," in which she urged women to take an active part in the legal system. She insisted that women not only had a right to engage in trial work but owed a duty to their less educated sisters to represent women in all tribunals. Strickland wrote:

Gradually as the years have passed and I have become more familiar with our courts and the administration of justice, the opinion has been forced upon me that not only is there need of women lawyers, but of women in all parts of our judicial system. In that very branch of government whose fundamental principle is that all men shall be tried by their peers, women, save in the most limited degree are called upon every day to submit their dearest rights of happiness, property and life to the judgment of persons differently constituted, mentally and physically, from themselves, and so widely separated by instincts, habit, thought, politics and social environment that the maxim of Charles Reade's hero, "Put yourself in his place" is impossible and any attempt thereto must from its inception prove a failure.

Despite what was thought of them, many early women lawyers were adhering to Strickland's view and, like Belva Lockwood, were distinguishing themselves in the courtroom. Almeda E. Hitchcock, an 1888 graduate of the University of Michigan Law School, was the first woman lawyer in Hawaii. The day she was admitted to the Hawaii bar, Hitchcock went to Waimea to argue a motion before the third judicial court. She told a friend that "the natives were all astonished to see a 'Wahine Loio' " (woman lawyer), and the remarks which she heard in passing were often amusing because they did not realize that she understood their language. When circumstances required it, Almeda Hitchcock was known to ride over two hundred miles on horseback to argue a case in an out-district circuit court. Her reputation spread and soon she was named interim sheriff of Hilo Island. One article describing the appointment noted: "When it is realized that the sheriff is to one of these islands practically what the Governor is to one of our States, the responsibility devolving upon this young girl can be imagined."

Similarly, Nevada's first woman attorney was a source of interest and amazement whenever she made an appearance in court. Laura Ray Tilden was admitted to the Nevada bar in 1893 at the age of twenty-two. The following year, when she won a burglary trial in neighboring California, her competence in the courtroom was major news in both states. A newspaper account printed by the Sacramento *Bee* and later reprinted by the Virginia City *Territorial Enterprise* reveals much about prevailing attitudes concerning women advocates:

Miss Laura Tilden, the young woman lawyer who recently hung out her shingle in Sacramento, scored her first victory in the Superior Court this morning, after which she was most cordially congratulated by many of the old practitioners who had dropped in to see how she would handle her case. Miss

Tilden is young and rather pretty. She has a clear pleasing voice which was distinctly heard throughout the courtroom. Some people thought that she would be flustered when she rose to address Judge Catlin. But she was not. She was by no means ill at ease, and made the customary salutation, "May it please your Honor," as though she had been accustomed to doing it every day. . . . She had piled up in front of her a lot of law books and papers, and was evidently prepared to make a hard legal battle if necessity required.

During this same period Chicago's Kate Kane Rossi boasted that by 1890 she had "either prosecuted or defended in every crime known to modern times except treason and piracy;" and that she has represented clients "from every quarter of the globe, of every hue and every religion except the followers of Zoroaster and Mahomet." In the late 1800s Nettie Lutes and Florence Cronise, sisters and law partners, were each such effective litigators that every year they handled more than fifty state and federal cases on the civil trial dockets for the Northern District of Ohio. Nebraska's Addie Billings regularly handled both civil and criminal trials noting that occasionally "a man comes into the office with work who does not want 'the woman' to meddle in his case, but such clients are exceptional." J. Ellen Foster was not only an outspoken temperance leader in Illinois but a well-known defense lawyer as well. In the 1880s her reputation was enhanced by her ability to secure a new trial for a woman client facing execution.

Most of the pioneer women lawyers earned their reputations and their skills in the courtroom. Clara Foltz and Laura De Force Gordon, the California women who successfully sued to gain admission to Hastings College of Law in the 1870s, each went on to become successful trial lawyers. Carrie Burnham Kilgore, Ada Bittenbinder, Ellen Martin, Frederika Perry, the mother-daughter team of Mrs. C. K. Pier and Kate Pier (they studied law together at the University of Wisconsin in the 1880s)*—all were known to be successful litigators.

For these early women lawyers, and for nineteenth-century lawyers in general, the nature of legal work was such that a single practitioner or a small group of lawyers handled whatever cases came to them with no real need for a division of labor. The general practitioner inter-

---

*In the 1970s the mother-daughter prosecution team of Lee and Penny Port made news in California's San Mateo County.

viewed the client, researched the law, drafted the legal documents, wrote the brief and argued the case in court. Women lawyers who were able to attract clients handled these same responsibilities themselves. But the advent of big business in the late 1800s brought about a fragmenting and eventual restructuring of the practice of law. Giant firms were created and separate tasks were given to lawyers with specialties. As historian Frank Ellsworth points out, lawyers during this period found that they had to understand developments in insurance, manufacturing, railroads, telegraph, telephone and the laws affecting these developments. Ellsworth claims that law was ceasing to be a learned profession and was itself becoming a big business. The result was that the era of specialization began and that the independent lawyer was a fading phenomenon.

Specialization had the unintended effect of relegating women lawyers to research and clerking jobs, putting them on the edge of the profession and outside the courtroom. Since the notion was, and to some extent today still is, that success in the courtroom depends on aggressiveness and flamboyance, women were considered particularly unsuited for the job. Lacking opportunities to prove their worth and practicing without the benefit of the contacts and mentors their male counterparts had, women had little chance to compete for courtroom glory. When jobs in specialized firms became available to them at all, and it was a rare circumstance when they did, they were typically in the back rooms, the libraries and the secretarial pools. So without the aggressive reputation or well-placed connections men had, women who insisted on trial careers found that their clients were usually other women or indigents or both.

Yet no matter how competently they represented these clients, women trial attorneys still were greeted with suspicion and scorn. Clarice Baright, a woman's bar leader with considerable courtroom experience, was challenged by a reporter for the New York *World* in 1916. Wasn't it true that women lawyers were flirtatious in court, unfairly hoping to win verdicts on their sex alone? Baright answered, "Those Judges look down from their bench, and their life job and assured position and see us, perhaps a little nervous, because everyone is trying to find something freakish about a woman lawyer. And they think we are trying to flirt with them . . . by the time you finish a case there isn't much the Judge doesn't know about your appearance. But I've never known a woman lawyer who got anything except by hard work." Baright is said to have been the first woman to try a case before an Army general court-martial. The New York *Times* noted: "In 1918 she appeared in a case at Camp Upton, Long Island, wearing khaki and a felt campaign hat and obtained the acquittal of a private on a larceny charge."

Kansas lawyer Tiera Farrow found unexpected success in the courtroom, but believed that on the whole her male colleagues saw her as just another woman "freak." A 1903 graduate of the Kansas City School of Law, Farrow recalled her fellow students frequently reminded her that "the great law documentor, Blackstone, classified women in a category with infants and idiots."

Farrow became an unlikely witness to a murder in 1915 when, after representing her client, Clara Schweiger, in a divorce matter, she watched in horror as Mrs. Schweiger pulled out a gun in the courthouse corridor and killed ex-husband Louis Schweiger in full view of a number of spectators. The event and the subsequent murder trial captured the attention of a national press in search of a sensational story:

For the first time in the history of Missouri, a woman attorney will conduct the defense in a murder case, when the trial of Mrs. Schweiger who shot and killed her husband in the courthouse is called. The woman attorney is Miss Tiera Farrow, young, good-looking and most feminine in appearance—not at all the sort of person one would connect with the wrangling of attorneys and the heated debates usually attendant upon murder trials.

Tiera Farrow decided she had no other choice but to plead her client temporarily insane. In her closing argument she made an emotional, if not melodramatic appeal to the jury, comparing the passion Clara Schweiger had for Louis Schweiger with that contained in all the great stories of love gone wrong—from Antony and Cleopatra to "Lord Byron and the Italian Countess." She ended by appealing to the jurors:

Gentlemen . . . after he had sipped the honey from this poor woman's life, he left her; when she could no longer physically appeal to him, his mind went elsewhere. Now, if that condition had been reversed in this case, do you think for one minute Mrs. Schweiger would have left him? Left him in a helpless manner, wrecked physically and mentally? No! A thousand times no!

The jury found Clara Schweiger guilty of manslaughter instead of murder and she was spared the death sentence. Tiera Farrow earned a reputation as an effective courtroom practitioner. She continued to do trial work and remained a strong supporter of women in the legal profession. In 1925 she helped to found a series of women's law classes in Kansas City. The Kansas City *Star* applauded her efforts, but could not help noting:

Women have not what is loosely called a "legal" mind. As a rule neither their inclinations nor their mental receptiveness are favorable to the acquisition of legal knowledge.

This would have surprised such women as Bessie R. Geffner, who not only successfully defended civil and criminal trials in New York, but sometimes went to unusual lengths to do so. Geffner was representing a client in a murder trial during a particularly muggy June in 1926, dressed every day of the trial in a heavy overcoat. "It was different then. I was eight months pregnant and the sight of a woman in court was unusual enough—a pregnant woman just wouldn't be tolerated. But what could I do? My client was being tried for murder and couldn't afford to hire anyone else. So I went to court in my coat. When the trial was over, the judge called me up to the bench and very sternly told me I was a disgrace. He ordered me to go home and have my baby."

Efforts to exclude women from criminal law and courtroom practice often began in law school. Tiera Farrow was told she could skip her criminal law classes at Kansas City School of Law "on the grounds the subject to be discussed might shock my maidenly modesty." Similarly, Margaret Hickey, the lawyer and journalist who helped to draft the civil rights section of the United Nations Charter, was excluded from classes when rape was being discussed, since her professor thought the subject an improper one for "a nice young woman." Upon graduating from law school, however, women found male attorneys keeping the "proper" business and estates cases for themselves, virtually assuring that women lawyers would be handling the very cases considered to be "too rough" for them.

This was particularly true for women such as Rose Falls Bres, who found herself in the early 1920s handling death-sentence appeals for a convicted murderer and then watching in horror as he was publicly hanged before a cheering crowd. Bres was so moved by the experience that she wrote a poignant account of her efforts to save the life of her client, Charles Brown Perelli. According to Bres, Perelli, a Brooklyn youth, "half crazed and with a crazy temper," had had minimal assistance of local counsel in Florida, where he was convicted of the first-degree murder of a cab driver in 1923. Perelli's family and a number of New York newspapers suspected the conviction had more to do with anti-Italian Catholic prejudice than with the evidence adduced at trial. One New York City tabloid, the *Evening Graphic,* appealed to readers to contribute to a legal defense fund for Perelli. But since most of the donations came from people as poor as Perelli himself, only $300 was raised. Nevertheless the *Graphic*'s editors convinced Bres, who was admitted to practice both in New York and in Florida, to take the case. It was to be a race with state officials, who were hoping to capitalize on the popular sentiment in Florida for Perelli's swift execution. Bres brought two writs of habeas corpus in the United States Supreme Court challenging Perelli's sanity at the time of trial and the state's policy of keeping Perelli in solitary confinement for more than a year, refusing him the right to bathe and exercise:

A Deputy Sheriff stated this was necessary because of the "crazy temper" of Perelli and the fears of keepers for their own safety. But, whatever the reason, surely there was never a more pathetic figure than the youth in his small barred cage on a floor where there were no other prisoners, where exercise was impossible, save walking possibly three or four steps back and forth, where through a barred window across the hall came the only light, the setting sun in its brief sweep across this space.

Bres's second writ of habeas corpus was based on changes in Florida law that occurred between the time of sentencing and the scheduled date for execution. While Perelli had been sentenced to be hanged, Florida now was executing prisoners by electric chair. Just two hours before the scheduled execution, the U.S. Supreme Court ruled Perelli's original sentence was "illegal, null and void." It was delivered over the telephone to the superintendent of the Raiford death house. Perelli quickly was resentenced by the original trial court, and the governor of Florida made extraordinary efforts to see that the execution was promptly carried out.

For Rose Falls Bres the ultimate irony was that Perelli had been scheduled to die on Easter weekend. Unable to take any further appeals or obtain any additional stays, Bres stayed in Florida just long enough to attend her client's execution and to bitterly describe the carnival atmosphere:

The jail at DeLand stands opposite the Courthouse which is in a large open square. Word had been sent all up and down and roundabout that there would be a hanging there on Monday morning and so the crowd began arriving early from the surrounding towns on the East Coast, from midstate, from adjacent communities, came those with the desire to see a man hung, "a Dago and a Catholic." When Perelli walked onto the scaffold, which was erected at the side of the jail, he stood high above the fence which would have obstructed the view of the curious from the street and open square. And there in that arena huddled more than two thousand men, women and children. It was a barbaric picnic party . . .

Movies picture very often the death watch, the last moments of a man condemned, but even the thrill-producers of movies are not permitted to picture an actual hanging, so that in this execution there was the real hundred percent thrill of witnessing the twitching for nearly thirty minutes of a young man, hung by the neck by "due process of law."

In 1937 Helen L. Buttenwieser, one of the first woman associates for a large Wall Street law firm, sought to move to New York's Legal Aid Society. While women attorneys such as Rose Rothenberg and Anna Moskowitz Kross had been involved in criminal cases since the early 1900s, Buttenwieser was to learn that she would only be considered for positions in the civil division of Legal Aid. "Women simply were not permitted to handle criminal cases—the idea was that it would be too upsetting for women to see what was going on in the criminal courts. After I had been with Legal Aid for about six or eight months, a court attendant came in to announce a lawyer was needed in Part One of the criminal court. I stood up to go with him but he said, 'No, not you.'

I persisted so he let me into the courtroom, but then I had to be screened by the judge. 'Are you married?' he asked. I told him I was. 'Do you have any children?' 'Yes.' 'Well then, you can stay.' Here I was in my midthirties, and unless I gave the right answers to these questions, I was not going to be allowed to handle a sodomy case."

In the 1940s Cecelia Goetz, who had graduated at the top of her law school class, sought a job as a trial lawyer for the government. "The prejudice against women was there even in the departments headed by well-known liberals. It was quite a blow to learn, for example, that no women, or blacks, were being hired for the Antitrust Division of the Justice Department." When Goetz, now a federal bankruptcy judge, sought a job as a prosecutor in the Nuremberg trials, her request initially was not taken seriously. "You're much too attractive," she was told. "When I persisted they then told me it would be impossible, since they had no facilities for me to live in during the trials. I remember asking what about the nurses and the secretaries and the clerks? Where are you putting those women and why can't I stay there?" When Goetz still met with resistance she decided to make a direct appeal to Telford Taylor, the chief U.S. prosecutor at Nuremberg. "Fortunately he did not share such antifeminist views and he immediately directed that I be appointed to the prosecution team. Nevertheless, in order for me to be processed, Taylor had to sign a 'waiver of disability' form—the disability being the fact I was a woman." In 1948 the New York *Sun* did a profile of Goetz's work at the Krupp trial in Nuremberg:

Cecelia admits she works under handicaps. All the original documents are written in German. All the witnesses are hostile. The political and economical set-up is entirely new to her. Learning about artillery and tanks is a terrific grind. Then being a woman isn't too much of a help either. . . . Listening to her reading part of the opening statement in the hushed courtroom, marriage and children don't seem to fit into the picture. . . . The British delegation were particularly impressed. At the first opportunity they swarmed over to congratulate her on her striking performance.*

---

*The first woman prosecutor to participate in the German war crimes trials was WAC captain Irma Von Nunes, a skilled trial attorney from Atlanta. In 1931 Von Nunes was interviewed by an Atlanta newspaper which reported, "Little Miss Von Nunes wears her hair cut like a boy's, affects an almost masculine garb and declares that marriage, like jail, is a good thing, but that she prefers to see other people in both."

Chicago attorney Carole K. Bellows recalls tremendous resistance to women practicing criminal law. In the 1950s when Bellows was a second year law student at Northwestern University, her professor asked his students to remain in their seats so that they could hear a short lecture from a member of the Chicago Bar Association who was eager to recruit criminal lawyers. "The young male lawyer entered the room. His eyes fell disapprovingly on the four women among the 90 or so men. 'I'm here to recruit investigators for the committee which represents indigent defendants in criminal cases. It is not necessary for any women to stay here. We can't use them.' Suddenly I wanted to be a bar association criminal law investigator. I protested vehemently. The young lawyer said he'd check with his committee. A few days later I was told flatly, 'No women will be allowed to participate in the investigations.' "

On the prosecution side, former New York congresswoman Geraldine Ferraro recalls being turned down for a job with the Manhattan District Attorney's office because she admitted she was planning to be married. "They said I would get pregnant and it would be a waste of their training." Feminist lawyer Lynn Hecht Schafran notes that when the current Manhattan district attorney Robert M. Morgenthau was United States Attorney for the Southern District of New York in the mid-1960s he did not hire women for the criminal division.*

By contrast, in 1944 Laura Miller Derry, a Kentucky lawyer, found herself defending a capital court-martial precisely because she was a woman. During World War II, Derry, along with a number of other attorneys in Louisville, was on call to give free legal advice to soldiers at nearby Fort Knox. Derry was surprised to learn that a Private Finn, a soldier who had been charged with raping a girl outside a local nightclub, had specifically asked that she represent him. "It was a very serious charge. I remember having heard somewhere that twenty-two soldiers were executed in England and in France after being convicted of rape. In the Army the only penalties were a death sentence or life imprisonment. I was not an expert in criminal law so I could not imagine why I was being summoned, but when I got the call from the stockade I went to see Private Finn, an Errol Flynn look-alike, who was

*Today over one-third of the prosecutors in the Manhattan DA's office are women.

seated on a slab bench in his cell." Finn, who was married and had a child, insisted that having a woman lawyer would help his case. Derry repeatedly told him she was not the expert in criminal law he ought to have, but Finn still wanted Derry to handle his defense. "As I was leaving the cell, he must have seen the look on my face because he called after me, 'Look, I'm satisfied if you are.' "

After having heard Finn's account of what had happened and doing some investigating on her own, Derry was convinced her client was innocent. "For more than two weeks before the trial I literally dropped everything to prepare for that case. It was a full court-martial, which meant the judges were eleven officers ranging in rank from major to colonel." The trial lasted more than three days. When it was over, Finn was acquitted and Laura Miller Derry was reported to be the first woman to successfully defend a client in a capital court-martial. "I knew how unusual it was for a southern woman to be handling a trial of this magnitude before a court-martial board. The president of the board was extremely cordial but I felt I had to be more than very well prepared, I felt I had to be a lady at all times. Now when I look back at the trial it occurs to me that I never once even said the word 'rape.' It was important to me then to be seen as a dignified woman."*

California's Gladys Towles Root never had that problem. Not only were sex crimes cases her specialty but the last thing Root wanted to do was present a dignified appearance in the courtroom. Insisting that she missed her calling—"I should have joined a circus"—Root made it a practice never to wear conventional dress in the courtroom, even when that courtroom was the United States Supreme Court. No one could have anticipated the reaction of the Justices when Root showed up for oral argument "in a tight-fitting bronze taffeta dress hemmed with brown velvet, bronze ankle-strap shoes, a topaz ring the size of a silver dollar and a pin [with a stone weighing] one hundred and ninety carats at her bust. Over the dress was a monkey fur cape, all white. Her huge hat was of the same material as the dress and her hair was dyed to match the topaz . . ." "These are my working clothes," Root explained. "If I wore the sports dress or tailored suit that the average

*Derry, a strong supporter of women in the law, went on to become president of the National Association of Women Lawyers.

person wears, I'd be miserable. I couldn't do my best." It is no wonder that reporters described her as "the most spectacular showman to appear on the local scene since Aimee Semple McPherson."

Like a number of her male counterparts, Gladys Towles Root believed a successful trial practice was built on aggressive lawyering and flamboyant courtroom tactics.* She started that practice immediately after law school in an office four blocks from the Skid Row section of Los Angeles. Root hoped to attract clients off the street, but when the practice was slow in starting, she began taking cases for indigent prisoners at a local jail. She quickly earned a reputation for being a skilled and dedicated lawyer. Her biographer notes that one derelict admirer was moved to "poetry":

Root-de-toot, toot-de-toot
Here's to Gladys Towles Root,
Her dresses are purple, her hats are wide,
She'll get you one instead of five.

In 1931 Root accepted the case of a young Filipino man who was prohibited by law from marrying his Caucasian girlfriend. She was successful in challenging the constitutionality of the California statute, and that case, along with a number of acquittals in sensational rape trials, brought Root to the attention of the press and public.

Through the years Gladys Root continued to dye her hair to match her clients' favorite colors and to make unforgettable entrances into California courts. Her style paid off. At the height of her career Root's law firm was handling more than 1,600 cases each year. And as part performer–part reformer, Root was speaking out on behalf of racial equality, humane treatment for sex offenders, and increased opportunities for women attorneys. "The chief critics of women lawyers are from the old school . . . old-timers. Many a male lawyer when defeated by a woman will blame it on that mystic factor they call feminine intuition. This is his excuse. In plain language, he faced too much perception and intelligence and logical thinking . . ."

---

*Root's antics were not always successful. In 1964 she was indicted by a federal grand jury on charges that she induced her client to give false testimony in the celebrated trial for the kidnapping of Frank Sinatra, Jr.

Roslyn Goodrich Bates, a Los Angeles attorney and women's bar leader, believed Root would have succeeded in the legal profession without the costumes and special effects, but like most observers Bates couldn't resist describing the Gladys Towles Root "look":

Mrs. Root is very competent and very thorough. . . . In one jury case she changed coats three times in one day. She makes 75 courtroom appearances monthly and is fantastically garbed for each. To repeat the same dress would be the equivalent of committing a cardinal sin. She favors black chantilly lace, multicolored sequins, pink ostrich plumes, red suede, various shades of velvet, woolens adorned with dozens of ermine tails. . . . Her hats are gigantic. A trial judge once ordered her to remove one. She did and exposed the court to hair done up in pin curls. "Put it back on," His Honor shouted . . . her hair has been dyed green, pink, lavender, mint, magenta—every color in the rainbow.

Gladys Towles Root died in 1982 and probably will be remembered more for her talent for spectacle than for her ability in the law— although both were formidable. She noted that all too often she would find herself the only woman trial lawyer in the courthouse. Root's need to put on a show in court may have been a matter of personal style, but in part it may also have reflected her feelings of separateness and isolation in what was virtually an all-male domain. If Root took on the traditional woman's appearance and soft-spoken style, the risk was that she would seem too passive. If she took on the traditional male role, she would be viewed as overly aggressive and "mannish." In the long run it may have been easier to be a spectacle than to have to choose either persona. According to Lynn Hecht Schafran, the director of the National Judicial Education Program to Promote Equality for Women and Men in the Courts, a project sponsored by the NOW Legal Defense Fund, women trial lawyers, even today, must cope with the continuing problems of "status set" and "double bind."

Schafran notes that sociologists use the term "status set" to describe the situation that prevails when a class of people sharing one key status, e.g. lawyer, share one or more matching statuses, e.g. male, and society endorses this as the appropriate match. "In our society lawyer-male is a deeply entrenched status set. As a result women lawyers are caught in a 'double bind.'" As Schafran describes it, "the woman lawyer is castigated as too weak to be effective if she displays feminine traits

. . . too pushy and abrasive if she asserts herself forcefully, although the same style would be deemed admirable in a man."*

Therefore, Schafran believes that

When a lawyer or judge for whom "litigator-male" is a deeply rooted norm encounters a "litigator-female" his status-set expectations are violated and he focuses on the litigator's femaleness rather than on her professional competence.

The man's discomfiture may express itself in a wide range of responses from calling the woman "young lady," "sweetheart" or some other inappropriate term to the extreme reaction of a Texas judge who recently asked 5' 2" Dallas lawyer Mannette Dodge to turn around and face the courtroom and then said, "Ladies and gentlemen, can you believe that this pretty little thing is an assistant attorney general?"

Such comments, which women lawyers report occur all too frequently in court, were labeled by Watergate prosecutor Jill Wine Volner in 1974 as "sexual trial tactics." Wine Volner (now Wine Banks) gained instant fame when she was assigned to cross-examine Rose Mary Woods, President Richard Nixon's personal secretary, about the eighteen-and-a-half-minute gap in the tape recording of a conversation between the President and his chief of staff H. R. Haldeman three days after the Watergate break-in. Woods had testified that she mistakenly stepped on the "record" button during a telephone conversation, thereby ruining the tape. Wine Volner recalled:

I asked her to demonstrate how she had managed to keep her foot on the pedal while reaching six feet behind her for the telephone. Right there in the courtroom, before hundreds of witnesses, her attempt to show me how she had done it failed.

Her foot came off the pedal and the demonstration tape stopped dead. No part of it had been erased. That was undoubtedly the highlight of my legal career, as it would have been for any trial lawyer. Perry Mason may do it every night on television but drama like that just doesn't happen very often in real-life courtrooms.

---

*Rhode Island's attorney general Arlene Violet presents a good example. Prior to taking office, Violet had been representing poverty-level clients in court while serving as a member of a religious order. Her vigorous trial tactics brought little admiration; instead, she was derisively dubbed "Attila the Nun."

Wine Volner reported that her first encounter with sexual trial tactics occurred while she was with the U.S. Department of Justice's Organized Crime Division. Opposing counsel insisted on referring to her, the government lawyer, as "the young lady." "Since I was inexperienced, I didn't know what to do so I ignored it—and very quickly realized that was precisely the right approach. The jury was becoming sympathetic to me and antagonistic to him." During a trial in Detroit, Wine Volner remembers the defense counsel commenting on her perfume in front of the jurors and putting his hand on her elbow at every bench conference. "I couldn't figure out the jury's reaction to these tactical demonstrations of chivalry so I decided to play it safe and put an end to them. Besides, they were very offensive to me. At the next bench conference when my opponent put his hand on my elbow I turned to him and said loudly enough for the judge to hear, 'Get your hands off me and don't ever touch me again.' The judge almost fell off his chair but the lawyer never touched me again. And I won the case."

By the time she had joined the Watergate prosecution team, Wine Volner knew exactly what to do when she encountered yet another instance of sexual trial tactics. "I told Mr. Wilson (John J. Wilson, counsel for H. R. Haldeman) I'd appreciate it if he wouldn't make such comments and that if he didn't stop I'd have to lower myself to his level and respond in kind."

But as Lynn Hecht Schafran points out, "In each of these incidents, the burden was on [Wine Volner] to decide whether she would be helped or hurt by a forceful response, and obviously she has superb instincts. However, a judge sensitive to the negative impact of such sexual trial tactics on a woman litigator's credibility and authority, and the double-bind implications for her of whatever action she might take, would have stopped 'the young lady' tactic with a comment like, 'Counselor, if by "the young lady," you are referring to your opponent, please note that in my courtroom lawyers are called counselor or by their names.'" Schafran has traveled extensively throughout the United States to give such training to judges on how to spot sexual trial tactics and how to deal with them when they arise.

One judge who is willing to admit that there is a disparity of treatment of men and women in the courtroom is Robert N. Wilentz, chief justice of New Jersey, who at the urging of Newark judge Marilyn Loftus in October 1982, created a thirty-one-member Task Force on Women in the Courts. Task force members interviewed judges and lawyers, analyzed rulings and statistics and distributed questionnaires to members of the New Jersey bar. In November 1983 the task force issued its findings:

Judges "sometimes appear" to give less credibility to lawyers, witnesses, experts and probation officers who are women than to their male counterparts.

Eighty-six percent of the lawyers surveyed who are women said their peers made hostile remarks or demeaning jokes about women. Two-thirds of these women said judges did the same.

More than half of the women questioned said lawyers who are men received more fee-generating court appointments for guardianships, receiverships and condemnations.

Seventy-eight percent of the lawyers surveyed who are women said they felt they were "treated disadvantageously" by judges in courtrooms and chambers and at professional gatherings because of their sex.

Chief Justice Wilentz in releasing the report reminded his fellow judges that "there's no room for the funny joke and the not-so-funny joke, there's no room for conscious, inadvertent, sophisticated, clumsy, or any other kind of gender bias and certainly no room for gender bias that affects substantive rights. There's no room because it hurts and it insults. It hurts female lawyers psychologically and economically, litigants psychologically and economically, and witnesses, jurors, law clerks and judges who are women. It will not be tolerated in any form whatsoever."

Three recent cases in point. In May 1982 trial lawyer Elizabeth C. Kaming successfully moved to have an entire panel of jurors excused because of the blatantly sexist remarks of opposing counsel in Nassau County Supreme Court. In March 1983 the New York State Commission on Judicial Conduct determined that state supreme court judge Anthony Jordan be admonished for calling lawyer Martha Coppelman "little girl" in open court. In July 1985 the New York State Commission on Judicial Conduct admonished district court judge Warren

Doolittle for courtroom remarks "inappropriate and offensive" to women attorneys. These included terms of endearment and speculation about how well the women might look in a bikini.

Judge Loftus notes, "When you tell people stories of what often happens to women in court they think you're talking about the old days. Then you tell them it happened yesterday or that afternoon and they don't believe it. They think that at least in a courtroom everything is supposed to be equal."

For trial lawyers like Katherine Timon the thrill of courtroom practice overrides the misgivings she has about the treatment of women in the courtroom. "It is not easy to be called 'sweetie' in court and have the judge look the other way or be referred to as a 'fluff-head broad' outside a grand jury, but in the end what that really does is toughen you up and improve your edge. And something interesting is happening these days too—the jurors are no longer surprised when a woman does a competent job in court. Opposing counsel who still think the courtroom is a male preserve are years behind the very jurors they are hoping to impress."

As Robin Reisig pointed out in her *American Lawyer* article "The Improbable Rise of Pamela Chepiga," women such as Chepiga, who "had fairly dismissed the notion of becoming a litigator" because they didn't view their personalities as being "sufficiently outgoing, aggressive or combative" are achieving enormous success as litigators. Chepiga moved from the litigation department of Hughes Hubbard & Reed to the U.S. Attorney's office, where in little more than five years she tried fifteen corruption and securities fraud cases, getting convictions in all but one of them. In December 1982 she was named chief of the securities and commodities fraud unit. Chepiga's courtroom style may represent the way young women will handle the dilemma of double bind—by ignoring the gender roles and being themselves. "I had viewed litigation as an exercise in debate. It isn't. It's advocacy. When you've prepared your case and it's a cause you believe in, you can absolutely turn on in the courtroom."

Katherine Timon agrees, but believes there are certain lawyers, like herself, who are especially cut out for courtroom work. "I like the competition. I like the drama. I like the idea of getting my point across. A trial is like a shot of adrenalin for me and there's always a depression when it's over—even if I've won. Trial lawyers understand that in each other. They know it's a high like nothing else. And whether you're patting yourself on the back, saying 'I did it,' or sinking in your chair wondering 'Where did I screw up?,' you can't wait for the next one to begin. I don't blame the men for wanting this all for themselves but that's just not happening anymore. Every woman trial lawyer I know is out there encouraging other young women to follow."

8

WOMEN IN MAJOR LAW FIRMS

When United States Supreme Court Justice Sandra Day O'Connor graduated with honors from Stanford Law School, only one large California law firm would offer her a job—and that was as a stenographer.

When Democratic vice-presidential candidate Geraldine Ferraro graduated with honors from Fordham Law School she survived four grueling interviews with Dewey, Ballantine, Bushby, Palmer & Wood, the Wall Street law firm, only to be told on the fifth and final interview, "We're sorry but we're not hiring any women this year."

When United States Secretary of Transportation Elizabeth Dole attended Harvard Law School, a favorite joke among her classmates was, "Question: What's the difference between a female law student and garbage? Answer: At least garbage gets taken out."

When former United States Secretary of Housing and Urban Development Carla Hills was an antitrust litigator, she sensed that if she wanted to continue in the courtroom, she would have to disguise the fact that she was pregnant. Hills deliberately lost weight and wore loose-fitting suits to cover her condition.

These are the lawyers the press frequently refers to as "super-women." More often than not they have attended the right schools, joined the right clubs and sought jobs at the right law firms. They have reached the top of the legal profession through the same combination of intelligence, skill, hard work and good fortune that successful male attorneys have always used—but with one important difference. Each of these superwomen has had to contend with the effects of gender-based prejudice and discrimination while attempting to build a successful career.

The dual pressures of trying to get ahead and get along have made these successful women lawyers all the more sensitive to the fact that there are so few of them in positions of wealth and power.

Stanford law professor Barbara Babcock recalled that when she was appointed chief of the U.S. Justice Department's civil division in 1980, in which she was to manage a staff of seven hundred employees and a budget of $23 million, "Interviewers repeatedly asked me how I felt about getting the job because I was a woman. I told them it's a lot better than not getting the job because I'm a woman." Considering that as late as 1980 she still was being questioned about her capabilities as a woman lawyer, Babcock believes successful women attorneys ought not to become complacent about some of the recent advances they have made in the profession: "The fact that some women who are gifted or are selected as tokens get into positions of power does not mean anything for the equality principle."

Statistics bear out Babcock's concerns, for while women seem to be making important gains in entry-level positions, they still are not making a significant impact on the prestigious and powerful areas of the law. In 1984 the *National Law Journal* updated its biannual survey of hiring practices at the one hundred largest law firms in the United States. As it had predicted two years earlier, the results of the *Law Journal*'s city-by-city review indicated the numbers of women were increasing considerably at these prestigious "blue-chip" offices. At the associate level—the first stage of employment, in which attorneys work for a five-to-seven-year period before going either "up" to partner or "out" of the law firm altogether—women comprised one-fourth to one-third of all lawyers. Chicago's giant law firm, Sidley & Austin, which employs more than three hundred and fifty attorneys, reported that 30.9 percent of the associates were women. At Houston's Vinson & Elkins, women made up 28.6 percent of the total. The Cleveland firms of Jones, Day, Reavis & Pogue, and Squire, Sanders & Dempsey each employed women in 30 percent of its associate positions. Numbers on the West Coast were even higher with firms such as Los Angeles's Gibson, Dunn & Crutcher, the city's largest, claiming that 35 percent of its associates were females.

As sociologist Cynthia Fuchs Epstein has noted, figures such as these are significant for women attorneys, since "these firms constitute a network of legal institutions not matched anywhere in the world. Their clients are the largest corporations, commercial banks, and investment houses, and a few rich men and women. They derive a good deal of their power from their ability to 'make' law in this country by influencing legislation and the way it is implemented, as well as by working on many precedent-setting cases. While the names of Wall Street lawyers are not generally known to the public, they regularly contribute legal talent to the highest levels of government and in turn draw upon Washington's leading political leaders."

Noting that the Wall Street lawyer increasingly is not a man in a gray pin-striped suit, Epstein points out: "A little more than a decade ago, a mere forty women were to be found in the wood-paneled offices, so much like gentlemen's clubs, of New York's largest and most prestigious law firms. In a change nothing short of revolutionary, the number of women on Wall Street has jumped, and today there are more than six hundred women in the three dozen select firms clustered along the elegant midtown sections of Park and Madison Avenues and in the canyons of Manhattan's financial district."

Shortly after the *National Law Journal* reported its findings, *Newsweek* magazine analyzed the current job prospects of women law graduates and confirmed that "on Wall Street and La Salle Street the giant law firms that take only the brightest and most energetic young lawyers now hire women in large numbers." Supporting that view was employment counselor Laura Colangelo, who said that in New York it is relatively easy for a "headhunter" to place women in Wall Street law firms, since "at the entry level there is no discrimination." But no one disagrees that at the partner level women are not significantly increasing their numbers in the large and powerful law firms. Based on the statistics provided by the *National Law Journal* the typical large law firm still can count the number of its women partners on one hand.

Sidley & Austin, for example, had, compared to other prestige firms, a relatively high proportion of women partners—6.2 percent. But in actual numbers this is 11 females out of 177. More characteristic is New York's Shearman & Sterling, which had 34.5 percent women associates but only two women out of 115 partners. Similarly, Morgan, Lewis & Bockius in Philadelphia, with 28 percent women associates had two women partners out of 148.

Most of these women partners reached that level only in recent years.* While Sullivan & Cromwell hired its first woman associate in 1930 (Yale Law School graduate Elizabeth Beam Osborne), it did not have a woman partner until 1982 (Margaret K. Pfeiffer). Milbank, Tweed, Hadley & McCoy hired its first woman associate, Ione Parker Barrett, in 1935, but did not have a woman partner, Carolyn Cochran Clark, until 1977. Cahill Gordon & Reindel hired its first woman associate in 1943 but did not have a woman partner until 1981. Shearman & Sterling's first woman associate was hired in 1944 but it was 1979 before the firm had a woman partner. Carter, Ledyard & Milburn hired a woman associate in 1942 but has yet to have a female partner.

Since the nineteenth century, women have been trying to break down the barriers at these large corporate law firms, but except in the limited areas of trusts and estates and "blue-sky work" they have met with little success. Because jobs in the private sector were so difficult to obtain, many women who were interested in business and financial careers looked to the government for employment. In 1886 the New York *Tribune* reported that the Treasury Department was the first government agency to hire women professionals: "The occasion arose during the late civil war, and was entirely a question of expediency and even necessity, in order to fill the large number of vacancies made by the enlistment of the employes. As a result two women in Treasury, one a section chief, the other a law clerk for the Internal Revenue Bureau, were earning $1,800 annually—a considerable sum for a woman [to be earning] in the 1880s."† While the *Tribune* never

---

*A notable exception was Soia Mentschikoff, believed to be the first woman to become a partner at a major Wall Street firm when in 1944, at the age of twenty-nine she joined Spence, Hotchkiss, Parker & Duryee.

†Many years later Helen Carloss, a lawyer for the Internal Revenue Service, who had made countless arguments on behalf of the government before the U.S. Supreme Court, was memorialized at her death in 1949 as having been a brilliant advocate in the tax field.

identifies her by name, it does report that one woman in particular had a superior reputation in the law:

Another conspicuous example of ability, and also in quite a new line, is that of a woman employed in the Law Division of this bureau, and who prepares the briefs for the Solicitor of Internal Revenue in the various cases arising out of violation of internal revenue laws. She is considered one of the best law clerks in the bureau, and is engaged upon the most difficult and complicated compromise cases. Her remarkable power of grasping important points of a case and presenting them in clear and concise language is shown by the fact that she prepares her briefs from first notice; that is, the first abstract is the one submitted to the Solicitor, no other copy being made. In order to do this she thoroughly studies the case before putting her pen to paper. In an important case five days are often spent in careful, laborious study of it. The result is a clearness of statement and a logical presentment of the evidence which is justly considered remarkable. The briefs in the case of the whisky frauds in Grant's time were prepared by her, and it is a satisfaction to add that she receives the same salary as men doing the same work.

Women who believed that a superior showing in law school would guarantee them a place in the blue-chip bar soon learned that academic excellence would never be enough. In 1905 Alice Dillingham graduated first in her class at New York University Law School. Nevertheless, not one of the Wall Street law firms would consider hiring her because she was a woman. Eventually she took a $10-a-week job with the Legal Aid Society, only to find that men who had shown considerably less ability in her law school class were making four times that salary in the commercial firms. Similarly, in 1918 Lady Willie Forbus graduated first in her class at the University of Michigan Law School. Anxious to join a firm, Forbus immediately was discouraged by the dean of the law school, who insisted there were no jobs available even though she was valedictorian. He promised Forbus that if "she wanted to work for a law firm, she would make a good stenographer." Forbus ignored the advice, becoming instead an influential private practitioner in the state of Washington.

The problem for the establishment bar was that occasionally it found itself in need of the expertise of these gifted and talented women. In such circumstances, firms would ingeniously devise ways of using the

talents of the woman attorney without supplying her with correspond-
ing recognition or income. While Lady Forbus and others decided
against going the stenographer route, many able women law graduates
had little choice but to take whatever jobs the law firms offered.

One of New York's earliest woman lawyers managed to turn her
"stenographer's and typewriter's" experience into an advantage. In
1898 the New York *Tribune* reported that Lavinia Lally, while employed as a secretary, had been preparing papers in a corporate law
firm's "most important case." Then, the *Tribune* noted that "the firm
with which she had long been associated dissolved. Its clients were
chiefly wealthy corporations. In settling up the affairs of the firm, it was
discovered that she was the only person who had an intimate knowledge of the cases involved. In this manner she is virtually stepping into
a practice that she herself unconsciously made." But Lally was the first
to realize that it was circumstance, not recognition of her ability, that
was bringing this measure of financial success: "Despite that she is
making the law pay, and her future seems promising, Miss Lally does
not hesitate to say, 'I wouldn't encourage any woman to enter the
practice of law for a livelihood.' "

The editors of the legal magazine *Law Notes,* a turn-of-the-century
journal, seemed to agree that women never would be successful in the
law:

The simple truth of the matter is that women as a class are not endowed by
their Creator with either the physical or mental attributes which fit them for
a legal career. There may be a few marked exceptions, but the average intelligent, cultured and educated woman is no more fit for the practice of law than
the ordinary male is for the position of leading soprano in a church choir
. . . women are doing nobly their part of the world's work in countless lines
of human endeavor, but as lawyers they never were and never will be a success.

Clara Foltz, California's first woman lawyer, practiced law in New York
City for a period of ten years. She shared Lavinia Lally's view that
restrictive hiring practices in the East made it virtually impossible for
women to practice law successfully, but she continued to encourage
their entry into the profession nonetheless:

I think the main reason the women lawyers of New York have not made the progress to which their ability and industry entitle them, is chiefly due to the fact that they have been intimidated by the ill-concealed, often rude opposition of the legal fraternity. The New York bar is extremely conservative, often to the verge of rudeness. Its women lawyers, happily, unlike too many of its men, cannot forget their birth and breeding, consequently they shrink from the tendency of their brothers at law to regard them as freaks, rather than their mental equals. . . . I advise every woman who has academic training, a strong analytical mind and a natural bent for the law, to study and practice it.*

Rose Young, writing for the New York *Evening Post* in 1913, noted that a number of women lawyers had developed areas of expertise that were of interest to the large commercial law firms. But when these firms wanted such specialists to assist them on their cases, they hired them as researchers—or even as outside counsel—but never as associates. As Young pointed out:

In this State some of the leading men lawyers have women assistants or turn over certain divisions of their work to women lawyers on the outside, a number of whom are expert specialists. Bertha Rembaugh specializes in bankruptcy proceedings and though not confining her practice to it, does a great deal of this class of work assisted by her partner Miss Mary Rutter Towle. Edith J. Griswold has been a recognized patent expert for many years. Martha U. Overland is retained by one of the large law firms on account of her expert knowledge of interstate commerce.

Though women were appreciably demonstrating their ability to handle all aspects of corporate law, the discrimination against them continued, giving only a very few an opportunity to prove themselves. In 1917 the *Women Lawyers Journal* reported one particularly glaring example of prejudice:

A well-known firm of law publishers has refused to give credit to one of the brilliant women lawyers of this country for work that she has done in connection with the publication of a valuable law book, which she and a distinguished man professor of law are writing together. The excuse offered by the firm is

---

*Just as western women had had less difficulty gaining admission to law schools, they seem to have had greater success in obtaining commercial cases. In 1913 Sarah Harrington Soren from Arizona appeared as sole counsel for a mining corporation in the U.S. Supreme Court. It was reported "her argument is said to be the most brilliant ever presented to that court by a woman."

that it would detract from the success of the book to have a woman's name appear on the cover.*

With the advent of World War I, women lawyers expected that opportunities would open up for them. Their optimism was perhaps best expressed by this item that appeared in the *Women Lawyers Journal:*

In Boston and New York women lawyers are being asked to volunteer their services to handle the cases of men who are enlisting in the army. Many women who have heretofore occupied obscure places in their profession, owing to the prejudice entertained by some persons against employing women lawyers, will now find that not only can they serve their country by coming forward and assisting the men who are doing army duty but that larger fields will be opened to these women in the matter of the active practice of law.

But even in the war years women were not welcome at establishment law firms. The legal work they performed consisted mainly of serving on draft boards and advising committees supporting the war effort.

After the war, with passage of women's suffrage, women attorneys were again hopeful that their time had come. But once again they were refused entry into corporate and commercial law firms. Law student Fannie Lichtblau took to verse to describe her frustration in seeking employment at the large law firms:

> Oh, tis not oft that I with rage and hatred am burning
> And seldom do I itch (with unfemale vigor) to massage
>   someone's jaw,
> But, oh, how my heart toward the aforesaid act goes yearning,
> When someone asks (with smile malicious)
> Do you *really* intend to practice law?

The following year, in 1924, Wall Street hired the woman who is believed to be its first female associate—Catherine Noyes Lee. Lee, a magna cum laude graduate of the New York University Law School

*Women have distinguished themselves in legal publishing for quite some time. In 1784 the Session Laws of the state of New York were published by Elizabeth Holt of Poughkeepsie. Her name appears on these old folio laws for the seventh session of the legislature and for the first meeting of the eighth Session.

and the daughter of U.S. Court of Appeals judge Walter C. Noyes, was employed by the prestigious law firm of Cadwalader Wickersham & Taft. She specialized in estate and matrimonial cases and became a partner in 1942.

One of the earliest women associates on Wall Street was Helen L. Buttenwieser, who was employed by Cravath Swaine & Moore from 1936 to 1937. It had been a requirement that law school graduates who had not first obtained their bachelor's degree clerk with a law firm for one year. Buttenwieser, who was the niece of New York's governor Herbert Lehman and daughter of a prominent investment banking family, was permitted to clerk for one year with the Cravath firm— then known as Cravath, De Gersdorff Swaine & Wood. "As you can imagine, my being there caused some very strong reactions," Buttenwieser recalls. "First of all, it was customary for associates to share an office but I had the 'privilege' of being put into a small room all by myself. I sensed this fear that I might contaminate the men if I worked too close to them. After about six months they finally let a man sit in the same office with me."

Buttenwieser delights in noting that the custom of the day was for new associates to carry the briefcases of the senior associates and partners. "No one ever suggested that I do that. The atmosphere at Cravath was such that it took about three more months before I could persuade the men not to jump up and put on their jackets when I walked into the library. They thought it was improper for me to see them sitting in their shirts and suspenders."

Buttenwieser's eagerness to handle litigation met with much resistance. When she finally was assigned a court case she discovered it had been especially chosen for her because the partners thought it would be amusing to have a woman defending a lawsuit that involved a sexually suggestive advertisement. "They gave me that case just to see how embarrassed I would be. But I went ahead with it, and I simply refused to react as I know they hoped I would. One of the things I have never been able to understand is this need businessmen and lawyers have to go off into corners and tell each other these dirty jokes, where you could guess the punch lines anyway or to make more of a suggestive subject than is necessary."

Buttenwieser recalls blatant discrimination in private clubs. "I remember having to attend a business meeting at the Yale Club. Women were allowed in only if they entered through a side door that led to the elevators. It wasn't considered proper for a woman to be in the main area—you could only stand on the edges of the room. Well, I just walked in, and here I was standing in the middle of the floor when a young page came over to me and said, 'Pardon ma'am, but you can't stand here.' I asked him why not, and he said, 'I don't know why, but I was told to tell you ladies aren't allowed on the carpet.' My answer was to ask him to go back to whoever gave him those instructions and tell him to come here and move me if he'd like."

In retrospect Buttenwieser believes the experience of working for a large prestigious law firm like Cravath was a benefit to her and the firm as well. "I got to learn a lot of good law there—and let's face it, Cravath got itself a bargain. By the 1930s it had managed to hire a woman and a Jew—and they only had to keep me for a year!"

Not surprisingly Buttenwieser's experiences were exceptional. For other women, the Depression years were the most difficult of times to find employment. Honors law school graduate Sadie Turak recalls, "The Depression gave law firms still another excuse for not hiring us. At every single interview, I was asked how I could possibly expect to be considered when there were men out there with families to support. It was bad enough I wasn't going to get a job with any of those law firms—on top of it they insisted on making me feel guilty, too." Turak ended up taking a $5-a-week job that had her working unusually long hours. "Even with the low pay and hard work I really felt lucky to have a job. Did I mention that as a condition of getting hired I had to promise that I would never, ever, look into the top drawer of the senior partner's desk? I never did find out what he had in there."

In describing the period, the New York *Times* noted that up until World War II, "About the only women employees in the offices of the Wall Street law firms—the major leagues of the legal profession—were receptionists, switchboard operators, secretaries and cleaning women."

A few women were employed by large law firms and corporations during World War II to make up for the loss of men who were called into service, but they made little impact on the regular hiring practices of the profession. Catherine Tilson, a New Haven lawyer, credits the war with providing her an opportunity to work for a prestigious Connecticut firm, but notes that when the war was over, the men resumed their careers as though they had never left, and women such as herself never made partner.

In a few token instances women did manage to succeed in corporate law during the 1940s. Elizabeth Doogan, who was hired by the U.S. Life Insurance Company as an attorney in charge of the legal and claim department in 1943, was elevated after the war to senior officer and counsel of the corporation. Daphne Robert, the 1943–44 president of the National Association of Women Lawyers, was a member of the legal staff of the Coca-Cola Company, specializing in trademark, copyright and unfair competition law, and continued to be employed by the company after the war.

But Dorothy Kenyon, who had served as a commissioner in New York City before being elevated to the bench, believed that women were making little headway in reaching the top levels of the profession and she bitterly expressed her concerns in an article for the New York *Times* in 1950:

The real bottleneck nowadays remains the law office. It is to the lawyer what an internship is to the doctor—a sine qua non for the development of a skill. The better the law office the greater the chance for development of skill. Many a promising young legal mind is stopped in her tracks by the reception she receives in the average hard-boiled law office. "What use can we possibly make of you? You'd make a fool of yourself and us in court. We can't work you late at night as we do the boys. What would the clients say? You may be a disturbing element, falling in love with people and vice versa. We'll have to install you in a law library out of sight. In the unlikely contingency that you turn out to be good you'll probably marry as soon as we've finished training you and we'll have had all that trouble for nothing. Thank you, no, we'll play it safe and take a boy."

Recalling her own experiences and those of her classmates, Kenyon wrote:

It's a lucky and nervy girl who can break through these barbed-wire entanglements and serve her law apprenticeship in an even reasonably good law office. It is still the rare exception to crash the gates of the gilded firms, the law factories that possess a monopoly of the big-business clients. I well remember the brilliant young editor-in-chief of the Law Review of a fine law school who long after all the other honor students (boys) of her class had been signed up by these gilded firms was still drearily making the rounds and peddling her highly superior wares in a market that wanted none of her.

In 1950, when Harvard Law School finally opened its doors to female students, there was anticipation once again among women that this move would, as a consequence, lead to greater acceptance by the blue-chip law firms. But despite the belief expressed in Arthur Sutherland's history of Harvard Law School that once women were admitted they found "appropriate employment after graduation," the women graduates and such recognized authorities as Erwin O. Smigel, the sociologist who in 1957 published his now-famous study *The Wall Street Lawyer*, provide a much different view. Smigel found discrimination against women law graduates from Ivy League law schools to be so pervasive as to have virtually eliminated them from consideration for employment:

While most large law offices now do have some women in their organization, very few become partners. This researcher came across only one woman partner practicing in New York City branches of the large law firms. An analysis of a directory of women lawyers reveals that of 1,755 female attorneys in New York in 1957 only 18 list themselves as working in large New York offices.

Moreover, Smigel pointed out that "the bias against women is so strong that one firm still elects to employ male stenographers when it can get them."

During the 1950s Barbara Armstrong, writing for the *Harvard Law School Record*, reported that "90 percent of the lawyers who wish to engage a law clerk refuse even to interview women and . . . such openings as there are often call for stenography . . . a well-dressed, well-acquainted, well-endowed woman applicant arouses immediate suspicion in the law offices although all this is just what they pray for in a man."

Harvard Law School graduate Nancy Young agreed. In 1956 Young surveyed the careers of thirty-four women from the classes of 1953 to

1955 and concluded "it is still far more difficult for a woman attorney to find a position today than it is for a young man even though he may not have as good an academic record . . . the barriers remain highest in the city firm which is often bound by tradition, precedent and a wary eye to the reactions of the clients with substantial retainers."

Alarmed by the restrictive practices of these large law firms, New York Supreme Court justice Samuel Hofstadler, addressing a bar association dinner in 1957, lashed out at the legal profession's continuing refusal to provide equal opportunity to women. "In a field as highly specialized as the law, competence and ability grow with opportunity. Women in our profession are denied the development of their potentialities," he said, when they are categorically refused consideration for employment. Hofstadler challenged the notion that academic excellence and intellectual ability were the criteria upon which job interviewers were judging prospective applicants. He claimed that if this actually was an important measure of suitability for employment, women would be represented in great numbers at the prestigious firms. And, warning that the profession was being deprived of the enormous talents of these female law graduates, Hofstadler urged his colleagues to "reject forever this vestigial treatment of women." That same year, Mary R. Cowell, president of the New York Women's Bar Association, deplored as "a common occurrence" the closing of law firm doors to women, claiming that even when women do get employment, they find "few opportunities for advancement." Cowell said that "the chances for a woman lawyer to attain partnership status are still slim," and insisted women lawyers were being paid far less than male colleagues who were doing the same work for the same hours in the same law firms.

Further warnings came from Nancy Young, in her survey of the careers of her classmates:

When they are employed women are generally expected to work in certain fields—probate, estate planning and tax. A number of other areas are completely closed to them. Few women, as an illustration, can expect a niche in the litigation section of a large firm. One warning which comes from many girls sums it up: "Beware of the firm looking specifically for a woman lawyer. They want you for work they cannot get any man to do.

United States Circuit Court of Appeals judge Ruth Bader Ginsburg provides a stunning example of the treatment of women lawyers in the 1950s. Ginsburg, the first tenured woman law professor at Columbia University Law School, was on Harvard's law review before transferring to Columbia Law. When she graduated in 1959 Ginsburg tied for first place in the class. Not one law firm would hire her. As the New York *Times* pointed out: "At first, when the rejection notices started coming in, she thought something might be wrong with her, but then, she said, 'when I got so many rejections, I thought it couldn't be they had no use for me—it had to be something else.' So she got, upon graduation, a job clerking for a Federal district judge—whereas, as anyone familiar with the subject knows, and as she refrained from pointing out, a man with those grades from that school could have gotten a clerkship in a Federal appeals court, if not the United States Supreme Court."

Similarly Rita Hauser, now a senior partner at New York's Stroock & Stroock & Lavan, discovered that not even a Fulbright fellowship, a doctorate and an honors law degree could get her employment on Wall Street. "It was really galling, the firms had this policy against women and it was impossible to change them." Hauser recalls being told by the New York law firm Cleary, Gottlieb, Steen & Hamilton to forget about an international practice, since women couldn't be expected to travel. She went to the Justice Department instead and later became influential in Republican Party politics.

In 1968 President Richard M. Nixon offered Hauser the job of U.S. Representative to the United Nations Commission on Human Rights, a position that allowed her to maintain her private law practice as well. She had been the "rainmaker"* for her six-person law firm and had a solid reputation in international law. But Hauser's impressive credentials still did not guarantee her a place in a Wall Street firm. Jill Abramson, in a profile she did of Hauser for *The American Lawyer*, notes the events that led to Hauser's joining a leading New York firm:

In 1972 Charles Moerdler, a partner at New York City's Stroock & Stroock & Lavan, was trying to lure Rita Hauser, a friend and fellow GOP activist to his firm. He was having trouble convincing "the elders," a group of senior

---

*A partner who attracts business into a firm.

partners, then in their sixties, who ruled the firm, that Hauser was worth a lateral partnership offer. Despite her credentials, which included 12 years in practice, a close relationship with then-President Richard Nixon, a four-year stint at the United Nations, and a sturdy base of international clients, the elders were skeptical. Stroock had never had a woman partner or a sizable international practice. The senior partners wondered whether Hauser was aggressive enough to build a big practice. "Gentlemen," Moerdler says he informed them, "she has bigger balls than all of you put together."

Twelve years later, it is laughable to anyone at Stroock that there were ever doubts about Hauser's aggressiveness. "She is a human buzz saw," says a top member of the firm's executive committee.

Margaret Taylor, now a civil court judge in New York City, was one of the few women able to land a position with a large law firm in the 1950s and early 1960s—Wall Street's Cahill, Gordon & Reindel. Taylor, "a WASP raised in Oregon," and an honors graduate of Reed College, earned her law degree at New York University. "Early in life I realized I wasn't going to be named the Snowball Queen of Klamath Falls. Where I came from, that was about the best a girl could hope for—and after that housewife and mother. It just wasn't for me. I didn't want to be like other girls—I was the kid who wanted to play football with the boys. Becoming a lawyer then was one way I could do that."

Taylor, who looks back on her antifeminist views in the 1950s with embarrassment and amazement, believes that a lack of role models coupled with the prevailing views about women contributed to her attitudes: "If you weren't a woman lawyer like I was, working in a big firm like I was, you basically had to be a boring nobody." Although she traveled extensively—"not many women did that then"—and worked on a number of celebrated cases, Taylor remembers now having been treated to "lots of 'honey,' lots of jokes, lots of flirting," that she made herself ignore. "I was so intent on proving that I wasn't like other women that it never occurred to me to fight back." She explains, "You have to understand the climate then. There were so few women lawyers working in the large Wall Street law firms. And everywhere the ideal woman was a housewife and mother who was glad to be staying home with the kids. If you wanted a career, you were so different—and not in a good sense. Some women made a point of talking about their husbands and children to make themselves seem more 'normal.' But I knew this was a man's profession and the harder you worked and the less you acted like a woman—whatever that meant—the better off you were going to be. That's how you survived. The idea wasn't to change things around—that never seemed possible—it was to make yourself fit in.''

Taylor, who wears slacks under her judicial robes, having sworn off dresses years ago, found her attitudes and beliefs changing dramatically in the late 1960s and 1970s: "I went from one of the worst Queen Bees around to just one angry feminist." She recalls teaching a clinical law course at New York University in 1972: "I would sit in court and watch my third-year women law students defend criminal cases. Here were all the sexist remarks from opposing counsel and court clerks that I used to put up with and ignore. But somehow when they were directed against my students it affected me in a much different way—I was outraged. It was all right there—you could see how a woman's effectiveness in court is undermined when this conduct is tolerated. It was the turning point for me."

The 1970s were the turning point for many women in the law. The revolutionary spirit of the college campuses extended to the conservative law schools and the even more conservative corporate law offices. Two significant results were the changes in attitudes about the right of women to seek employment on Wall Street and the recognition that law school placement offices had a duty to ensure equal employment opportunities for their female students. Rather than simply hoping that change would take place, women law students began demanding their rights. In the fall of 1969 women at New York University, disturbed by the treatment they were receiving from law firm recruiters, decided to join with Columbia University Law School women in taking action. Among their complaints was that firms were either refusing to interview qualified women or were asking such outrageous questions at the interviews that it was clear they had no serious intention of making job offers. Diane Blank, then a second-year law student, complained that Shearman & Sterling was interviewing law review men but refusing to schedule appointments for women with similar qualifications. NYU's placement office informally asked Shearman & Sterling to relent, and the firm did, but there was no question in the minds of the women interviewed that they were being seen only as a courtesy.

Legal historian Doris Sassower pointed out in an article for the *American Bar Association Journal* in 1971 that

the law school placement offices have been the scene of a great deal of prejudiced thinking about women, not just by prospective employers. Placement office personnel frequently "slot" women lawyers into specific types of jobs and accept coolly the unwillingness of prospective employers to hire women.

The situation was soon to change. The New York University women began monitoring their school's recruitment policies and as Sassower noted: "A pilot study in 1970 of sex-based discrimination in the legal profession by the Women's Rights group at New York University Law School revealed practices that seem strange in a profession that each Law Day reaffirms its belief in equal treatment under the law. What of equal treatment *in* the Law?"

She went on to report:

Six years after Title VII of the Civil Rights Act of 1964 declared a national policy against job discrimination on account of sex, the N.Y.U. group's survey records these actual remarks made by some of the nation's lawyers to women applying for their first job in a law office:

"We don't like to hire women."
"We hire some women, but not many."
"We just hired a woman and couldn't hire another."
"We don't expect the same kind of work from women as we do from men."
"Women don't receive $—— salary, or more than $—— salary."
"Women don't become partners here."
"Are you planning on children?"

The study also reported that the actual personnel practices of these law firms matched the attitudes expressed at the interviews. For example, there was no promotion of women to partnerships or top administrative levels, women were used only for work not involving client contact, they were excluded from policy-making boards and committees and from employer's social events or firm meetings held in places excluding women.

At the same time, Columbia Law School established an Employment Rights Project, which was supported with federal Equal Employment

Opportunity Commission funding. Attorney Harriet Rabb was named
as its director. Working with the NYU and Columbia women, and
aided by law school professor George Cooper and attorney Howard J.
Rubin, Rabb and the project filed discrimination complaints with the
New York City Commission on Human Rights against ten major New
York law firms, claiming each had established "a pattern and practice"
of discriminating against women law students in New York City. The
ten firms named were: Royall, Koegel & Wells; Cravath, Swaine &
Moore; Roth, Carlson, Kwit, Spengler, Mallin & Goodell; Aranow,
Brodsky, Bohinger, Einhorn & Dann; Carter, Ledyard & Milburn;
Gilbert, Segall & Young; Shea, Gallop, Climenko & Gould; Shearman
& Sterling; Sullivan & Cromwell; and Winthrop, Stimson, Putnam &
Roberts.

In filing the complaints, the project relied heavily on the evidence
compiled by NYU's Diane Blank, who had been interviewed by Sullivan & Cromwell, and by Columbia's Margaret Kohn, who had failed
to receive an invitation to be interviewed at the offices of Royall, Koegel
& Wells. In Blank's case the recruiter from Sullivan & Cromwell
admitted that his firm was biased against women and boasted that
when women lawyers were employed by the firm they purposely were
assigned to "blue sky" work. Margaret Kohn, described as "the second-
best applicant interviewed at Columbia," was never seriously considered for employment by Royall, Koegel & Wells even though three
male students from Columbia with equal or lesser qualifications were
hired by the firm.

Following a lengthy investigation, in 1971 New York City Human
Rights commissioner Eleanor Holmes Norton, herself an attorney,
charged Royall, Koegel & Wells practiced sex discrimination in the
"recruitment, hiring, promotion and treatment of women lawyers,"
adding that this one law firm had been singled out because if charges
were sustained against one of the ten, "the rest are far easier." Commissioner Norton agreed with the project's attorneys that "almost without
exception women with qualifications equal to or better than male
applicants were rejected and that females were never advanced to
partnership." Norton indicated also that women lawyers were being
limited to working in a single division dealing with trusts and estates

and that the firm paid the fees of male partners for membership in a private club that not only refused women as members but required them, when guests, to eat in a separate dining room.

Both the Blank and Kohn complaints developed into class-action lawsuits filed in the federal district court in New York: *Kohn* v. *Royall, Koegel & Wells* and *Blank* v. *Sullivan & Cromwell*. Following the New York City Commission on Human Rights complaint, Margaret Kohn similarly filed with the federal Equal Employment Opportunity Commission. The EEOC issued Kohn a permission-to-sue letter, and she immediately filed a civil rights action on behalf of herself and women in the law who were similarly situated. Royall, Koegel & Wells, now Rogers & Wells, finally lost on the issue that they had systematically discriminated against women in hirings. Five years after Margaret Kohn brought her original complaint, Rogers & Wells agreed to a hiring formula that guaranteed female law graduates a percentage of the firm's associate positions.

The *Blank* case also proceeded as a civil rights class action in the federal district court in Manhattan and it too had a successful conclusion. To the amazement of both sides, the judge randomly selected to hear the case was none other than the Honorable Constance Baker Motley, then the only woman in the federal courts in New York who before taking the bench was a celebrated civil rights lawyer for the NAACP Legal Defense Fund.

No sooner had Judge Motley certified *Blank* v. *Sullivan & Cromwell* as a class action than the law firm moved to disqualify her on the grounds of personal and extrajudicial bias against the defendant and in favor of the plaintiff and her cause. In a stinging memorandum opinion Judge Motley refused to remove herself from the case:

It is beyond dispute that for much of my legal career I worked on behalf of blacks who suffered race discrimination. I am a woman and before being elevated to the bench was a woman lawyer. These obvious facts, however, clearly do not, ipso facto, indicate or even suggest personal bias or prejudice. . . . The assertion, without more, that a judge who engaged in civil rights litigation and who happens to be of the same sex as a plaintiff in a suit alleging sex discrimination on the part of a law firm, is, therefore, so biased that he or she could not hear the case, comes nowhere near the standards required for recusal. Indeed, if background or sex or race of each judge were, by definition sufficient grounds for removal, no judge on this court could hear this case, or many others, by virtue of the fact that all of them were attorneys, of a sex, often with distinguished law firm or public service backgrounds.

Sullivan & Cromwell appealed Judge Motley's decision but the U.S. Circuit Court of Appeals agreed with her view that she was entitled to hear the case. The recusation motion was only one aspect of this bitter and protracted lawsuit. At one point Sullivan & Cromwell claimed it had been entrapped by Diane Blank, since it was certain she never had had any intention of joining the law firm. At another point the judge felt it necessary to condemn the "acrimony" that had developed between the lawyers, citing a letter in which Sullivan & Cromwell's attorneys referred to Blank's counsel as a Yahoo. But when Harriet Rabb, the attorney for the plaintiffs, began to question the firm about partnership earnings and other internal matters, Sullivan & Cromwell decided it was time to settle. The law firm, and in fact all the law firms cited in the original NYC Human Rights Commission complaint, agreed to hiring guidelines that assured women places at the associates level and assured that women would not be required in the future to possess "higher attributes" than male applicants.

Similar lawsuits and actions began springing up throughout the United States. At the urging of women students, the dean at Boalt Hall (University of California at Berkeley) agreed to bar a recruiter whose firm had a stated bias against women lawyers. In Illinois, women law students filed a complaint with the Equal Employment Opportunity Commission, charging the University of Chicago Law School had discriminated against its women students in placement efforts. When the prestigious Covington & Burling in Washington, D.C., refused to move its weekly luncheons from a private club that prohibited women, the law firm's position was publicized in *Washingtonian* magazine under the eye-catching headline, OINK, OINK. The position on luncheon meetings changed. In 1979, after protracted litigation, Houston's giant and politically powerful law firm, Fulbright & Jaworski, was forced to settle a sex-discrimination suit. While all documents in the case were sealed, Stephen Brill writing for the *American Lawyer* noted that the complaint contained a number of allegations of discriminatory treatment of women lawyers, among them that the firm's first woman associate "was instructed to do her own typing and was on at least one occasion requested to assist the typing pool."

Not all complaints concerned recruitment and hiring practices. Janis McDonald, an attorney for the Atlantic Richfield Oil Company in Los Angeles, was on a business trip in Europe in 1981 when a senior vice president "commanded" that she "meet him in his hotel room for nonbusiness purposes." Rather than take action against the executive, ARCO placed McDonald on probation and told her "to find other work." In a lawsuit brought on her behalf by EEOC, McDonald alleged the incident was "part of a continuing pattern of sexually-harassing behavior." The *National Law Journal* reported that ARCO eventually settled the case "with Ms. McDonald receiving close to six figures."

In 1983 Constance Charles Willems, a partner in the prestigious Louisiana law firm of McGlinchey, Stafford, Mintz, Cellini & Lang and then president of the Louisiana Association for Women Attorneys, spearheaded a legal battle on behalf of lawyer Margaret Gaines Bezou's effort to build a top-level career for herself. At issue was Bezou's belief that it was important for her to move to Washington, D.C., to take a job with the National Labor Relations Board. Bezou was involved in a bitter divorce case and both she and her husband, a New Orleans physician, sought custody of their daughter. The court, upon learning that Margaret Bezou planned to work for the NLRB and would not be staying home with the child, ruled in favor of the husband, although he was never asked to give up his busy medical practice. In making its ruling, the court called Margaret Bezou "a busy self-centered lawyer in pursuit of a legal career in a strange city . . . she is interested first and foremost in herself and in furthering her professional career." Willems, on behalf of the Women Attorneys Association filed an amicus curiae brief with the Louisiana Supreme Court in which she argued that "public policy requires a reversal of the trial court's decision thereby affording to professional working wives and mothers the same opportunity for professional fulfillment that professional husbands and fathers have enjoyed for years."

Margaret Bezou eventually regained custody of her daughter but as Willems notes, "This did not happen in the distant past. We filed these papers in 1983. Anyone who thinks the fight for equality in the law is over ought to remember this."

The most celebrated case concerning equal opportunity for women in the legal profession is *Hishon* v. *King & Spalding* in which the U.S. Supreme Court ruled that Title VII of the Civil Rights Act of 1964 prohibits a law firm from denying partnership status to an associate on the basis of sex.

In 1972 Elizabeth Anderson Hishon was hired as an associate at Atlanta's King & Spalding, one of the South's most well-known law firms, which has among its partners former U.S. Attorney General Griffin Bell. Hishon had attended all the right schools—Wellesley and Columbia Law, and had earned all the right honors; she was a Harlan Fiske Stone scholar at Columbia, and had just the right genteel South Carolina background to make her a suitable choice for the nearly century-old law firm.

Connie Bruck, writing for the *American Lawyer*, noted that in the South, King & Spalding has "more blue-chip clients and more political connections than any other firm." "They have always managed to attract people who are not only very good lawyers but come from good families, marry well and belong to the right clubs," says one Atlanta lawyer. "We call them the Ritzy Crackers."

The only other women to have been employed by King & Spalding prior to Hishon's hiring were Anita Mulkey, who in 1944 was taken on by the firm as its only "permanent associate," meaning there was no chance for promotion to partner, and Mary Ann Sears, a graduate of the University of Georgia Law School, who was hired in the mid-1960s to work on a special project. When it was completed, Sears says she "didn't even think of applying to be an associate there, it was out of the question, it was just understood."

In the seven years Elizabeth Hishon was employed by King & Spalding she claims she always received favorable evaluations from her superiors. She was assured she was at the top of her class of associates and had every reason to be optimistic about her chances for making partner. But when the partnership decisions were made, Elizabeth Hishon was twice passed over for consideration. Under the unwritten but traditional "up or out" rule existing at most major law firms, Hishon had no choice but to leave the firm.

Her next move was to file a discrimination complaint against King & Spalding with the Equal Employment Opportunity Commission and to file suit in federal court in Atlanta, claiming that the law firm used unexpressed and discriminatory factors in making the decision to pass her over for partner and that she had never been judged on the actual quality of her work as male associates had been. King & Spalding predictably disputed Hishon's right to sue, and in the first round at federal district court, Judge Newell Edenfield agreed with the law firm's position. Ruling against Hishon, Judge Edenfield wrote: "In a very real sense a professional partnership is like a marriage . . . to coerce a mismatched or unwanted partnership too closely resembles a statute for the enforcement of shotgun weddings."

Hishon appealed to the U.S. Court of Appeals for the Eleventh Circuit, but it too agreed that partnership decisions did not come within the purview of the 1964 Civil Rights Act. Hishon and her lawyers, joined by the U.S. Justice Department, petitioned the United States Supreme Court for a writ of certiorari—permission to bring the case before this highest court. The petition was granted, and in October 1983 lawyers for both sides presented their arguments. Court watchers, sensing the mood of the Justices, seemed certain that this time there would be a different outcome: Hishon appeared to have a winning case.

The New York *Times* reported: "The Supreme Court gave a skeptical hearing today to the argument by a major law firm that the Federal law against employment discrimination does not apply to a law firm's decision on which young lawyers should become partners." It went on to describe the Court's scorn while listening to arguments on behalf of King & Spalding, and cited Justice O'Connor's "tone of strained patience."

King & Spalding had reason to be worried. Only a few months earlier it showed remarkably poor judgment in announcing plans at the firm's summer outing in North Carolina to hold a wet T-shirt contest involving the female summer associates. When the partners were persuaded that the event might be inappropriate they turned it, incredibly, into a bathing suit competition. The *Wall Street Journal* reported that "as he bestowed first prize on a third-year law student from Harvard University, one of the firm's partners said, 'She has the body we'd like to see more of.' " The newspaper noted:

Lawyers at King & Spalding dismiss the incident as an example of the rollicking good times that characterize the firm's social events and contribute to an unusually high esprit de corps among the firm's lawyers.

But some participants in the impromptu bathing-suit event say that they felt humiliated and that they didn't protest only because they were candidates for year-round jobs with the firm. They say they were stunned that the contest occurred because King & Spalding was the defendant in a sex-discrimination suit.

In May 1984, as many had predicted, the U.S. Supreme Court ruling on the *Hishon* case was that professional partnerships do come under the federal antidiscrimination laws. Chief Justice Warren E. Burger wrote: "A benefit that is part and parcel of the employment relationship may not be doled out in a discriminatory fashion . . ." The decision meant that Hishon now had the right to proceed to trial to prove that she had in fact been a victim of discrimination at King & Spalding.*

Interestingly, while women's bar associations and other feminist organizations applauded the decision, a number of women lawyers privately expressed the view that it would bring little change. One Wall Street associate said, "I suspect we will see a few more women making partner. But I'm afraid the real result of *Hishon* may just be that firms will keep a more careful watch on their women associates—not in an effort to promote them but to better justify their decision not to make these women partners."

Corporate lawyer Barbara M. Levi was also guarded in her optimism. "I would like to believe *Hishon* will make a difference. But then, I can't help thinking this won't end it, the decision is just one more step along the way. I remember reading somewhere that when Betty Southard Murphy was named head of the National Labor Relations Board in the 1960s she said that in order for women to be equal they have to be excellent. That's still true today."

---

*The trial never took place. Shortly after the Supreme Court ruling, Hishon and King & Spalding reached an out-of court-settlement. The parties refused to discuss the terms but Hishon did not return to the firm.

9

WOMEN ON THE BENCH

The significance of Sandra Day O'Connor's appointment to the United States Supreme Court in 1981 managed to overshadow national statistics gathered that same year that indicated how seriously underrepresented women are in the judiciary. When O'Connor became the first woman Justice, only 5.4 percent of all federal judges were women and fewer than 5 percent of all state court judges were women. Of more than 20,000 judicial positions in the United States only 900 were held by women.

When asked why the judiciary has been so slow to add females to its ranks, one prominent woman judge said she was certain she knew the answer. "Male lawyers still only grudgingly accept women in the courtroom—they have very little tolerance for women making decisions that might seriously affect them and their clients. For years they have relied on knowing the judge personally and . . . socializing on the golf course or at some private club. You put a woman on the bench and there is a lot less certainty about who she is and how she will decide a case. I still find tremendous resistance. And many women judges find that once they join the bench they are limited in the kinds of cases they are assigned and how they move up through the judicial system."

Women attorneys have little doubt that it is their gender, not their lack of ability or judicial temperament, that is the reason for unusually low numbers of women on the bench. While women formally began practicing law shortly after the Civil War, by 1900 only five women in the United States had served in any judicial or quasi-judicial capacity. Two decades later that number had risen only by ten. Even when women won the vote and the right to sit on juries, the percentages of women on the bench did not substantially improve. In 1930 only twelve states had at least one woman judge. In 1950 there was at least one woman judge in thirty-nine of the states. It was not until 1949 that a woman was appointed to the federal district court, 1965 before a woman was chief justice of a state supreme court and 1979 before every state in the union had had at least one woman serving in some judicial capacity. And with no woman on the United States Supreme Court until 1981, there was little impetus for lower courts to change their restrictive policies. Attorney and former congresswoman Bella Abzug, long a champion of women in positions of power, was outraged by the lack of women on the Supreme Court. "When President Richard Nixon had four separate opportunities to name a woman to the United States Supreme Court and didn't, he implied he couldn't find one good enough. I said then the problem was that he couldn't find a woman bad enough."

The nation's first woman judge was Esther McQuigg Morris, who in 1870 was named justice of the peace of South Pass City, Wyoming, a frontier mining town. Although Morris had not been trained as a lawyer, she managed to render no less than seventy legal opinions in a term of eight and one-half months. At the time of her appointment, Morris, a woman well in her fifties and said to be almost six feet tall, was working in South Pass City as a milliner. She had been instrumental in drafting and gaining passage of the 1869 Women's Suffrage Bill, which made Wyoming women the first in the world to win equal suffrage. When the bill was signed into law, P. S. Barr, who had vehemently opposed its passage, resigned his office as justice of the peace, sarcastically suggesting a woman might better fill the office. To his amazement the county commissioners took him at his word, and

Esther Morris, the woman who was to be called "the mother of equal rights," got the job.

Mae Urbanek, a Wyoming writer who did a profile of Esther Morris for *The Women Who Made the West,* gives a vivid description of America's first woman judge at work:

Things hadn't been too peaceful in South Pass City of late. Indian trouble around the area had resulted in several people being killed and more wounded. Governor Campbell had troops dispatched and rifles and ammunition were issued to civilians in South Pass City so they could defend themselves . . . [Judge Morris] held court seated on a slab bench in her log cabin and ordered all "shooting irons" to be left outside. She wore a calico dress with a green necktie and matching ribbons in her hair. Around her shoulders was a worsted shawl to keep out the chill of a Wyoming winter.

Ironically, Morris's first case involved former Justice of the Peace Barr. Having regretted his decision to resign his office, he now was refusing to give up the post. Judge Morris ruled that because she herself was involved in his decision she would have to remove herself from the case. The crowd of miners and shopkeepers who had come to see the woman judge was impressed by the wisdom of that first decision and by a number of others that followed.

But Barr was not the only one who hated the idea of Esther Morris serving as justice of the peace. An even stronger, and louder, opponent was Esther's husband, John Morris, who ran a saloon in South Pass City. According to Urbanek, John Morris objected to his wife's accepting the office and he made a scene about it in the courtroom. Judge Morris fined her husband for contempt of court, and when he refused to pay his fine, she sent him to jail. Justice first, then after that the law, was her motto. When lawyers quarreled in front of her she often said, "Behave yourselves, boys." Morris served as justice of the peace for less than a year, but during that time she received international acclaim. She performed scores of marriages and tried a wide range of cases, everything from claim-jumping to assault. One lawyer said of her, "To pettifoggers she showed no mercy, but her decisions were always just." Of herself, Morris is reported to have said, "Circumstances have transpired to make my position as Justice of the Peace a test of women's ability to hold public office and I feel that my work has been satisfactory, although I have often regretted that I was not better qualified to fill the position. Like all pioneers, I have labored more in faith and hope."

Because of the informal and unstructured nature of frontier courts like Morris's, it is impossible to know for certain just how many women may have held the post of justice of the peace or other low-level judicial positions before the turn of the century. For example, while she is not generally mentioned in legal histories, a brief item in the 1881 *Chicago Legal News* indicates that a Mrs. Schuchardt survived challenge to her appointment as master of chancery in Union County:

Judge Harker of the Circuit Court paid her the compliment that she was the most competent master in his circuit but held that as she was a woman she could not legally hold the office. She appealed to the Appellate Court, composed of Judges Casey, Baker and Wall, and they, without giving any reason, or writing an opinion, affirmed the judgment of Judge Harker. Mrs. Schuchardt again appealed and took the case to the Supreme Court, and on last Tuesday that court, by Judge Scholfield reversed the judgments of the two courts below, and held that a woman could hold the Office of Master in Chancery.

In reporting the story, the newspaper's editor, the outspoken Myra Bradwell, could not resist comment: "One by one the old rules of law which prevented women from standing side by side upon an equality with man are being removed by the liberal enactments of the law-making power and the construction of our courts."

It was reported that in 1884 Ada Lee, a Port Huron woman who had recently graduated from the University of Michigan Law School, "was nominated for the Office of Circuit Court Commissioner by the Republican, Democratic and Greenback parties with no solicitation for the nominations; and she was duly elected, receiving the entire vote cast in the county." Lelia J. Robinson wrote that Lee

performed the duties of this office, and held it until the expiration of her term, despite the fact that thirteen suits were begun to oust her, during which time two hundred and seventeen cases were tried before her. This brave little woman, who has not yet seen a quarter of a century, has earned her own living and education, being without either home or money.

In the late 1880s two more women, both of whom were ardent suffragists received judicial appointments. The first of these was Marilla Young Ricker, the first woman lawyer in New Hampshire. She obtained her legal education in Washington, D.C., and in 1883 when she took the D.C. bar, she ranked highest of the nineteen applicants. Ricker "was said to give evidence of possessing more extensive legal knowledge than had ever been displayed by any other candidate." One year later she was appointed United States Commissioner, handling a large number of cases in the District. Ricker continued to practice law and specialized in criminal defense work. The New Hampshire *Daily Democrat* made mention of Ricker's regular Sunday visits to prisoners and her tireless efforts for penal reform. It noted she frequently made applications for pardons and releases for prisoners and "quite early in her legal career [she] made the test of the 'poor convicts act' under which she believed great injustice was done in the fines usually imposed supplementary to confinement . . ." Ricker was successful in contesting the fines and they were held to be illegal.

While lauded for her work on behalf of prisoners, Marilla Ricker was better known for her feminist and suffragist views. Beginning in 1870 and continuing every year until her death, Ricker would appear before the selectmen of the town of Dover and, as a law-abiding and tax-paying citizen, demand the right to vote. Each time she was prevented from casting a ballot, she vowed she would only pay her taxes under protest and would be back to vote the following year. Ricker joined pioneer lawyer Belva Lockwood on the Equal Rights Ticket in the 1880s (as a candidate for Vice President), long before women's suffrage was achieved, and in 1910 she placed her name in candidacy for the New Hampshire Governor's race. A staunch critic of hypocrisy in government, Ricker never stopped publicly expressing her views. Toward the end of her career she turned to poetry to scathingly refute President Woodrow Wilson's claim that "the present depression in business is merely psychological." Ricker wrote:

Let your hopeful bosom give a
   psychologic throb,
Ask some psychologic brother for a
   psychologic job,
If your savings have been scattered
   in a psychologic crash,
Pay the grocer and the butcher
   with some psychologic cash—
And you speedily will find yourself in psychologic health
And possessed of an embarrassment of
   psychologic wealth.

Marilla Young Ricker died in 1920.

In 1886 Carrie Burnham Kilgore, the woman who had fought for the right to study and practice law in Pennsylvania, was named a master of chancery in Philadelphia. Orphaned at the age of eleven, Kilgore managed to support and educate herself entirely on her own earnings, first as a domestic and later as a teacher. In 1864 she had the distinction of being the first woman in the state of New York to earn an M.D. degree—but Kilgore decided she had a greater interest in law than in medicine. She was a passionate supporter of the suffragist movement and gave stirring speeches on the rights of women before the Pennsylvania legislature. After her terms as master of chancery were completed, one journal noted: "Mrs. Kilgore has won the respect and the confidence of the bar and the courts and the character of the business intrusted to her proves that she has gained the confidence of the public." Apparently Kilgore never tired of challenges. In 1909, at the time of her death, she was actively involved in a new pastime—hot-air ballooning. The New York *Times* reported that at the age of seventy-two, Mrs. Kilgore was the veteran of several recent and dangerous trips.

At the turn of the century many women blamed the lack of opportunities for women in the judiciary on the fact that women still did not have the vote and therefore were less able to garner political support. In this period only a few more women were appointed to the bench. These included Helen Jaeger, who served as a police judge in Tacoma, Washington; Catherine Waugh McCulloch, twice appointed justice of the peace of Evanston, Illinois; Othilia Beals, justice of the peace in Seattle, Washington; Frances Hopkins, temporary probate judge of Jefferson County, Missouri; Lydia Beckley Pague, a county court judge in Eagle, Colorado; and Reah Whitehead, a justice of the peace in Seattle, Washington. Whitehead, who before taking the bench was a prosecutor in King County, Washington, is reported to have taken part in the first case on record in the United States in which a felony case was prosecuted and defended by women lawyers. In *State of Washington v. Raymond* in 1913, Reah Whitehead and defense lawyer Leola May Blinn tried the case to a hung jury of ten women and two men.

As the suffrage movement intensified and women were close to getting the vote, efforts to increase the number of appointments of women to the bench increased as well. One of those urging that women be considered for judgeships was Grace I. Rohleder, a Washington, D.C., attorney and writer:

With all due veneration for the opinions that have been written by our learned judiciary, it may be fairly stated without any fear of contradiction or ground for argument the decisions and interpretations of the laws of this land . . . have emanated from men, from the male viewpoint for the upkeep of a world designed and maintained for the good of man and with only a man's idea or conception of what constituted the good of man. They lived up to their responsibilities as they saw them. . . . The trouble with the system lies just here. No man . . . can provide the woman's viewpoint.

Rohleder went on to note:

Our courts as presently organized are almost exclusively male. Male judges, male clerks, male sergeants, marshals, policemen—even the official court stenographer—all male. A woman who perhaps is the innocent victim of a man's passion if she be held to testify against him is consigned in nine cases out of ten to a male jailor; when the case comes to trial she is examined by a male attorney and brought before a male judge to be tried according to the male standard. Under such conditions is it any wonder that there are few convictions under the Mann White Slave Act? After having lived through the first experience could any woman support herself through the ordeal suggested above and be able to convince a judge and jury of men that she has been sinned against rather than sinning?

Rohleder's view was becoming increasingly popular among women and women's organizations.

In 1914 Mrs. O.H.P. Belmont, a prominent suffragist, reminded the members of the Women Lawyers' Association what their goals should be:

We are told all occupations are open to women. But appointments which depend upon political power manage in a mysterious way to fall only to men. Yet some of us have such confidence in our women lawyers that we have become very bold and now we want women judges. . . . And when we capture these plums we're going out to gather more. . . . Now why should the great city of New York lag behind in these matters? With women making good as lawyers, as probation officers as fire inspectors, as investigators along all lines, why shouldn't we have women judges?

As some women activists had predicted, the likelihood of women's suffrage led to an increase in the number of women nominated to the bench, although not suprisingly most of these were appointments to divorce and children's courts. The first such nomination was that of Kathryn Sellers to the juvenile court of Washington, D.C., in 1918.

Prominent among this group of newly appointed judges were Camille Kelley of Memphis and Mary Bartelme of Chicago, who captured the attention of the press with their sympathetic and sensitive rulings regarding young people.

Judge Kelley, who was appointed to the juvenile court in Tennessee in 1921, estimated that after ten years on the bench she had handled 25,000 cases officially and had been involved in another 25,000 "unofficial adjustments." *Holland's* magazine reported that Kelley's jurisdiction permitted her to try all types of cases with the exception of rape and murder, but she "conducts the preliminary hearing in regard to those to determine whether the defendant should be held for grand jury action. Both delinquent and dependent children pass through her court. The law is broad, giving her almost unlimited power where children are mistreated or neglected." In interviews, Judge Kelley said she did not believe in long sentences for adolescents because "They cut home ties and that usually is disastrous."

A strong proponent of child welfare laws, Kelley also claimed to be a firm believer in equal rights—"but not equal wrongs." She said, "My concept of a juvenile court is a strong arm to supplement home care and training, to supply it where it does not exist, and a place where parents may go for counsel concerning the life problem of their child. It is the arm of protection that holds the child in correct channels until it is strong enough to stand alone, and the protection of right training that heals the bruised concept of life. And it's the sweetest, most satisfying work in the world."

Judge Kelley was joined in that view by Mary Margaret Bartelme, a protégé of the Chicago lawyer Myra Bradwell, who had been appointed in succession public guardian of Cook County, judicial assistant of the juvenile court in Chicago, and in 1923, circuit court judge assigned fully to the juvenile court. Bartelme's comments were often quoted by the press. "There are no bad children, there are confused, neglected children, love-starved and resentful children. These are the ones who find their way into the court, and what they need most I try to give them—understanding and a fresh start in the right direction." Early in her career Judge Bartelme created programs to help adolescent girls. With the assistance of charitable organizations and social service programs in the Chicago area she arranged for the establishment of halfway houses for young women, even donating her own home on the West Side for the project. For her efforts reporters gave her the nickname "Suitcase Mary" Bartelme, since the judge insisted that each girl leaving the home be given a satchel filled with new clothes so that she would have a fresh start in life. In 1933, at the time of Bartelme's retirement, it was estimated that more than 2,000 girls had been helped through these halfway house programs.

During the presuffrage period there had been continuing argument about whether women were better suited to help their own by presiding over courts of inferior jurisdiction that often handled family matters or by seeking appointments to more prestigious benches. Grace Rohleder wrote: "The Juvenile Court is a recognized necessity and women are fast becoming a recognized necessity as judges for the juvenile court but that is not the law; that is social betterment work; when it comes to real law that is a realm exclusively for the male." Yet even she realized that until women had real political strength, appointments to the bench, when they occurred at all, would be limited to the "social betterment" courts and not the jurisdictions that wielded economic and political power.

One of those who appeared ready to challenge an exclusively all-male bench was Jean H. Norris, an accomplished New York lawyer with a cunning ability in politics. Norris was assistant secretary of the very powerful New York Democratic Party machine, Tammany Hall, a founder and president of the Women Lawyers' Association and a transfer tax attorney for the New York State comptroller. An expert on corporate tax matters, she wrote extensively on business law and on issues affecting women.

Norris had organized women's organizations in the past and was able to effectively unite this constituency when Tammany decided the time was right in 1919 to appoint the first woman to the New York bench. Norris's appointment received national attention, and in the years that followed, she proved herself to be a strong and capable jurist. But the *DeSena* case of 1927 brought an ignominious end to Judge Norris's judicial career.

Her problems began with the trial. Marie DeSena, a woman charged with the crime of vagrancy, was being represented by lawyer Peter L. F. Sabbatino. The trial had been adjourned for various reasons but was scheduled to proceed on May 18, 1927. On that day, the trial record indicates the following conversation between the judge and defense counsel:

THE COURT: Too late.

MR. SABBATINO (defendant's attorney): Will Your Honor set it down for two o'clock tomorrow? I was here Saturday from ten until one o'clock and my case was not reached.

THE COURT: I am sorry for that.

MR. SABBATINO: I have been here since ten o'clock.

THE COURT: So have I. You know what to do; plead her guilty and tell her to throw herself on the mercy of the Court.

MR. SABBATINO: The defendant says she is not guilty.

THE DEFENDANT: I am not guilty.

THE COURT: How long will it take you to try this case? You are going to be
    limited. This case has been pending since the 26th of April . . . I won't
    try this long case at four o'clock in the afternoon.
MR. SABBATINO: I ask that it be put down for two o'clock tomorrow.
THE COURT: How long will it take you to try this case?
MR. SABBATINO: Well about—
THE COURT: Never mind, "about."

The colloquy continued with Judge Norris showing increasing irrita-
bility. When Mr. Sabbatino told the judge that he had five witnesses
scheduled to testify for the defendant, she told him she would not let
him put all five on: "Twelve o'clock tomorrow, and I shall give you half
an hour."

The following day the trial began. Two police officers testified for
the prosecution and four witnesses testified for the defense.

THE COURT: Any more witnesses? Will you put the defendant on or not?
MR. SABBATINO: May I state what this witness will testify?
THE COURT: I won't have any more witnesses. Next case. Step aside.
MR. SABBATINO: I am obliged to put the janitress on.
THE COURT: No argument. Will you put the defendant on or not?
MR. SABBATINO: I cannot rest without putting in the full case.
THE COURT: Step aside.
MR. SABBATINO: I want to call the janitress of the house.
THE COURT (to defendant): Get up.
MR. SABBATINO: I will have to call the janitress.
THE COURT: Take the stand.
THE DEFENDANT: He is my counsel, I beg your pardon.
THE COURT: Will you stop arguing?
MR. SABBATINO: You will appreciate the importance of the janitress' testimony
    as soon as you hear it.
COURT ATTENDANT: Do as the Judge tells you.

Marie DeSena was convicted. Her lawyer appealed to the court of
special sessions and ordered a copy of the trial transcript to present to
the higher court. When Peter Sabbatino received the transcript he
noticed that all the damaging statements made by the judge were either
revised or missing. Sabbatino demanded that the stenographer issue a
true copy, but the stenographer refused. Sabbatino obtained a court

order, and before the return date specified by the court, the stenographer sent Sabbatino the original version.

The original confirmed what Sabbatino suspected. The transcript was filled with deletions and changes, all of which were made by Judge Norris. Instead of showing that the court demanded that the defendant plead guilty, the transcript was changed to read: "What is it counsel, do you wish to plead her guilty and throw herself on the mercy of the court?" Comments such as "Never mind 'about' " were omitted entirely.

Norris's actions were brought to the attention of Judge Samuel Seabury, who, following allegations of widespread corruption in the magistrate's courts in New York City, was empowered by then Governor Franklin D. Roosevelt to investigate judges and other government officials.

A hearing was held at which Judge Seabury reported that Judge Norris "testified before me that she never changed minutes in any case in any material respect—nothing that would change the import of the proceedings or affect the defendant's rights or affect a possible error committed by Magistrate Norris that might be the basis of an appeal." But by the end of the hearing it was clear that Norris was adding perjury to her list of misdeeds on the bench. Judge Seabury submitted his findings to the appellate division of New York's supreme court, concluding that Judge Norris was "unfit to continue to hold the office of City Magistrate, and should be removed therefrom."

Norris did not resign. Instead, she appeared for trial before the appellate division, represented by one of the best-known defense lawyers in New York, Martin Conboy. Conboy was able to convince the court to dismiss one charge on the ground that "there was no intentional wrongdoing, the evidence showing merely a mistake in judgment," but that was all he could do for Norris.

The court found that:

In the DeSena case Magistrate Norris changed or attempted to change official records in material respects, to the prejudice of the defendant, in an endeavor to eliminate from the record on appeal remarks and rulings by her as a magistrate which presented evidence of unjudicial and unfair conduct at the trial and thus to prevent the substantiation in the appellate court as to what had in truth occurred. . . . During the course of the hearing an issue was tendered, met and tried as to whether Magistrate Norris forced the defendant DeSena to take the witness stand in violation of her constitutional rights. We find that the evidence preponderates in proving this charge.

In the end the appellate division ruled that several charges had been proven and that "taken together they show unfitness for judicial office and constitute cause for removal." Norris was forced to relinquish her post.

Regrettably, Norris was not the only woman judge involved in controversy during this period. In 1928 Brooklyn Law School graduate Amy Wren was appointed a United States Commissioner—one of the first women in the nation to hold such a position. Wren had practiced law for nearly twenty years before joining the New York State Attorney General's office, but resigned because she said that "the more serious duties of the office were given to men."

A Republican district leader in Brooklyn Heights, Wren was active in the suffrage and equal rights movements, and her involvement in politics appears to have greatly helped her in obtaining appointment to the federal post. After taking the oath of commissioner, Wren became a source of interest to the press and public. One newspaper noted: "The courtroom in which Commissioner Wren presides is somewhat duller and uglier than other courtrooms but her mod clothes, her bobbed, marcelled hair and the animated expression of her face relieve the gloom."

The circumstances surrounding Commissioner's Wren's resignation remain a mystery, since there were no hearings on the matter, as there were with Judge Norris. What is known is that Wren held the post for little more than a year and then claimed she was leaving the court because of political chicanery. The New York *Times*, however, reported that Wren had been accused of accepting a $30 fee to sign a bail release for a defendant charged with violating the liquor laws.

Fortunately for women seeking equal access to the judiciary, the Norris and Wren incidents were isolated cases. In the years that followed, women performed extraordinarily well in state and federal courts. The fine work of women such as Edith Atkinson, the first woman judge in Florida; Mary O'Toole, the first woman municipal court judge in Washington, D.C.; and Anna Kross Moskowitz and Justine Wise Polier in New York overcame whatever notoriety arose due to previous scandals.

One woman who received a good deal of positive attention was Genevieve Rose Cline, the first female to be appointed to the United States Customs Court. Her appointment by President Calvin Coolidge in 1928 was hailed by women's organizations as "not only a tribute to Miss Cline's work . . . but also a recognition of all women lawyers."

Cline, who was raised in Warren, Ohio, moved to Cleveland in 1905. One year after she passed the Ohio bar in 1921, President Harding appointed her appraiser of merchandise in Cleveland, a position that required interpretation of customs and tariff laws. She served as appraiser until 1928 when Coolidge nominated her to be the first woman on the U.S. Customs Court. There was immediate opposition to her proposed appointment, much of it coming from New York's Customs Bar Association, since Cline was expected to be sitting in New York. Members of the association had no other candidate in mind, but ignoring Cline's six years experience as Appraiser of the Port of Cleveland, they complained she had "no judicial experience and no extensive experience in legal practice." Despite their opposition the nomination went through.

After Genevieve Cline was sworn in, she addressed the courtroom, which was filled with women supporters:

I do want to say not only for myself but in behalf of my sister members of the bar, I thank you and want to assure you that I shall meet all absolutely fairly as *man to man* in the court.

The woman who broke more barriers in the judiciary than any other was Florence Ellinwood Allen, who, it is generally agreed, would have been appointed to the United States Supreme Court in the 1940s had she not been a woman. Allen was a political activist who vigorously campaigned for suffrage and women's rights. Her mother, one of the first students at Smith College, frequently advised her daughter that

the key to success was to "make your point and sit down." Florence
Ellinwood Allen was raised and educated in Ohio, was elected a member of Phi Beta Kappa at Case Western Reserve University, and was
also an accomplished pianist. After college she traveled abroad to study
music and was employed as a music correspondent for the Berlin
Musical Courier and the German *Times.* Upon returning to the
United States, Allen became music critic of the Cleveland *Plain Dealer*
and taught classes in Greek and German. Allen decided to study law
at the University of Chicago Law School, and when she began classes,
discovered she was the only woman enrolled. She was to recall that her
fellow law students resented her presence, and when she excelled they
attributed her success to her having an unnaturally "masculine mind."
At the close of her winter quarter at law school Florence Allen was
ranked second in the class. She decided, however, to transfer to the
New York University Law School, which she discovered had a friend-
lier attitude toward women students. Allen completed her studies with
high honors in 1913, again ranking second in her class.

Despite the fact that Allen's law school record was outstanding and
her father had many influential lawyer friends in Cleveland, she could
not get a job with any law firm in Ohio. Allen remembered that
interviewers would give one excuse or another for not hiring her, with
one attorney pointing to some snowflakes floating past his window and
saying, "Why, I wouldn't think of sending a woman down to the
courthouse on a day like this."

In September 1914, Florence Allen decided to set up her own law
practice and to volunteer to take cases for the Cleveland Legal Aid
Society. In her first case, Allen represented a woman who had been
abandoned by her husband and was suing him for support. It netted
her a fee of $15. Five years later Allen was sufficiently well known in
Cleveland to be offered the post of assistant prosecutor of Cuyahoga
County. After several months she was put in charge of the grand jury
and proudly claimed that "during my first year we drew up 823 indict-
ments."

Allen now knew enough about law and politics to consider a run for
the court of common pleas. Taking advantage of the constituency of
women's groups she had developed around the state through her suffrage lectures, Allen campaigned vigorously for the job. Only ten weeks

after the adoption of the constitutional amendment giving women the vote, Florence Ellinwood Allen was elected to the court—the first woman to attain such a high-level position by the ballot. The job did not come without problems. "No sooner was I elected," Allen remembered, "than the other justices of the court of common pleas decided a divorce division of the court should be established with me in charge of it. This did not appeal to me. I did not care to spend my life hearing and deciding divorce controversies. Since I was unmarried, I thought these eleven men, most of them married, were better qualified than I to carry their share of this burden." She refused the assignment, and the reorganization plan was discontinued. Allen prided herself on working as hard or harder than the best male judges. Between January 1921 and September 1922 she disposed of 892 cases of which 579 involved actual civil or criminal trials.

Her most dramatic case involved a first-degree murder trial. A number of the men in her courtroom were searched and found to be carrying loaded weapons. Allen recalled: "One day a letter was delivered to me at the court. It was written on dirty smudgy paper and had no signature. My name was at the top of the page and every member of the jury was listed below. The letter said; 'The day Motto [the defendant] dies, you die.' On the smudgy paper were printed several black outlines of a hand." Unaware of the significance of the "black hand," Allen seemed remarkably calm to the court officers, who were treating the note with the seriousness they believed it deserved. Motto was in fact found guilty, and in passing sentence, Allen became the first woman judge in United States history to sentence a defendant to death.

Throughout her career, Allen would be asked about the *Motto* case and whether ordering an execution was compatible with the nurturing role of women. She responded by telling interviewers something about the jurors in the case:

I saw in the corner of the jury box a man crying as if his heart would break. He had joined in the verdict and evidently considered it just, but he was so moved at ordering the death of a fellow human being that he could not keep back the tears. . . . Whether it is a man or a woman, the human being is an emotional creature and in this case the woman (foreman of the jury) delivered the verdict without evident emotion while the man was weeping violently.

In 1922 Florence Ellinwood Allen won election to the Ohio Supreme Court, the first woman to be elected to a court of last resort. Her first case was *Reutner v. the City of Cleveland*, in which she ruled on proportional representation issues. While on the court Allen was again asked about the possible conflicts she might have combining the roles of woman and judge. She answered, "I don't cook or sew or shop, for the simple reason that I haven't the time or energy for these things, any more than the men judges have."

In 1928 Allen was reelected to the supreme court by a 350,000 vote majority. Her popularity and achievements in Ohio politics had paid off. Six years later President Franklin Roosevelt appointed Florence Ellinwood Allen to the United States Court of Appeals for the Sixth Circuit, which made her the first woman ever to sit on a federal appeals bench. Allen's jurisdiction covered the states of Ohio, Michigan, Kentucky and Tennessee. The only higher court in the nation is the United States Supreme Court.

Her fellow justices on the sixth circuit were appalled by the President's decision. In her autobiography, *To Do Justly*, Allen recalled that "none of the judges favored my appointment. I am told that when it was announced, one of them went to bed for two days." Letters of welcome and congratulations came from some but not all the members of her panel. Allen was determined to ignore their discomfort, but noted that her fellow judges would refuse to look directly at her during deliberations. She attacked her work on the federal appeals court as strenuously as she had in the state courts, working an almost around-the-clock schedule. When Allen discovered that she was not being assigned patent cases as the men judges were, she demanded them and got them. She also was a member of the panel called upon to decide the constitutionality of the Tennessee Valley Authority.

In 1949 women's groups began pressuring President Harry Truman to appoint a woman to the United States Supreme Court. It was obvious that Florence Ellinwood Allen was their choice—no other woman came close to having her judicial background. Eleanor Roosevelt gave her support, saying she "could see no reason why a woman should not be appointed," and indicating that Allen was the right woman for the job. But according to legal historian Beverly B. Cook,

"When India Edwards, director of the Women's Division of the Democratic National Committee, asked the President to appoint Allen he said he was willing but he would have to 'talk to the Chief Justice about it and see what he thinks.' Later Truman told Edwards: 'No, the Justices don't want a woman. They say they couldn't sit around with their robes off and their feet up and discuss the problems.'"

Allen was disappointed at not getting the nomination. She recalled that when her name was dropped from consideration she forced herself, on the advice of a fellow judge, to greet the press and to enter the courtroom with a smile.

Allen continued to serve on the Sixth Circuit, becoming chief judge in 1959. In October of that year she reached the mandatory retirement age of seventy-five and became a senior judge with part-time duties. She died in Waite Hill, Ohio, in 1966.

The exclusion of women from the judiciary and from private clubs has been a concern of women's groups for decades. Interestingly, on one occasion these exclusionary practices turned into an advantage for women attorneys. It was in 1925 in the now famous Texas case of *Johnson v. Darr*. At issue was a trust and title dispute involving a number of parties including the fraternal organization Woodmen of the World and involving two tracts of land in El Paso, Texas. At the trial-court level plaintiff J. M. Darr and others were successful. On intermediate appeal however, judgment was reversed in favor of the appellants, Woodmen of the World. When the case came to the state's highest court, the Texas Supreme Court, all its judges had to disqualify themselves because all were members of Woodmen of the World. The result was that Texas governor Pat Neff was forced to appoint a special three-member court composed of women attorneys—the only lawyers in the area who were not members of the fraternal organization. He named Hortense Ward, who had been Texas's first woman lawyer, the special chief justice and Ruth Brazzil and Hattie L. Henenberg the special associate justices.

News of the all-women court spread throughout Texas. As *Law Student* magazine reported:

The courtroom was filled with lawyers and women when the special judges took their seats upon the bench. They first conferred with Governor Neff in his office, where they received their commissions, which were adorned with the gold seal of the State.

Chief Justice Cureton of the Supreme Court administered the oath to the women. It is the same oath Mrs. Miriam A. Ferguson as Governor took and provides that the official must swear she has never fought a duel. None of the women raised her right hand as is customary among men taking an oath of office. They did not seem to be flurried by the experience.

In separate written opinions the justices affirmed the ruling of the intermediate appellate court and gave judgment to Woodmen of the World.

But the lesson of *Johnson* v. *Darr* seemed to have been lost on Texas officials. Despite having proven their ability, none of the women received any other appointments to the bench, and it was not until 1934 that a woman was nominated for a full-term judgeship. The distinction went to Sarah T. Hughes, a lawyer and state representative for four years who received an appointment to the district court in Dallas. Hughes had had a varied career. She was a member of Phi Beta Kappa at Goucher College, and after graduation she taught biology and chemistry at the Winston Salem Academy in North Carolina. After two years of teaching, she decided she wanted to become a lawyer like her cousin Walter Douglas and she enrolled at George Washington University Law School to accomplish that goal. Hughes worked her way through law school by serving as a police officer in Washington, D.C. State Senator Claude Westerfield opposed her appointment to the bench, claiming that "a married woman ought to be home washing dishes." Hughes's nomination nevertheless was approved.

Sarah Hughes later recalled that she had received a similar reaction when she had tried to find employment in Dallas after she graduated from law school in 1922. No firm would hire her, and as a result, her first law job consisted of sitting at a receptionist's desk and answering telephones for male lawyers.

By 1961 Sarah Hughes had served as a state trial judge for twenty-six years and was known for her energy and hard work. Vice-President Lyndon Johnson and House Speaker Sam Rayburn were anxious for

Hughes to receive an appointment to the federal district court in Texas. Joseph Goulden in his book *The Benchwarmers* notes that although Hughes was considered "the star of the Dallas trial bench," opposition to her nomination as a federal judge came from a variety of sources, not the least of which was the American Bar Association, which claimed Hughes was unqualified because of her age. (She was sixty-five at the time.) According to Goulden, then Attorney General Robert Kennedy told Speaker Rayburn of the growing opposition and said he was inclined to agree, since regardless of Judge Hughes's capabilities, he did not want the Administration to set a precedent for breaking the age rule. "Sonny boy," Rayburn is reported to have said, "in your eyes most folks look too old." The appointment went through and Goulden noted in 1977 that "thirteen years later Sarah T. Hughes runs as active a trial calendar as ever—even though she is in her late seventies—and is regarded as one of the top judges in the state."

In a long and varied career Judge Hughes was perhaps best known for administering the oath of office to Lyndon Johnson on Air Force One following the assassination of President Kennedy in 1963. She remembered, "When Mrs. Kennedy came into the compartment, Vice-President Johnson told her to stand on his left and Mrs. Johnson on his right. I leaned over and said, 'I loved your husband very much.' Mr. Johnson turned to her and told her who I was, that I was a district judge who had been appointed by her husband. Then I read the oath of office which somebody had handed me and the Vice-President repeated it after me." The New York *Times* in its page-one reporting of the event noted: "As Judge Hughes read the brief oath of office her eyes, too, were red from weeping." The photograph of her administering the oath was reprinted in nearly every major newspaper throughout the world. Judge Hughes died in 1985.

She had been one of a growing number of women who finally were obtaining judgeships in state courts in the 1930s and 1940s. Among the firsts were Ruth F. Hale, chancery court of Arkansas; Anna J. V. Levy, juvenile court of Louisiana; Emma Fall Scofield and Sadie Shulman, district court and municipal court respectively of Massachusetts; M. Eleanor Nolan, municipal court in Minnesota; Matilda Pollard, justice of the peace of Nevada; Idella Jeness, municipal court in New Hampshire; Louise B. Taylor, magistrate's court in South Carolina; Reva

Beck Bosone, police and traffic court in Salt Lake City, Utah; and Ruth O. Williams, county court in Virginia. On the federal level, Carrick Buck in 1934 was appointed a district court judge in the Hawaii territory. Two years later Marion J. Harron of California was seated on the U.S. board of tax appeals, following the lead of Annabel Matthews, who in 1928 was the first woman to serve on the tax court.

Despite Florence Ellinwood Allen's appointment to the federal appeals court in 1934, no women served on the federal district court until Burnita Shelton Matthews was nominated by President Harry Truman in 1949. Matthews, born in Mississippi in 1894, came to Washington, D.C., to obtain her law degree in 1919 and a master's degree in patent law in 1920. While still a law student she picketed the White House in a demonstration for women's suffrage. After law school Matthews went into private practice. Her clients included the National Women's Party and feminists such as Maud Younger, Mrs. O.H.P. Belmont and Ruby Black, for whom she secured a ruling from the State Department creating the precedent that a woman who has not changed her name upon marriage need not assume her husband's name to obtain a passport. Additionally, Matthews drafted the law removing the disqualification of women as jurors in the District of Columbia, the Arkansas and New York statutes eliminating the preference for males over females in inheritance, the Maryland and New Jersey acts giving women teachers equal pay with men teachers for performing equal work, the South Carolina law allowing married women to sue and be sued without joinder of their husbands, and the 1931 and 1934 amendments to the federal statute extending citizenship rights of women.

Matthews also taught an evidence course at the Washington College of Law of American University and wrote extensively on the rights of women in the law. Matthews often recalled the resistance she faced when it was learned that she was being appointed to the federal bench, but she chose to ignore the criticism. After a long and brilliant career she retired in 1968. In tribute, the Washington *Post* wrote in an editorial:

The announcement that she will retire on March 1 has some special poignancy. She was a hard-working conscientious judge who took cases as they came, never ducking one because it would be difficult to decide or because the trial should be long and tedious. Some of the judges with whom she worked from time to time tried to convince her that she was carrying more than her share of the load. She was, and she kept on doing it because she never wanted it said that a woman could not keep up with the men. Presiding daily over major criminal and civil trials, she established that a woman can do the job as well as a man—and that was what she had set out to do many years ago in Mississippi when she gave up a career in music for one in law.

Legal historian Larry Berkson points out that one year later, in 1969, Shirley Hufstedler was the only woman serving on the United States Court of Appeals and was the only woman since Florence Ellinwood Allen to have been appointed to that position. Only three women, Sarah Hughes, Constance Baker Motley and June L. Green, were serving on the federal district court.

As late as 1977, Sixth Circuit Court of Appeals judge Cornelia G. Kennedy, in a speech she gave at the National Women's conference in Houston, noted:

Every Federal judge when appointed receives a commission signed by the President. It is a very impressive document as befits the importance of the position. The document is worded in such a way that a personal pronoun is used in several places. The plates from which these commissions are engraved include the words "his" and "him." On those rare occasions when a woman is appointed, "his" or "him" must be erased and "her" lettered in by hand. I think that symbolizes the long-standing attitude with regard to judicial appointments.

President Jimmy Carter is largely credited with attempting to change this situation. During his presidency he appointed forty-one women to the federal bench—more than all previous administrations combined. By insisting that merit standards be used as mandated by the 1978 Omnibus Judgeship Act and by deemphasizing political affiliations, Carter effectively opened up the appointments process to qualified women. His actions were important in setting the stage for the last breakthrough—the appointment by President Ronald Reagan of the first woman to the United States Supreme Court. It was reported that of one hundred and five judicial nominees confirmed by the United States Senate during the first term of the Reagan Administration, only seven were women, including Justice Sandra O'Connor.

.   .   .

Changes at the state court level have moved almost as slowly. The first woman chief justice of a state court was Lorna E. Lockwood, who in 1965 came to be known as "the grand dame of Arizona jurists." Lockwood was born near Tombstone at the turn of the century and was the only woman in her class when she graduated from the University of Arizona Law School in 1925. She had been inspired to practice law by pioneer woman attorney Sarah Soren, who maintained a thriving practice in Globe.

After law school Lockwood went into private practice, then served in the Arizona state legislature before working as a state assistant attorney general. In 1951 she was appointed to the Maricopa County superior court and began handling a variety of civil and criminal cases. Lockwood remembered that the first case she presided over was the trial of a defendant charged with raping a four-year-old girl. Although she was certain of the defendant's guilt, the jury didn't agree, and Lockwood was furious at their acquittal. Six years later she was the first woman judge in Arizona to sentence a man to death. In reporting the event, one newspaper wrote: "She faltered noticeably when she informed the man who had murdered his former wife that he must die for his crime. She swallowed hard and bowed her head as she told him, 'May God have mercy on your soul.' "

In 1960 Judge Lockwood was elected to the Arizona Supreme Court —the first woman to be seated on a court of last resort in the United States. She remembered vividly her first day as a supreme court judge. When she arrived at the courthouse and drove into her parking space marked SUPREME COURT JUSTICE, the guard rushed out, saying, "Lady, lady, you can't park there. Those are for justices." "It took some doing," she said, "but I persuaded him I was entitled to it, even if I was a woman."

Lockwood's name was twice suggested by Arizona senator Carl Hayden for appointment to the United States Supreme Court, but the nominations went instead to Abe Fortas and Thurgood Marshall. Justice Lockwood died in 1977, leaving it to another Arizona woman judge to become the first woman on the United States Supreme Court.

.   .   .

In 1975 Susie M. Sharp became chief justice of the state of North Carolina. Sharp, a native of Reidsville, had been a champion debater in high school and college and had received strong encouragement from her parents to pursue a career in the law. After graduating from the Greensboro College for Women, she entered the University of North Carolina Law School as one of the first women to enroll at Chapel Hill.

Her first days at law school were difficult. "The boys that didn't ignore me treated me rudely. They would leave little anonymous notes on my chair containing citations to certain North Carolina cases. For example, one day I received a note about a case and I went hurrying to the library to read it. It turned out to be a decision upholding the right of a husband to use reasonable force to beat his wife." Sharp was outraged. "The notes continued for a little while longer, but when they realized I meant business and had no designs on them, I stopped being a good joke." The last note left on her chair indicated the beginnings of a changing attitude: "If you're going to stay, get some rubber for those high heels." She admits her shoes made a racket when she raced down the hall to get to class.

Susie Sharp graduated with high honors and was a member of the law review and the Order of the Coif, an honorary society. After law school she went into private practice with her father, James Sharp. "He was 100 percent supportive and pushed me into courtrooms to get trial experience. But at first the clients only wanted 'Mr. Jim' to represent them, no one ever asked for 'Miss Susie.' " To Sharp's great disappointment, when someone finally did ask for her, it was because "he heard there was a woman lawyer in town and he wanted to see what one looked like," not because he wanted to retain her.

Sharp argued her first appeal in Raleigh, an event of great interest to the North Carolina newspapers. "But the client, who stayed home, thought my father was arguing his case, not me. When he saw the newspaper articles he demanded I be taken off the case. Of course it was too late, by then the damage was done. But I won the appeal so we didn't hear any more about it."

The Sharp family was active in Democratic Party politics, and in the late 1940s Sharp served as vice chairman of the state organization. She became involved in the governor's race, serving as campaign manager in Rockingham County and easily delivering the votes Kerr Scott needed for victory. When the governor expressed an interest in appointing a woman to North Carolina's superior court—the first woman judge in the state—Sharp was the obvious choice: a party faithful with extensive courtroom experience.

The press and public were stunned by the news of Sharp's appointment. One journalist asked his readers: "What if she were forced with trying a case of rape? Wouldn't that be too much for her delicate sensibilities?" In a style that was to become characteristic of Judge Sharp throughout her career, she sent a written reply to the newspaper: "In the first place, there could have been no rape had not a woman been present, and I consider it eminently fitting that one be in on the 'pay-off.'"

Sharp never changed that view. She still believes the numbers of women in the judiciary are shockingly low and grossly unfair to women litigants. "You take the average support case. In all my years on the bench I worked with many fine gentlemen, judges I greatly admired and respected. In every other area of the law I was able to understand and trust their views. But when it came to a women's issue like custody and support—there wasn't a one of them I could really count on."

As a superior court judge, Sharp had the opportunity of riding circuit, a physically demanding job that had her presiding in sixty-four counties throughout the state and provided her with tremendous state-wide exposure. Thirteen years later, in 1962, Governor Terry Sanford appointed Susie Sharp to North Carolina's supreme court. Her immediate reaction on joining the bench was that "it seemed like going to a Cloister." She "missed the excitement of the trial court."

Ten years later, when she was at retirement age and the senior member of the supreme court, Sharp was in line for chief justice, since in North Carolina it is tradition for the senior judge to be the preferred candidate in the election of the chief justice. Sharp's fellow justices urged her to go ahead and run, and in January 1975 Susie Sharp became the highest-ranking judge in the state. Judge Sharp is now retired, but in looking back on her career, she said, "Government touches people more perceptibly in the courtroom than at any other point in their lives, and its impact upon them depends upon the spirit of those who administer the law. While most of the cases a judge tries do not shake the cosmos very much, they shake the litigants greatly. The truth is that no human being is equal to the task of judging another because no man can ever fully understand another—not even himself. A judge does not necessarily understand criminals just because he has tried a thousand of them. The only consolation a judge can find is that somebody must do some preliminary judging on earth, and when he has done the best he could, if he had kept a concern to be kind and patient, even with the small affairs of momentarily helpless people, then perhaps he has done as well as anybody could have done."

In 1977 Rose Elizabeth Bird was named chief justice of the state of California, a controversial appointment, since she was only forty years old at the time and well-known for her strongly liberal views. Bird remembers that as a law student, she wanted to be a good trial attorney. "I had been discouraged at Boalt Hall [University of California at Berkeley] from going into trial work because it was the belief of most of the professors that women were emotionally not suited for that type of work." Bird worked for a time as a public defender, and recalls, "One of my first cases involved taking a file into San Jose Municipal Court. I entered the courtroom and the judge ordered me out immediately. He was so unfamiliar with women practicing law that he thought I was a bail bondsman and he didn't allow them to enter his courtroom." Justice Bird claims that she never really experienced sexual discrimination until she joined the bench. "For a system that was like a secular religion, a priesthood, it was very, very difficult to accept a younger woman coming into a position of authority. There are small examples of it, really trivial on the surface, but they exemplify the problem. For example, I remember when the Oakland Raiders case was written up in *Newsweek*, Justice Richardson had written the majority opinion and I wrote a dissenting opinion. Justice Richardson was referred to as 'Justice Richardson' and I was referred to as 'Rose.' "

Since her appointment in 1977, Bird has been the target of no less than eight attempted recall campaigns that she claims were "basically a harassment process" against her as symbolic head of the California judicial system. In his campaign for the gubernatorial race, California's conservative governor George Deukmajian claimed, "Rose Bird has done more damage to the California Supreme Court in the administration of justice than any of her predecessors." She seems unconcerned despite the growing "Bye-Bye Birdie" bumper stickers and placards popping up throughout the state. And in answer to her other critics who claim Bird is soft on crime, she replies, "We incarcerate more individuals on a per capita basis in California than any nation in the world other than the Soviet Union and South Africa. Of the number of cases that come up through the appellate system, 90 percent of all of the criminal convictions are affirmed, and of the other 10 percent or less that are not, over 90 percent of those go back for retrial. So we're not releasing anybody. It's a very tough system." But, she says, "When you're upholding the Constitution you're not being pro-defendant or pro-prosecution. You're doing your job and following your oath of office."

In 1977 Rosalie Wahl was the first woman appointed to the Minnesota Supreme Court. In 1981 Marie Garibaldi joined New Jersey's highest court. New York finally had a woman on its highest court in 1983 when Judith Kaye was appointed to the court of appeals, and Ellen Ash Peters became chief judge of Connecticut's supreme court in 1984. Currently at least ten more states, among them Alabama, Arkansas and Wisconsin, have women justices on their highest courts.

Women running for election for judicial office are starting to succeed at the polls. One of the most interesting races for the bench occurred in 1977 when Moria Krueger, a public defender in Madison, Wisconsin, successfully challenged Judge Archie Simonson in a recall election that was to make headlines throughout the world.

Krueger, a graduate of the University of Wisconsin Law School and the first juvenile defender in Dane County had been annoyed by Judge Simonson's remarks in the past. But when the judge gave a sentence of probation to a teenage boy who had sexually attacked a young girl in a high-school stairwell, suggesting that the young man reacted "normally" to provocative dress and a climate of sexual permissiveness, Moria Krueger worked with women's organizations throughout the state to demand Simonson's recall. Demonstrations were held on the streets of Madison at which Simonson was hanged in effigy, petition drives were carried out in bars and restaurants, and speeches were made throughout the county. Contributions of money and offers of help for the recall began pouring in. Judge Krueger remembers that "the more Judge Simonson tried to justify his views to the press, the worse he sounded. At the very beginning it seemed that only women would be outraged by his remarks, but we found men were appalled by his judgment too."

In the end 27,000 people voted to support the recall. Simonson was out and Judge Moria Krueger was in, with a margin of 6,000 votes.

Krueger currently is on the board of directors of the National Association of Women Judges, the organization that was founded in 1979 to alleviate what founder Joan Dempsey Klein calls "the very lonely, very isolated lives of those women judges who may be the only one on their bench in that locale or state. Often they are treated rather shabbily or are subject to subtle discriminatory practices in assignments and these judges find the NAWJ helps them to discuss mutual problems and feelings and to gain self-confidence."

Despite the appointment of NAWJ charter member Sandra Day O'Connor to the United States Supreme Court, former NAWJ president Gladys Kessler describes the current situation concerning appointments of women to the bench as "pretty desperate." In 1983 she noted that "about 13 percent of those in the legal profession are women. Five percent of the state appellate judges in the country are women. Two percent of the state trial judges in the country are women and on the federal bench, approximately 11 percent of the court of appeals judges are women and only 6.9 percent of the district court judges are women. As you can see, the numbers are very small. And we have to remember that those numbers took a quantum jump in the last five years. In particular, on the federal bench probably 90 percent of the appointments were made in the last six years."

At NAWJ conventions, stories of sexism on the bench abound. "When you're called 'sweetie' or 'honey' in a room full of lawyers it kind of makes your heart stop," remarked Martha Craig Daughtrey, a criminal appeals judge from Tennessee. Appellate division judge Geraldine Eiber of Queens recalled the joys of presiding over the very same courtroom in which years earlier a male judge leaned over the bench and said to her client, "Why did you go and get a woman to defend you? What do you want to do, go to jail for the rest of your life?" Also recalled was the 1955 Washington *Post* photograph of the newly sworn U.S. Customs Court judge Mary Donlon cheerfully doing needlepoint "to soothe her nerves." Appellate judge Joan Dempsey Klein of California remembered being passed up for a promotion in the judicial system because the prevailing attitude was, "Why does a married woman need to go on to a higher court?" "I wanted to tell them, 'You really think I came on to the bench for pin money, don't you?' "

And fondly recalled was the devastating reply Birdie Amsterdam, a retired New York judge, gave members of a judicial screening panel many years ago when they asked how she could possibly want to work in a court that wasn't equipped with ladies' rooms for judges. "Gentlemen," the very elegant Amsterdam coolly replied, "I have learned how to steel myself so that I no longer require a bathroom between the hours of nine and five."

Are women judges different from their male counterparts? A number of studies indicate that currently they are. In 1982 *Judicature* magazine devoted an entire issue to several profiles of women on the bench. It found that women judges tend to be younger, more liberal, less interested in politics, less wealthy than male judges, and that they possess a higher degree of scholarship and academic talent on average than the men. Historian Beverly B. Cook, who has done several analyses of women judges, found that at the same time they were sitting on the bench, 38 percent of all female trial judges were doing all or most of their own housework as well. As reporters were fond of pointing out during her confirmation hearings in the Senate, even Sandra Day O'Connor, as an appeals judge, was pushing her own grocery cart in the supermarket. Whether these practices make women more sensitive to the everyday responsibilities of average citizens or prevent them from concentrating their full talents on the law is yet to be known. But as appellate judge Gladys Kessler reminded her sister jurists:

I think that we have a moral obligation to achieve more. . . . Whether we are working to eradicate gender bias in child custody decisions, or to ensure that the poor have lawyers and access to the courts, or to make the pace and schedules of a Wall Street law firm more responsive to those with child-care obligations, we have a responsibility to "make a difference" in the legal system and the administration of justice. My hope is that when historians assess the impact of this early wave of successful women entering all corners of the legal profession, they will not find us wanting.

10

THE INVISIBLE BAR

In the more than three centuries women have been practicing law in America, they have, with relatively few exceptions, been invisible—to history, to the legal profession and to each other. With so little documentation of their experiences, it was a natural consequence that their struggles would be minimized and their accomplishments ignored.

In recent years women have become increasingly vocal about their achievements as well as their ambitions, and this, coupled with the extraordinary rise in the numbers of women joining the bar, promises to bring about dramatic changes in the coming decades. In the last thirteen years the number of women practicing law in the United States increased nearly tenfold, from 12,000 to 116,000. In the last twenty years the proportion of women in law schools nationwide rose from 4 percent in 1964 to nearly 40 percent in 1984. The American Bar Association estimates that if the trend continues, by the end of this century women will constitute half of all the attorneys in the nation.

It is tempting to point to these significant gains and to believe that the battle for equality is almost over. But history indicates otherwise. At nearly every stage of their development women attorneys incorrectly believed that once they themselves had proven their competence, acceptance for women in the next generation would be assured. As early as 1870 Chicago attorney Myra Bradwell was boasting that "the time will come, and shortly too, when women will not have to obtain legal knowledge and the right to use it under such difficulties." Twenty years later Boston attorney Lelia J. Robinson pointed to the strides women lawyers were making and said confidently that they soon would have the same successes as their male colleagues. In the 1920s feminist lawyers, heady with the passage of the women's suffrage amendment, predicted it would be only ten years or less before they had managed to "blot out of every law book in the land, to sweep out of every dusty court-room, to erase from every judge's mind that centuries-old precedent as to women's inferiority and dependence and need for protection, substituting for it at one blow the simple new precedent of equality." In the 1940s, with the men going off to war, women lawyers believed they would finally have an opportunity to exhibit their skills in the high-level positions they were taking over in law and government. But as New York County surrogate Marie M. Lambert notes about her experience with the Wall Street law firms, "We proved we could do it all. But when the men returned we were put in the back offices again and assigned the less important cases. Never mind that we had done an outstanding job, our usefulness was over and our accomplishments were ignored."

Clearly the high expectations of these generations were never met. In part the problem was their belief that they had only to prove their worth in order to be welcomed by the bar. What they failed to realize, largely because they had no written history and far too few role models, was that they long ago had proven their competence and that there really were unspoken, undefined, invisible barriers that were keeping them from attaining positions of power and importance in the legal profession. As long as they continued to believe that proving their individual excellence was necessary, they would never be mobilizing the strength of their numbers to effect change. Texas attorney Frances ("Sissy") Farenthold perhaps best understood this when she announced her candidacy for governor in 1972. She recalled members of her own family flinching at the notion of a woman running for high state office. Farenthold, a respected lawyer who was a Phi Beta Kappa graduate of Vassar College and held an honors law degree from the

University of Texas, resented having to justify her entry into a race against two male opponents with lesser qualifications whom she caustically described as "law school dropouts." Farenthold said she was "working for the day when the unqualified woman, black or Chicano can join the unqualified white man in politics." More women need to understand that although the statutory prohibitions and restrictive admissions policies have been removed, discrimination against them still exists and is still widespread, only now it is taking far more subtle forms. Women have entree to the major law firms as associates but as the *Hishon* case indicated, they still have little chance of making partner. Women attorneys may be well regarded in the seemingly less important, less prestigious positions within the profession but they still are regarded as intruders in the worlds of banking and finance and in the inner circles of power.

In the early part of the nineteenth century, feminists complained that there were only a few acceptable occupations for women outside the home: housekeeping, sewing, cooking, domestic nursing, teaching in a "dame" school, and working in a shop. We must guard against a parallel circumstance today whereby women are limited to practicing in those areas of the law that center on marriage, children, family, work on behalf of the poor and other "safe" specialties.

We must recognize too that the entry of substantial numbers of women into the law will not necessarily mean that women will move on to the higher levels of the profession. Women are likely to be relegated to a second tier—in much the same way that educators in the elementary school grades are for the most part women, and teachers of higher grades, and principals, primarily are men. The forces that once kept women out of the law altogether simply have shifted now to keeping them out of powerful positions within the law. It is important for women attorneys to know their past and to understand that the struggle for equality is nowhere near completion, for as Belva Lockwood pointed out over a century ago, "We shall never have equal rights until we take them, nor respect until we command it."

ACKNOWLEDGMENTS

With so little having been written about the history of women lawyers in the United States I came to rely on the resourcefulness and interest of scores of historians, librarians and professors, and on interviews with hundreds of women lawyers who openly shared their thoughts and experiences with me. I am grateful to all the people and institutions listed in the acknowledgments and the reference notes, and I thank them for joining me in this effort.

Karen Abrams, Washington, D.C.; Pam Abrams, New York; Bella Abzug, New York City; Boyd Addlesperger, Mansfield-Richland County Library, Ohio; Elizabeth Alexander, P. K. Yonge Library of Florida History, Gainesville; Sadie T. M. Alexander, Philadelphia; Barbara S. Allar, University of Colorado School of Law, Boulder; American Bar Association, Chicago; Pearle Appelman, New York; Charlotte Horwood Armstrong, New York City; Association of the Bar of the City of New York; Isabella Athey, Museum and Library of Maryland History, Baltimore; Mary Ann Bamberger, University of Illinois at Chicago; Rebecca Barber, Wyandotte County Museum, Bonner Springs, Kansas; Eleanore Barrows, M. G. Gallagher Law Library, University of Washington, Seattle; Marie A. Beary, New York; Margie Becker, New Bloomfield, Pennsylvania; Leo Berger, New Haven, Connecticut; Sy Berger, Oradell, New Jersey; Carole K. Bellows, Springfield, Illinois; Marge Belyea, Dover Public Library, New Hampshire; Larry Berkson, American Judicature Society, Chicago; Beverly D. Bishop, Missouri Historical Society, St. Louis; Edward M. Bonney, Maine State Bar Association, Augusta; Patricia Boyle, Detroit; Charles Breitel, New York City; Mary Jane Brittain, Iowa State Bar Association; Robert E. Brooks, Library, Yale Law School; Philippa Brophy, New York City; Ellen Kuniyiki Brown, Baylor University, Waco, Texas; Jack Brown, *Chicago Daily Law Bulletin;* Ronald L. Brown, New York University School of Law; Sara Bruce, Hastings College of the Law, San Francisco; Roberta Good Brundage, St. Louis; Ruth Brunson, University of Arkansas Law School, Little Rock; W. Hamilton Bryson, University of Richmond School of Law, Virginia; Pam Bugosh, Portland, Maine; Helen D. Burns, Jefferson County Historical Society, Port Townsend, Washington; Richard

Burtt, Northeastern University Law School; Helen L. Buttenwieser, New York City; Anne Caiger, University of California at Los Angeles; Louise R. Camp, University of New Mexico School of Law, Albuquerque; Ellen Campbell, Ashland County Historical Society, Ohio; Catherine Carter, Florida; Denise Carty-Bennia, Northeastern University Law School; James B. Casey, The Western Reserve Historical Society, Cleveland, Ohio; Kathleen Casey, New York City; Robert Cason, State of Alabama Department of Archives and History; Catalyst Library, New York City; Leah F. Chanin, Walter F. George School of Law, Mercer University, Georgia; Ruth Harvey Charity, Virginia; Mary Charles, New York City; Beverly Sitrin Coleman; Margaret Collins, New York; Robert Collins, New York; Thomas O. Collins, Jr., Louisiana State Bar Association, New Orleans; Beverly Blair Cook, Milwaukee; Irene Cooley, Boston University Law School; Constance J. Cooper, The Historical Society of Delaware; Richard Crockett, Virginia; Robert D'Ambrosio, Villanova University Law School, Pennsylvania; Forrest Daniel, State Historical Society of North Dakota, Bismarck; Anne Davidow, Detroit; Julia Davis, Idaho Historical Society; Grace Day, Missouri; Gene DeGruson, Pittsburg State University Library, Kansas; Laura Miller Derry, Kentucky; J. Roger Detweiler, State Bar of Nevada; Frederick O. Dicus, Historical Society of Streator, Illinois; Anne P. Diffendal, Nebraska State Historical Society; Virginia R. Dochterman, Iowa State Historical Department; Clifford Dougherty, George Washington University Law School, Washington, D.C.; Eric S. Drake, Dickinson School of Law, Pennsylvania; Ruth Dubois, Maryland; Geraldine Eiber, New York; Betty Ellerin, New York City; J. David Ellwanger, District of Columbia Bar Association; Catherine T. Engel, Colorado Historical Society; Cynthia Fuchs Epstein, New York City; Marjory W. Epstein, Birmingham, Michigan; Nancy S. Erickson, Ohio State University College of Law; Roberta G. Evans, University of Chicago Law School; Katherine Robinson Everett, North Carolina; Maralyn Fairberg, New York; Charlotte Horwood Faircloth, New York City; Laura L. Farris, Washington, D.C.; John Feinblatt, New York City; D. X. Fenton, New York; Geraldine Ferraro, New York; Lana S. Flame, New York City; W. Louise Florencourt, Washington, D.C.; Sue Follon, Iowa Commission on the Status of Women; Karin Ford, Idaho State Historical Society, Boise; Donna Fossum, Rockville, Maryland; Barbara Cornish Fountain, Virginia; Michael Franck, State Bar of Michigan, Lansing; G. Kent Frandsen, Indiana University School of Law, Indianapolis; William F. Fratcher, University of Missouri School of Law, Columbia; Stephen S. Freeman, New York; Lucy N. Friedman, New York City; Hilda Gage, Pontiac, Michigan; Jonathan Galassi, New York City; Philip E. Gauthier, University of Denver College of Law; Bessie Ray Geffner, New York; Helen R. Gilloon, Pasadena Historical Society, California; Stephen G. Gleissner, Wichita-Sedgwick County Historical Museum, Kansas; Catherine R. Glover, New York; Cecelia Goetz, New York City; Meg Goodyear, Connecticut Historical Society, Hartford; Anna Mae Goold, J. Reuben Clark Law School, Brigham Young University, Provo; Jack Goor, New York; Paula M. Gribbs, Detroit; Marilyn Grant, State Historical Society of Wisconsin; Martha Griffiths, Michigan; Rosemary Gunning, New York; Howard R. Hall, Boston University School of Law; Ronnye Halperin, New York City; Rebekah Hamilton, Chicago Bar Association; C. Elaine Hammons, Oklahoma; Howard Hansen, Stoughton Historical Society, Massachusetts; Vivian Hansen, Humboldt Free Public Library, Iowa; Dorothy L. Harder, Washburn University of Topeka School of Law, Kansas; Virginia Hardison, The Florida Bar; Charles Harris, Delaware State Bar Association; Lois Hatten, Pioneer Museum and Haggin Galleries, Stockton, California; Frae Hay, Wyoming; Pamela Haylock, New York City; Lois Heddens, Floyd County Historical Association; Paul T. Heffron, Library of Congress; Kevin Hegarty, Tacoma Public Library, Washington; Victoria L. Herring, U.S. Department of Justice, Iowa; Elizabeth Heyman, New York; Anne H. Hiemstra, Michigan; Robbye Hill, Washington University, St. Louis; Raymond W. Hillman, Pioneer Museum and Haggin Galleries, California; Jean Hinkle, Humboldt County Historical Association, Iowa; Carl Hogendorn, North English, Iowa; Eileen Host, West Publishing Co., Minnesota; Larry Houchins, Mississippi State Bar; C. L. Howard, Delaware Supreme Court; Lucy Somerville Howorth, Cleveland, Mississippi; Eileen L. Husted, State Bar of Arizona; Mary Hynes, Harvard University Law School; Richard Ingles, Syracuse University College of Law, New York; Kathleen Jacklin, Cornell University Libraries, Ithaca, New York; Bruce R. Jacob, Stetson University, Florida; Mary-Elizabeth Schlosser Jacques, New York; Larry Jochims, Kansas State Historical Society, Topeka; D'Arcy W. Jones, Department of Archives and History, Office of the Secretary of State, Georgia; Barbara Jordan, University of Texas at Austin; Deborah Jordon, New York City; Fran Kaiman, New Jersey; Elizabeth C. Kaming, New York City; Marge Karowe, New York; Thomas P. Kelly, William Mitchell

College of Law, Minnesota; Florynce Kennedy, New York City; Carol J. Kenner, Women's Bar Association of Massachusetts, Boston; Anne R. Kenney, Thomas Jefferson Library, University of Missouri; Jean L. King, Ann Arbor, Michigan; Ida Klaus, New York City; Joan Dempsey Klein, California; Mary Jane Knight, Hawaiian Mission Children's Society; Marjorie Fine Knowles, University of Alabama Law School; Eva Koben, New York City; Jane Lahr, Delhi Public Library, Iowa; James Laird, Wyoming State Archives, Cheyenne; Carl A. Lane, New Jersey Historical Society, Newark; John Lankalis, New York City; Barbara M. Levi, New York; Linda S. Levi, New York City; Myrna Felder, New York City; Eleanor M. Lewis, Sophia Smith Library, Smith College; Roger D. Liddicker, Lombard Historical Society, Illinois; Arthur Liman, New York City; Celya Lindberg, University of San Diego School of Law; Ruth Lindsay, University of Arkansas School of Law; John M. Lindsey, Temple University School of Law; Alice B. Lonsdorf, University of Pennsylvania Law School; Angel Lopez, Oregon State Bar, Portland; Sterling Lord, New York City; Ruth N. Lunde, Rockford Public Library, Illinois; Jack Lyle, Indiana State Bar Association; Margot McClain, Maine Historical Society, Portland; Lexie MacDonald, Historical Society of Old Newburyport, Massachusetts; Kenneth MacFarland, Albany Institute of History and Art, New York; Derek McKown, Warren County Historical Society, Pennsylvania; Pat V. Madsen, Gonzaga University School of Law, Washington; Constance M. Mandina, City University Law School at Queens College, New York; Jewell Mann, Oklahoma; Beryl Manne, Washington University, Missouri; Gladys Margolis, New Hampshire Bar Association; Frances A. Marshall, St. Clair County Library, Port Huron, Michigan; Rosemary Masters, New York City; Alan Matheson, Arizona State University College of Law; Harlene Matyas, Chicago; Frances I. Messer; Lynn Metz, Knox College, Illinois; Miriam Miller, Rutgers School of Law, Newark; Patricia Miller, Northwestern University School of Law; Sondra Miller, New York; Elizabeth Monocrusos, Museum and Library of Maryland History, Baltimore; Karen Monroe, Washington College of Law; Maurice I. Montgomery, Rock County Historical Society, Wisconsin; Betty Moore, Woodrow Wilson School of Law, Georgia; Anthony Morella, Washington College of Law; Dorothea Dixon Morello, New York; Haley A. Morello, New York; Joseph J. Morello, New Jersey; Ned Morello, New York; Margarita J. Morello, New York; John Morris, *Harvard Law School Record;* Claire E. Morrison, National Association of Women Lawyers; Rita L. Moss, Southern Illinois University at Carbondale; Constance Baker Motley, New York City; Frank Motley, Indiana University School of Law, Bloomington; Mary-Elizabeth Murdock, Sophia Smith Library, Smith College; Joanne Wharton Murphy, Ohio State University College of Law at Columbus; Clifford Muse, Moorland-Spingarn Research Center, Howard University; John Nagy, New York; Linda Nanos, New York; National Association of Women Lawyers; New York County Lawyers' Association, New York State Bar Association; Lynda L. Nygren, Albany, New York; Patricia O'Mahoney, National Association of Women Lawyers; Brian Owen, *Chicago Daily Law Bulletin;* Patricia Scollard Painter, Michigan; Andrea I. Paul, Nebraska State Historical Society; Frank O. Paull, Jr., Marquette County Historical Society, Michigan; Elaine Peabody, San Diego County Law Library; Doris M. Perry, Allen County–Fort Wayne Historical Society; Charles Petluck, New York; Eleanor Pierce, Hawaii State Bar Association; Harriet F. Pilpel, New York City; Marcia Poell, Kansas Bar Association; Lee Port, California; Susan Powers, New York City; Jane Praeger, New York City; Susan Westerberg Prager, University of California School of Law at Los Angeles; Roy R. Profitt, University of Michigan Law School; Nancy Pryor, Washington State Library, Olympia; Mary Jo Pugh, Bentley Historical Library, University of Michigan; Peggy Pullman, Effingham Regional Historical Society, Illinois; Paul P. Purta, Washington College of Law, Washington, D.C.; Queens County Women's Bar Association; Karen Ramos, Stockton–San Joaquin County Public Library, California; C. Elizabeth Raymond, Nevada Historical Society, Reno; Lili Axinn Reinis, New York; Rhode Island Bar Association, Providence; Jeanne Roberts, Historical Society of Pennsylvania, Philadelphia; Helen Robinson, Connecticut; Sharon Robinson, Schomberg Center for Research in Black Culture, New York Public Library, New York City; Wilhelmina Jackson Rolark, National Association of Black Women Attorneys; Libby Sachar, New Jersey; Barefoot Sanders, Texas; Lynn Hecht Schafran, New York City; Schlesinger Library, Radcliffe College; Joseph Schneider, Chicago; Sandy Schoenfein, New York City; Hilda Schwartz, New York City; Nelson Seitel, *New York Law Journal;* Susie M. Sharp, North Carolina; Ethel Shay, Historical Society of Streator, Illinois; Elizabeth Shenton, Schlesinger Library, Radcliffe College; LePoint C. Smith, Bolivar County Library, Mississippi; Sophia Smith Library, Smith College; Martha M. Snow, Oklahoma Bar Association; Janet Snyder, Metropolitan State

College, Denver; Edith Spivack, New York City; Virginia Stevens, Cornell Law School, New York; John Charles Sullivan, Cambridge Historical Society, Massachusetts; Edwin C. Surrency, *American Journal of Legal History,* Temple University School of Law; Terry Swanlund, Harvard Law School Library; Elinor Porter Swiger, Chicago; Margaret Taylor, New York City; Linda Thatcher, Utah Division of State History, Salt Lake City; Jane Thieberger, New York University Law School; Katherine Timon, New York; Virgil E. Tipton, Jr., Illinois State Bar Association; Sadie Turak, New York; Jeannette E. Tuve, Cleveland State University, Ohio; U.S. District Court Library, Southern District of New York; U.S. Supreme Court Library; Vicki Van Heuvlen, Oregon Historical Society, Portland; Joanne M. Ventura, New Jersey State Bar Association, Trenton; Diana Vincent-Daviss, New York University Law School; Valerie Viola, New York City; Lucy Wagner, Texas Tech University School of Law, Lubbock; Elinor Wakefield, San Joaquin County Historical Society, California; Cora T. Walker, New York City; Mary Ellen Waller, New York; Nancy R. Walseth, Oregon; Janine Warsaw, *Trial Diplomacy Journal,* Glenview, Illinois; R. L. Watts, Howard University Archives, Washington, D.C.; Herbert Wechsler, Columbia University Law School; Kenneth G. Weinberg, Cleveland, Ohio; Karen Colby Weiner, Women Lawyers' Association of Michigan; Joan L. Weisberg, New Jersey; Mabel Welch, South Texas College of Law, Houston; Westhampton Free Library, Long Island; Carol Westphal, Joliet Public Library, Illinois; Valerie White, Vermont; Ruth Widdicombe, Rock County Historical Society, Wisconsin; Constance Charles Willems, Louisiana; Carol A. Williams, Ontario County Historian; Jan Wilson, State Bar of Arizona; Virginia Wise, Harvard Law School Library; Women's Bar Association of the State of New York; Gwen Y. Wood, University of Georgia School of Law; Harold Worthley, Congregational Library, Boston; Julia Young, Bentley Historical Library, University of Michigan; Mary H. Zimmerman, Michigan; Loretta M. Zwolak, Historical Society of Pennsylvania, Philadelphia.

NOTES

1. THE FIRST WOMEN LAWYERS

PAGE

3   "The first woman lawyer": Information about Margaret Brent was obtained from the following sources: Caroline Sherman Bansamer, "A Colonial Dame," *Harper's* magazine, June 1898; "Margaret Brent," Maryland Department of Information; Grace Darin, "Margaret Brent and the Early Seeds of Feminism," Baltimore *Evening Sun*, July 28, 1971; Sophie H. Drinker, "Women Attorneys of Colonial Times," *Maryland Historical Magazine*, 1961; Mary E. W. Ramey, "Chronicles of Mistress Margaret Brent," 1915, pp. 1–12.

8   "History records": Drinker, "Women Attorneys of Colonial Times," p. 335.

8   "In 1783": Rayford Logan and Michael P. Winston, eds., *Dictionary of American Negro Biography* (New York: W. W. Norton, 1982), p. 244.

8   "In 1795": Barbara Mayer Wertheimer, *We Were There: The Story of Working Women in America* (New York: Pantheon, 1977), p. 36.

8–9   "She had warned her husband": Letter dated March 31, 1776, in L. H. Butterfield, ed., *The Adams Papers*, 2d ser., vol. 1 (Cambridge: Harvard University Press, 1963), pp. 369–370.

9   "By 1828": Eleanor Flexner, *Century of Struggle* (Cambridge: The Belknap Press of Harvard University Press, 1975), p. 55.

9   "Angela Davis points out": Angela Y. Davis, *Women, Race and Class* (New York: Vintage, 1983), p. 39.

10   "Nevertheless their activism": Flexner, *Century of Struggle*, p. 47.

10   "We hold these truths": Elizabeth Cady Stanton, Susan B. Anthony and Matilda Joslyn Gage, *The History of Woman Suffrage*, vol. 1 (New York: Fowler & Wells, 1881), p. 70.

10–11   "They want to fill": Flexner, *Century of Struggle*, p. 82.

11   "The *Chicago Legal News*": *Chicago Legal News*, February 27, 1869.

11   "In June 1869": Information about Belle Mansfield obtained from the following sources: "Arabella Mansfield," Biographical Notes, Iowa Commission on the Status of Women; Louis A. Haselmayer, "Belle Mansfield," *Women Lawyers Journal*, Spring 1969; Lelia J. Robinson, "Women Lawyers in the United States," *The Green Bag* 2, Boston: 1890, pp. 20–21; M. Romdall Williams, "Nation's First Woman Lawyer," *Iowan*, Fall–Summer 1966–1967; *Chicago Legal News*, February 4, 1871.

14   "She served as editor": *Chicago Legal News*, October 3, 1868.

14–15   "Have not some of the greatest": *Chicago Legal News*, November 7, 1868.

15   "With the same intensity": Herman Kogan, *The First Century: A History of the Chicago Bar Association 1874–1974* (Chicago: Rand McNally, 1974), pp. 26, 31–32.

15   "They certified": *Chicago Legal News*, February 5, 1870.

19   "Now Mrs. Bradwell": *Chicago Legal News*, vol. 4, 1871–1872, pp. 108–109.

21   "While waiting": Robert M. Spector, "Woman Against the Law: Myra Bradwell's Struggle for Admission to the Illinois Bar," *Journal of the Illinois State Historical Society*, June 1975, p. 238.

21   "She drafted": Herman Kogan, *The First Century*, p. 29.

21   "The *American Law Review*": *Chicago Legal News*, vol. 3, 1869–1871, p. 13.

21   "Lelia J. Robinson": Robinson, "Women Lawyers," p. 16.

22   "In 1866 she joined": Nancy A. Kopp, "Lavinia Goodell and Angie King: Wisconsin's First Women Lawyers," unpublished thesis, University of Wisconsin, 1981.

22   "If she would agree": Ibid.

23   "The *Chicago Legal News*": *Chicago Legal News*, January 1, 1876.

24   "There was little doubt": "Negro Suffrage and Women's Rights," *Wisconsin Magazine of History*, Madison: Wisconsin State Historical Society, 1920, pp. 228–229.

25   "The Wisconsin *State Journal*": Wisconsin *State Journal*, February 17, 1876.

25   "The Chicago *Tribune*": Chicago *Tribune*, February 16, 1876.

25   "The Milwaukee *Sentinel*": *Chicago Legal News*, April 26, 1879.

26   "The Janesville *Gazette*": Janesville *Gazette*, March 11, 1880.

26   "Just when Goodell's career": Robinson, "Women Lawyers," p. 24.

27   "Probably the most notorious": Information about Mary Gissen Leonard was obtained from the following sources: Fred W. Decker, "Letter to the Editor," *Oregon Historical Quarterly*, June 1977; Helen F. Althaus, "Women with the West in Their Eyes," *Oregon State Bar Bulletin*, July 1976, p. 8; Malcolm H. Clark, Jr., "The Lady and the Law: A Portrait of Mary Leonard," *Oregon Historical Quarterly*, June 1955.

31   "The first woman to try": Information about Belva A. Lockwood was obtained from the following sources: Julia Davis, "A Feisty Schoolmarm Made the Lawyers Sit Up and Take Notice," *Smithsonian Magazine*, March 1981; Terry Dunahoo, *Before the Supreme Court* (Boston: Houghton Mifflin, 1974); Mary Virginia Fox, *Lady for the Defense* (New York: Harcourt Brace, 1975); Robert McHenry, ed., *Liberty's Women* (Springfield: G & C Merriam, 1980), p. 250; *Chicago Legal News*, February 10, 1877; *Chicago Legal News*, May 11, 1878.

37–38   "These first were": The most complete and accurate state-by-state information about the first women lawyers and judges in the United States can be found in *Judicature*, the Journal of the American Judicature Society, December–January 1982. Where I discovered different "firsts" through my research, I made revisions accordingly.

2. THE FIRST WOMEN LAW STUDENTS

39   "During no previous period": Frank L. Ellsworth, *Law on the Midway: The Founding of the University of Chicago Law School* (Chicago: The University of Chicago Press, 1977), p. 2.

40   "Richard Lingeman": Richard Lingeman, *Small Town America* (New York: Putnam, 1980), p. 122.

40   "This decision was made": Paul E. Wilson, "The Early Years: The Bench and Bar Before 1882," in Robert W. Richmond, ed., *Requisite Learning and Good Moral Character* (Topeka: Kansas Bar Association, 1982), p. 35.

40   "As Kansas Supreme Court justice": John F. Fontron, Jr., "The KBA Story," in Richmond, *Requisite Learning*, p. 7.

41   "Julius Rosenthal": Kogan, *The First Century*, p. 85.

41   "In Kansas": John F. Fontron, Jr., in Richmond, *Requisite Learning*, p. 9.

41   "The Board of Law Examiners": Ibid.

41   "The usual practice": Oliver H. DeGroote, ed., *1863–1963 The History of Humboldt's First One Hundred Years* (Humboldt: Jacqua Printing, 1963), p. 209.

41   "In 1876": Kogan, *The First Century*, p. 43.

41   "Myra Bradwell suggested": Ibid., p. 30.

42   "And now young ladies": Judge Horatio Davis, speech delivered May 24, 1898; text supplied by the P. K. Yonge Library of History, Gainesville.

43   "The man over there": Flexner, *Century of Struggle*, p. 91.

43   "Ruth A. Gallaher": Ruth A. Gallaher, *Legal and Political Status of Women in Iowa* (Des Moines: State Historical Society of Iowa, 1918), pp. 22 and 39.

43   "Barbara J. Harris": Barbara J. Harris, *Beyond Her Sphere: Women in the Professions in America* (Westport: Greenwood Press, 1978), p. 98.

44   "a large heavy built": Diary of William B. Napton, May 5, 1870, p. 577; provided by the Missouri Historical Society, St. Louis.

44   "who gives": Sedalia *Daily Bazoo*, March 30, 1870.

44   "Yet within two years": Robinson, "Women Lawyers," p. 13.

44   "What a sad chapter": "Death and the Bar: The Woman Lawyer"; 1870 clipping from the Wilson Primm scrapbook maintained by the Missouri Historical Society, St. Louis.

44–45   "Little is known": Ibid.

45   "Professor William B. Napton": Diary of William B. Napton.

45   "His was an unlikely": Wilson Primm scrapbook.

45   "In the very opening": Ibid.

45   "Before her death": Sedalia *Daily Bazoo*, March 30, 1870.

46   "Mr. Russell, it is said": *United States Biographical Dictionary*, Missouri Volume, 1876, p. 111.

46   "If the question were left": Report from the faculty of the law department of Washington University to the Reverend William G. Elliot, president of the board, 1868.

46–47   "Two years ago": Undated and unidentified materials from the Phoebe Couzins Collection of the Missouri Historical Society, St. Louis.

47   "In Augusta, Illinois": Missouri *Republican*, November 25, 1878.

47   "In Whitewater": Missouri *Republican*, May 10, 1878.

47   "In St. Louis": Missouri *Republican,* October 26, 1873.

48   "Phoebe Couzins on 'Women as Lawyers' ": Ibid.

48   "The *Spectator* has": St. Louis *Spectator,* April 8, 1882.

48–49   "She told a number": Jeanne Madeline Weiman, *The Fair Women* (Chicago: Academy Chicago, 1981), p. 49.

49   "In 1898": Letter to Mrs. Blake from V. C. Whitney, dated January 18, 1898, St. Louis; supplied by the Missouri Historical Society, St. Louis.

49   "Couzins's mental state": St. Louis *Post-Dispatch,* May 12, 1909.

49   "Probably the last mention": *Women Lawyers Journal,* December 1913.

49   "Kepley, who was from Effingham": Robinson, "Women Lawyers," p. 14.

49   "After earning": Unless otherwise indicated, information about Ada H. Kepley was obtained from Hilda Engbring Feldhake, ed., *Effingham County, Illinois—Past and Present* (Effingham: Effingham Regional Historical Society, 1968).

49–50   "Kepley finally was admitted": James R. Parker, "Effingham County Bar," *Brief Histories of Some County Bars and Other Legal Organizations in Illinois,* Illinois State Bar Association, January 1977, p. 19.

51   "Dear Friend": Letter written by Ada H. Kepley dated May 2, 1923; obtained from Peggy Pulliam of the Effingham Regional Historical Society.

52   "It is not to be understood": *Green Bag* 1, September 1889, pp. 377–378.

52   "It was reported": Isabella Mary Pettus, "The Legal Education of Women," *Albany Law Journal* 61, 1900, p. 326.

52   "By 1880": Gallaher, *Legal and Political Status of Women in Iowa,* p. 50.

52   "In a survey": Robinson, "Women Lawyers," p. 17.

52–53   "At the beginning": Elizabeth Gaspar Brown, *Legal Education at Michigan 1859–1959* (Ann Arbor: University of Michigan Press, 1959), pp. 251–252.

53   "Bordin notes": Ruth Bordin, *The University of Michigan* (Ann Arbor: University of Michigan Press, 1967), p. 16.

53   "Sara Kilgore Wertman": Robinson, "Women Lawyers," p. 16.

53   "Probably the best glimpse": O. C. Burlingame, ed., *Lettie Lavilla Burlingame* (Joliet: J. E. Williams, 1895).

54–55   "the number of women": Brown, *Legal Education at Michigan,* p. 253.

57   "In 1878": Unless otherwise indicated, information about Clara S. Foltz and Laura De Force Gordon was obtained from Thomas Garden Barnes, *Hastings College of the Law: The First Century* (San Francisco: Hastings College of the Law Press, 1978), and Mortimer D. Schwartz, Susan L. Brandt and Patience Milrod, "Clara Shortridge Foltz: Pioneer in the Law," *Hastings Law Journal,* January 1976.

59   "Gordon, reported to be": Loree Cook, "Laura De Force Gordon, A Thesis Presented to the Faculty of the Department of History," San Joaquin Delta College, May 1977.

59   "This disinclination": Ibid., p. 4.

59   "While Mrs. Gordon": Stockton *Daily Evening Herald,* September 6, 1871.

59   "Laura is only having": Stockton *Daily Evening Herald,* June 14, 1878.

60   "Those Directors": Stockton *Daily Evening Herald,* January 14, 1879.

61–62   "The hearing excited": San Francisco *Chronicle*, February 25, 1879.

64   "I have never heard": O. T. Shuck, *History of the Bench and Bar in California* (Los Angeles: Occident Printing House, 1901), p. 831.

64   "Mrs. Gordon undertook": Robinson, "Women Lawyers," p. 26.

3. WOMEN IN THE URBAN LAW SCHOOLS

67   "In Philadelphia": Robinson, "Women Lawyers," p. 13.

67   "My application": *Women Lawyers Journal*, December 1915.

68   "In 1890": Robinson, "Women Lawyers," p. 29.

68   "In Boston": Ibid., p. 30.

69   "That year they received": "Law Gave Women a Hard Time," Boston *Herald American*, September 20, 1981.

70   "According to Ronald Chester": Interview with Professor Ronald Chester, New England School of Law, August 31, 1982.

70   "Further, Joseph Beale's": Boston *Herald American*, September 20, 1981.

70   "A more successful": Information about Portia Law School obtained from the Office of Alumni Affairs, New England School of Law.

71   "October 7, 1869": Dunahoo, *Before the Supreme Court*, p. 66.

71   "Lockwood, who at the time": Davis, "A Feisty Schoolmarm," p. 136.

72   "No. 432 Ninth St., N.W.": Dunahoo, *Before the Supreme Court*, p. 105.

73   "Ten years later": Robinson, "Women Lawyers," p. 27.

73   Information about law schools in Washington, D.C., was obtained from records maintained by the Washington College of Law. It includes the following: "Woman Dean of a Law College," Chicago *Times Herald*, September 11, 1898; "Mrs. Ellen Spencer Mussey, The Only Dean of a Law College," *Club Woman*, 1899; Jean S. Schade, "The Washington College of Law—A History From the Founding of the College Until Its Merger with the American University 1896–1949," Catholic University master's thesis, 1969; Certificate of Incorporation of the Washington College of Law dated April 2, 1898; Washington College of Law Program for First Annual Commencement May 31, 1899; "Six Bachelors of Law," Washington *Post*, June 1, 1899; *Kansas Woman's Journal*, December 1925.

76   "Columbia's George Templeton Strong": Allan Nevins and Milton Halsey Thomas, eds., *The Diary of George Templeton Strong* (New York: Macmillan, 1952), vol. 4, p. 256.

76   "Eleanor Flexner": Flexner, *Century of Struggle*, p. 18.

76   "One such woman": Unless otherwise indicated, information about the woman's law class at New York University and the New York University Law School was obtained from the library archives of the New York University Law School, which includes the following: *For the Better Protection of Their Rights* (New York: Washington Square Press, 1940); "Woman's Law Class Bulletin," June 16, 1915; Theodore Francis Jones, *New York University 1832–1932* (New York: Washington Square Press, 1933); Announcements for the Woman's Law Class; and Russell's Lectures, 1892.

77   "At a time": Robinson, "Women Lawyers," p. 31.

78   "those who study here": Isabella Mary Pettus, "The Work of the Woman's Law Class at New York University," *Women Lawyers Journal*, November 1911.

80   "Alice Dillingham, who died in 1985": Information about Alice Dillingham obtained
        in interview with her son, John Nagy, December 14, 1981.

81   "The number of women students": Isabella Mary Pettus, "The Legal Education of
        Women," *Albany Law Journal*, 1900, p. 328.

82   "She was noted": *Women Lawyers Journal*, January 1914.

83   "Libby Sachar": Interview with Hon. Libby Sachar, October 9, 1982.

84   "Lili Axinn Reinis fondly remembers": Interview with Lili Axinn Reinis, January 10,
        1982.

84   "By the 1930's": Interview with Helen L. Buttenwieser, June 9, 1982.

85   "But an administration": Interview with Susan Powers, June 18, 1982.

86   "In 1969 the committee": Epstein, *Women in Law*, p. 142.

86–87   "Lana S. Flame": Interview with Lana S. Flame, September 24, 1982.

4. LAST BASTIONS: THE IVY LEAGUE LAW SCHOOLS

88   "Although women had been": William J. O'Neill, *Everyone Was Brave: The Rise and
        Fall of Feminism in America* (Chicago: Quadrangle Books, 1969), p. 13.

89   "Graduates of the Law School": Yale College, *Courant*, May 3, 1873, cited in
        Frederick C. Hicks, *Yale Law School: The Founders and the Founders' Collection*
        (New Haven: Yale University Press, 1937), p. 14.

89   "Frank Ellsworth notes": Ellsworth, *Law on the Midway*, p. 4.

89   "Most important": Hicks, *Yale Law School: The Founders*, p. 18.

89–90   "Today, as sociologist": Epstein, *Women in Law*, p. 49.

90   "Restrictions or quotas": Ibid., p. 51.

90   "Helen M. Sawyer": Charles Warren, *History of Harvard Law School and of Early
        Legal Conditions in America*, vol. 2 (New York: Da Capo Press, 1970), p. 385.

90–91   "Hartford, Conn.": Frederick C. Hicks, *Yale Law School: 1869–1894, Including The
        County Court House Period* (New Haven: Yale University Press, 1937), p. 72.

92   "In 1890": Robinson, "Women Lawyers," pp. 12–13.

93   "Five other women": Information about Matilda Fenberg obtained from interview
        with her in *Yale Law Report*, Winter 1963, pp. 21–22.

94   "In the fall of 1927": Interview with Helen Robinson, January 19, 1982.

94   "Butler entered Kent Hall": Information about Elizabeth Butler obtained through
        records on file with the Alumni Office of Columbia Law School.

94   "Margaret Spahr": Information about Margaret Spahr obtained through records on
        file with the Alumni Office of Columbia Law School.

94–95   "There, after little discussion": Julius Goebel, *A History of the School of Law,
        Columbia University* (New York: Columbia University Press, 1955), pp. 290–291.

95   "Neither side": Ibid.

95   "A question involving": *Law Student Monthly*, School of Law, Columbia University,
        April 1920, p. 2.

95   "Not a bad argument": *New York Daily Register*, January 22, 1887.

96   "The resolution": Goebel, *A History of the School of Law*, pp. 290–291.

96   "Lucy Somerville Howorth": Interview with Lucy Somerville Howorth, October 28, 1981.

96   "At the time": Epstein, *Women in Law*, p. 51.

97   "For pioneers like": Interview with Ida Klaus, January 8, 1982.

100   "Rembar notes that": Charles Rembar, *The Law of the Land* (New York: Simon and Schuster, 1980), pp. 249–250.

100   "Rembar believes that Columbia": Ibid.

100   "For nearly eighty years": Arthur E. Sutherland, *The Law at Harvard: A History of Ideas and Men 1817–1967* (Cambridge: Harvard University Press, Belknap Press, 1967), pp. 319–320.

101   "Kenneth Weinberg": Interview with Kenneth G. Weinberg, April 14, 1982.

101   "Four years later": *Harvard Law School Record*, October 11, 1949.

102   "Matthews mentioned": *Harvard Law School Record*, October 11, 1950.

102   "Griswold's announcement": *Harvard Law School Record*, October 11, 1949.

102–103 "Not to be outdone": Ibid.

103   "One of the twelve": Interview with Beverly Sitrin Coleman, April 5, 1982.

103   "Louise Florencourt recalls": Interview with Louise Florencourt, April 12, 1982.

103   "Charlotte Horwood Armstrong": Interview with Charlotte Horwood Armstrong, April 12, 1982.

104   "we dressed in black": Epstein, *Women in Law*, p. 67.

104   "I got a mysterious": *Harvard Law School Record*, April 21, 1978.

105   "Rosemary Masters": Interview with Rosemary Masters, March 16, 1982.

105   "Roberta Good Brundage": Interview with Roberta Good Brundage, April 15, 1982.

5. REBELS AND REFORMERS

108   "As historian Eleanor Flexner": Flexner, *Century of Struggle*, p. 215.

108   footnote: Alexander Schlosser, *Lawyers Must Eat* (New York: Vantage Press, 1933), p. 201.

109   "Thus altho when": *Women Lawyers Journal*, July 1928.

109   "In a document": Frances E. Willard, "Hints and Helps in Our Temperance Work" (New York: National Temperance Society and Publication House, 1875).

109   "Foster, who began": Robinson, "Women Lawyers," p. 21.

109   "Ada Kepley, the first woman law graduate": Feldhake, "Effingham County," p. 303.

110   "In tribute": Rock County *Record*, April 2, 1880.

110   "In 1888": Robinson, "Women Lawyers," p. 25.

111   "The prohibition party": Nebraska *State Journal*, November 22, 1894.

111   "Minick was twelve years old": "Bride of Log Cabin Days Crowns Her Career at 91"; clipping on file with the Nebraska State Historical Society.

111   "Some judges are fair": Omaha *Sunday World Herald*, October 15, 1911.

112   "I am persuaded": Alice A. Minick, *One Family Travels West* (Boston: Meador, 1936), p. 266.

112   "Nation replied": Adela Rogers St. John, *Some Are Born Great* (New York: New American Library, 1975), p. 36.

112   "When Warren G. Harding": Unless otherwise indicated, information about Mabel Walker Willebrandt was obtained from the following sources: Thomas M. Coffey, *The Long Thirst: Prohibition in America, 1920–1933* (New York: Norton, 1975); and Dorothy M. Brown, *Mabel Walker Willebrandt* (Knoxville: University of Tennessee Press, 1984).

112   "Willebrandt was admitted": New York *Times*, April 9, 1963.

113   "Nobody in the Justice Department": Interview with Lucy Somerville Howorth, October 28, 1981.

113   "Despite the fact": New York *Times*, April 9, 1963.

113   "This was the specific aim": Interview with Anne Davidow, June 14, 1982.

115   "DeCrow, who had joined": Lois Decker O'Neill, ed., *The Women's Book of World Records and Achievements* (Garden City: Anchor Books, 1979), p. 705.

116   "Seidenberg was one of three": Ibid., p. 355.

116   "The New York *Times*": New York *Times*, June 26, 1970.

117   "Katherine Robinson Everett": Interview with Katherine Robinson Everett, September 23, 1983.

117–118   "In 1891": Margot Fruhe, "Ellen Martin," Lombard, Illinois, Historical Society, p. 1.

119   "Far from ordinary": Information about Mary Lease obtained from the following sources: Leta Bright, *Wichita Eagle & Beacon Magazine*, July 16, 1961; Lily Rozar, "A harridan and a goddess, she preached the Populist gospel," *Midway, Topeka Daily Capital*, June 29, 1969; "The Return of a Wanderer," *Wichita Eagle*, April 4, 1897; Kunigunde Duncan, "Mary Lease's Oratory Decisive in Election," unidentified article supplied by the Kansas State Historical Society; Dorothy Levenson, *Women of the West* (New York: F. Watts, 1973); Bob Butler, "Less Corn and More Hell!" Topeka *Daily Capital*, July 28, 1968.

123   "Conley, a native of Kansas City": Information about Lyda Burton Conley obtained from the following sources: Henry Van Brunt, "Three Sisters Defense of Cemetery Continued for Nearly Forty Years," Kansas City *Times*, June 1, 1946; I. T. Martin, "Living in a City of the Dead," *Kansas* magazine, 1906, p. 51; Bob Friskel, "Huron Cemetery Plans Wouldn't Please Sisters," unidentified article supplied by the Wyandotte County Historical Society; "The Objection of an Indian," Kansas City *Times*, October 24, 1906.

126   "Prior to World War I": "A Message to Lawyers," *Case and Comment*, October 1914.

126   "McCulloch had been warned": "Mrs. McCulloch First to Seek Public Office," *Morning Star*, March 20, 1938.

126   "Breckinridge also helped": McHenry, ed., *Liberty's Women*, p. 50.

126   "Her office was aptly": New York *Times*, September 3, 1934.

126–127   "At a time when": Harrison Tweed, *The Legal Aid Society, New York City 1876–1951* (New York: Legal Aid Society, 1954), p. 13.

127   "My first legal advice": New York *Tribune*, November 28, 1901.

127   "She said she studied law": Robinson, "Women Lawyers," p. 22.

127   "Oregon's Olive Stott Gabriel": Mary Zimmerman, ed., *75 Year History of National Association of Women Lawyers* (Lansing: Wellman Press, 1975), p. 51.

127   "Detroit's Martha Strickland": Martha Strickland, "Woman and the Forum," *The Green Bag* 3, May 1891, p. 240.

128   "The New York *Times*": New York *Times*, August 20, 1931.

128   "During this period": George Gregory Kiser, "The Socialist Party in Arkansas 1900 –1912," *Arkansas Historical Quarterly*, Summer 1981, p. 147.

128   "Two women attorneys": Information about Ida Hayman Callery and Caroline Lowe obtained from the following sources: The *Worker's Chronicle*, Pittsburg, Kansas, April 20, 1917; G. Gregory Kiser, "The Socialist Party in Arkansas 1900–1912," *Arkansas Historical Quarterly*, Summer 1981; A. W. Ricker, New York *Call*, April 15, 1912; May Wood Simons, "A Socialist Woman's Work," *The Coming Nation*, May 11, 1912; Grace D. Brewer, "Farewell Comrade Callery," *Appeal To Reason*, April 27, 1917; Mari Jo Buhle, *Women and American Socialism 1870–1920* (Urbana: University of Illinois Press, 1981), p. 154; Illinois *Miner*, April 27, 1923; Thomas A. Braker, "Caroline Lowe," biographical sketch for Pittsburg State University, 1976; letter dated January 1, 1975, to Professor Earl Bruce White from Robert L. Robertson obtained from the Library of Pittsburg State University, Pittsburg, Kansas; "Caroline Lowe," Pittsburg *Morning Sun*, May 20, 1976.

131   "Eastman wrote": Blanche Wiesen Cook, ed., *Crystal Eastman: Women and Revolution* (Oxford: Oxford University Press, 1978), pp. 7–8.

131–132 "These included the wealthy": June Sochen, *The New Woman in Greenwich Village 1910–1920* (New York: Quadrangle Books, 1972), p. 17.

132   "Ashley helped to found": "The Women Lawyers' Association," *Case and Comment*, October 1914.

132–133 "Many of our unjust": *Women Lawyers Journal*, May 1912.

133   "Max Eastman caustically": Edward T. James, ed., *Notable American Women 1607–1950*, vol. 1 (Cambridge: Belknap Press of Harvard University Press, 1971), p. 189.

133   "She also obtained": McHenry, ed., *Liberty's Women*, p. 226.

134   "Kenyon described herself": New York *Times*, February 14, 1972.

135   "Edith Spivack": Remarks made by Edith Spivack in address commemorating Women's History Month, March 21, 1984.

136   "In 1914": Isabel Giles, "The Twentieth Century Portia," *Case and Comment*, October 1914.

136   "Still she insisted": Cook, *Crystal Eastman*, p. 56.

136   "After graduating with honors": Interview with Harriet Pilpel, May 9, 1983, and Ben Gerson, "Renaissance Woman," *National Law Journal*, September 27, 1982.

138   "Three-term congresswoman": Bella Abzug with Mim Kelber, *Gender Gap* (Boston: Houghton Mifflin, 1984), p. 13.

138   "Similarly, when Democratic": Interview with Geraldine Ferraro, December 12, 1983.

138   "Several studies": Address by Hon. Geraldine Ferraro to the National Association of Women Judges, October 9, 1982.

138–139 "Lillian Rinenberg": Interview with Lillian Rinenberg, January 16, 1982.

139   "It is sometimes suggested": James J. White, "Women in the Law," *Michigan Law Review*, April 1967.

140   "In her revealing book": Helene Schwartz, *Lawyering*, (New York: Farrar, Straus, 1975).

141   "Shortly after Colorado attorney": *Case and Comment,* October 1914.

141–142   "More recently that view": *Oregon State Bar Bulletin,* June 1979, and interview with
               Nancy Walseth, July 8, 1982.

                    6. DOUBLE IMPAIRMENT: BLACK WOMEN LAWYERS

143   "Writer Angelina Grimke": Gerda Lerner, *The Grimke Sisters From South Carolina*
               (New York: Schocken, 1971), p. 162.

143   "Susan B. Anthony": Flexner, *Century of Struggle,* p. 147.

143   "Frederick Douglass": Ibid., p. 148.

144   "At an equal rights convention": Davis, *Women, Race & Class,* p. 83.

144   "As historian Eleanor Flexner": Flexner, *Century of Struggle,* p. 37.

144   "Jacqueline E. Jackson": Jacqueline E. Jackson, "But Where Are the Men?" in
               Robert Chrisman and Nathan Hare, eds., *Contemporary Black Thought* (Indianapo-
               lis: Bobbs-Merrill, 1973), p. 160.

144   "After the Civil War": Address before the American Equal Rights Convention, 1869,
               in Carol McPhee and Ann Fitzgerald, eds., *Feminist Quotations* (New York: Thomas
               Y. Crowell, 1979), p. 31.

144   "Couzins's view": Anna J. Cooper, *A Voice From the South* (Xenia: Aldine Printing
               House, 1892), pp. 75–79, cited in Flexner, *Century of Struggle,* p. 131.

145   "In 1890": Robinson, "Women Lawyers in the United States," p. 28.

145   "Charlotte E. Ray": Information about Charlotte E. Ray was obtained from the
               following sources: Letter dated February 22, 1983, from R. L. Watts, Moorland
               Spingarn Research Center, Howard University; Flexner, *Century of Struggle* p. 132;
               Sadie Tanner Mossell Alexander, "Women as Practitioners of Law in the United
               States," *National Bar Journal* 1, July 1941, p. 60; General O. O. Howard, Third
               Annual Report, Howard University, Washington D. C., July 1870; Phoebe Han-
               naford, *Daughters of America* (Augusta: True and Company, 1882), p. 643; M. A.
               Majors, *Noted Negro Women: Their Triumphs and Activities* (Chicago: Donohue and
               Henneberry, 1893), p. 184; Dorothy Thomas in Edward T. James, ed., *Notable
               American Women 1607–1950,* vol. 3, pp. 121–122; Walter Dyson, *Howard Univer-
               sity: The Capstone of Negro Education, A History 1867–1940* (Washington D.C.:
               Howard University Press, 1940), p. 237.

146–147   "While jobs for blacks": Richard Kluger, *Simple Justice* (New York: Knopf, 1975),
               vol. 1, p. 132.

147   "Newspapers frequently": *Case and Comment,* October 1914.

147   "In 1912": *Women Lawyers Journal,* November 1912.

147–148   "Howard Washington Odum": Kluger, *Simple Justice,* p. 391.

148   "Not only was": *Case and Comment,* October 1914.

148   "In 1918": Frances Hawthorne, "Who's Who in Iowa: Gertrude Rush," *The Iowa
               Bystander,* July 11, 1959, p. 1.

148   "By the 1940's": Alexander, "Women as Practitioners of Law in the United States,"
               p. 61.

148   "Alexander recalls": Interview with Sadie T. M. Alexander, July 6, 1982. Addi-
               tional information obtained from article written by her, "The Best of Times and the
               Worst of Times," for the *University of Pennsylvania Law Alumni Journal,* Spring
               1977.

150   "Anderson became": Alexander, "Women as Practitioners," p. 62.

150–151   "Richard Hammer": Richard Hammer, *Playboy's Illustrated History of Organized Crime* (Chicago: Playboy Press, 1975), p. 166.

151–152   "So quite reluctantly": Thomas E. Dewey, *Twenty Against the Underworld* (Garden City: Doubleday, 1974); additional information about Eunice Hunton Carter supplied by Hon. Charles Breitel in interview, July 11, 1983.

153   "Jane Mathilda Bolin": Alexander, "Women as Practitioners," p. 62.

153   "Similarly, Edith S. Sampson": Laura Miller Derry, *Digest of Women Lawyers and Judges* (Louisville: Dunne Press, 1949), p. 300.

153   "Smith was an outspoken": Mrs. E. D. Brown, Sr., "In Memoriam: Lena O. Smith," *Hennepin County Bar Journal,* 1967.

153–154   "Very few hotels": Interview with Bessie R. Geffner, January 16, 1982.

154   "Marian Sullivan, an expert": Interview with Marian Sullivan, July 14, 1982.

154   "Among them was": Interview with Ruth Harvey Charity, April 1, 1983.

156–157   "Constance Baker Motley": Unless otherwise indicated, information about Constance Baker Motley was obtained through an interview with her on May 25, 1982, and from materials supplied by the Sophia Smith Library at Smith College.

157   "Someone told me": Richard C. Lee, "Black Elm City Woman Rose to National Role," New Haven *Register,* February 21, 1982.

157   "That same year": *New York Law Journal,* May 18, 1982.

162   "One lawyer particularly attuned": Information about Florynce Kennedy obtained from her autobiography, *Color Me Flo: My Hard Life and Good Times* (Englewood Cliffs: Prentice Hall, 1976), and interview with her on July 7, 1982.

166   "Epstein quoted one woman": Epstein, *Women in Law,* p. 87.

166   "Denise Carty-Bennia": Interview with Denise Carty-Bennia, October 4, 1982.

167   "Carty-Bennia's view": Interview with Deborah Jordon, October 6, 1982.

168   "Born in 1936": Information about Barbara Jordan obtained from her autobiography. Barbara Jordan and Shelly Hearon, *Barbara Jordan: A Self-Portrait* (Garden City: Doubleday, 1979).

171   "The distinction": O'Neill, *The Women's Book of World Records and Achievements,* p. 368.

7. WOMEN IN THE COURTROOM

173   "Early in 1881": Anne C. Southworth, "Why Should Not Women Be Lawyers?," unpublished essay supplied by Howard Hansen, Stoughton, Massachusetts, Historical Society.

174   "The notion that law": Charles C. Moore, "The Woman Lawyer," Hartford *Daily Times,* May 17, 1886, reprinted in the *Green Bag,* December 1914, p. 526.

174   "The Association of Trial Lawyers": Beverly Blair Cook, "The Path to the Bench: Ambitions and Attitudes of Women in the Law," *Trial,* August 1983, p. 49.

175   "Matthews pointed out": Burnita Shelton Matthews, "The Woman Juror," *Women Lawyers Journal,* April 1927.

175   "Alice McClanahan": Alice McClanahan, *Her Father's Partner* (New York: Vantage Press, 1958), p. 97.

175   "McClanahan, who was": Ibid.

175–176   "When the girl lawyer": "A Woman Lawyer's Chances," *Case and Comment,* 1914.

176   "It is now more than thirty": Theron Strong, *Landmarks of a Lawyer's Lifetime* (New York: Dodd, Mead, 1914), cited in Patricia S. Painter, "Portia in Michigan 1870–1890," unpublished master's thesis, Wayne State University.

176–177   "Gradually as the years": Martha Strickland, "Women and the Forum," *Green Bag,* May 3, 1891, p. 240.

177   "She told a friend": Robinson, "Women Lawyers," p. 20.

177   "One article describing": Ibid.

177   "Laura Ray Tilden was admitted": Virginia City *Evening Chronicle,* July 24, 1893.

177–178   "Miss Laura Tilden": Virginia City *Territorial Enterprise,* February 1, 1894.

178   "During this same period": Robinson, "Women Lawyers," p. 16.

178   "In the late 1800s": Ibid., p. 23.

178   "Nebraska's Addie Billings": Ibid., p. 26.

178   "In the 1880s": Ibid., p. 21.

178   "(they studied law together)": Ibid., p. 24.

179   "Ellsworth claims": Ellsworth, *Law on the Midway,* p. 2.

179–180   "Baright answered": Schlosser, *Lawyers Must Eat,* p. 208.

180   "The New York *Times* noted": New York *Times,* January 9, 1961.

180   "Kansas lawyer Tiera Farrow": Unless otherwise indicated, information about Tiera Farrow was obtained from her autobiography, *Lawyer in Petticoats* (New York: Vantage Press, 1953), or from materials collected by Rebecca L. Barber, Curator of Collections of the Wyandotte County Historical Society in Bonner Springs, Kansas.

181   "This would have surprised": Interview with Bessie R. Geffner, January 16, 1982.

181   "Similarly, Margaret Hickey": Papers of Margaret Hickey, University of Missouri, Thomas Jefferson Library, St. Louis.

182   "This was particularly": Rose Falls Bres, "The Charge, Sentence and Execution of Charles Browne Perelli," *Women Lawyers Journal,* April 1927.

183   "In 1937": Interview with Helen L. Buttenwieser, June 9, 1982.

184   "In the 1940s": Interview with Hon. Cecelia Goetz, May 18, 1984.

184   "Cecelia admits": The New York *Sun,* January 21, 1948.

185   "Chicago attorney": Carole K. Bellows, "The Bar Necessities," *Student Lawyer,* May 1980, p. 42.

185   "They said I would": Interview with Geraldine Ferraro, December 12, 1983.

185   "Feminist lawyer Lynn Hecht Schafran": Lynn Hecht Schafran, "Women as Litigators: Abilities vs. Assumptions," *Trial,* August 1983, p. 40.

185   "By contrast": Interview with Laura Miller Derry, July 1, 1981.

186   "California's Gladys Towles Root": Unless otherwise indicated, information about Gladys Towles Root was obtained from her biography by Cy Rice, *Defender of the Damned* (New York: Citadel Press, 1964).

187   footnote: New York *Times,* July 30, 1964.

188   "According to Lynn Hecht Schafran": Interview with Lynn Hecht Schafran, April 12, 1983.

189   "When a lawyer or judge": Schafran, "Women as Litigators," p. 36.

189   "Such comments": Jill Wine Volner, "How One Woman Tamed the Watergate Tigers," *Redbook*, April 1976, pp. 86–88.

189   footnote: Tracy Breton, "Being a First Is Becoming A Habit," *National Law Journal*, December 17, 1984.

190   "But as Lynn Hecht Schafran points out": Schafran, "Women as Litigators," p. 39.

191   "In November 1983": New York *Times*, November 22, 1983.

191   "In May 1982": Interview with Elizabeth C. Kaming, August 3, 1983.

191   "In March 1983": *New York Law Journal*, March 1, 1983.

191–192 "In July 1985": New York *News*, July 24, 1985.

192   "Judge Loftus notes": "Sex Bias in the Courtroom," *American Bar Association Journal*, August 1983.

192   "It is not easy": Interview with Katherine Timon, December 12, 1983.

192   "As Robin Reisig": Robin Reisig, "The Improbable Rise of Pamela Chepiga," *American Lawyer*, April 1983.

8. WOMEN IN MAJOR LAW FIRMS

194   "When United States": Laurence Bodine, "Sandra Day O'Connor," *American Bar Association Journal*, October 1983, p. 1394.

194   "When Democratic vice-presidential": Letter dated November 8, 1981, to author from Geraldine Ferraro.

194   "When United States Secretary": Stacy Shapiro and Flora Johnson, "What's A Nice Girl Like You Doing in A Profession Like This?" *Student Lawyer*, May 1980, p. 18.

194   "When former United States Secretary": Connie Bruck, "The Impeccable Carla Hills," *American Lawyer*, April 1983, p. 84.

195   "Stanford law professor": Moira K. Griffin, "With More Women Becoming Lawyers," *Student Lawyer*, May 1980, p. 29.

195   "In 1984": Kathleen Sylvester, "Minorities in Firms: Women Gaining, Blacks Fall Back," *National Law Journal*, May 21, 1984.

196   "As sociologist": Epstein, *Women in Law*, p. 175.

196   "Noting that": Ibid., p. 176.

196   "Shortly after": "With Justice for Some," *Newsweek*, June 4, 1984.

196   "Supporting that view": Ibid.

197   "While Sullivan & Cromwell": Letter from Sullivan & Cromwell dated December 15, 1983.

197   "Milbank Tweed": Letter from Milbank Tweed Hadley & McCoy dated October 25, 1983.

197   "Cahill Gordon & Reindel": Letter from Cahill Gordon & Reindel dated November 9, 1983.

197   "Shearman & Sterling's": Letter from Shearman & Sterling dated October 19, 1983.

197   "Carter Ledyard & Milburn": Letter from Carter Ledyard & Milburn dated November 11, 1983.

197   "The occasion arose": New York *Tribune*, March 14, 1886.

198   "Eventually she took": *Washington Square News*, December 14, 1981.

198   "Anxious to join": Cynthia Whitaker, "The First Wave of Women Lawyers," *Washington State Bar News*, May 1981.

199   "In 1898": New York *Tribune*, July 2, 1898.

199   "The simple truth": New York *Tribune*, September 1, 1901.

200   "I think the main reason": New York *Tribune*, July 2, 1898.

200   "In this State": Rose Young, "Only Two States in this Country Deny Them the Right to Practice," New York *Evening Post*, February 15, 1913.

200   "A well-known firm": *Women Lawyers Journal*, June 1917.

201   "In Boston": *Women Lawyers Journal*, May 1917.

201   "Oh, tis not oft": Fanny Lichtblau, *Annual & Review*, Class of 1923, cited by Phyllis Klein in "Provocation or Why Female Law Students Commit Assault," unpublished thesis, New York University, 1981.

201–202   "The following year": Information about Catherine Noyes Lee supplied by Richard N. Crockett, retired partner, Cadwalader Wickersham & Taft in letter dated June 30, 1982.

202   "One of the earliest": Interview with Helen L. Buttenwieser, June 9, 1982.

203   "At every single interview": Interview with Sadie Turak, December 19, 1981.

203   "In describing the period": New York *Times*, June 22, 1970.

203–204   "Catherine Tilson": Shirley R. Bysiewicz, Anne I. Ballog, Anne Cleary Drangenis, "Women Lawyers in Connecticut," *Connecticut Bar Journal*, March 1975, pp. 123–129.

204   "Elizabeth Doogan": Zimmerman, *75 Year History*, p. 171.

204   "Daphne Robert": Ibid., p. 113.

204   "The real bottleneck": Dorothy Kenyon, "Case (By One of Them) for Women Lawyers," New York *Times*, February 19, 1950.

204–205   "It's a lucky": Ibid.

205   "But despite the belief": Arthur E. Sutherland, *The Law at Harvard: A History of Ideas and Men 1817–1967* (Cambridge: Harvard University Press, Belknap Press, 1967), p. 320.

205   "While most large": Erwin O. Smigel, *The Wall Street Lawyer: Professional Organization Man?* (London: The Free Press of Glencoe, Collier-Macmillan Ltd., 1964), pp. 46–47.

205   "During the 1950s": Barbara Armstrong, "2,997 Women Practice Law in U.S.," *Harvard Law School Record*, December 6, 1951.

205–206   "In 1956": Nancy Young, "Alumnae," *Harvard Law School Bulletin*, December 1956.

206   "In a field": New York *Times*, April 7, 1957.

206   "Cowell said that": New York *Times*, May 12, 1957.

206   "When they are employed": Young, "Alumnae," p. 13.

207   "As the New York *Times*": New York *Times*, January 26, 1972.

207   "Similarly Rita Hauser": Interview with Rita Hauser, March 7, 1984.

207–208 "In 1972": Jill Abramson, "Pushing Hard at Stroock & Stroock," *American Lawyer*, September 1984.

208   "Margaret Taylor": Interview with Hon. Margaret Taylor, May 21, 1983.

209   "Diane Blank": Epstein, *Women in Law*, p. 184.

210   "the law school": Doris L. Sassower, "Women in the Law: The Second One Hundred Years," *American Bar Association Journal*, April 1971, p. 332.

211   "Attorney Harriet Rabb": Epstein, *Women in Law*, pp. 184–185.

211   "The ten firms": New York *Times*, June 25, 1972.

213   "At the urging": Epstein, *Women in Law*, p. 187.

213   "In Illinois": Ibid.

213   "When the prestigious": Ibid., p. 195.

213–214 "While all documents": Stephen Brill, *American Lawyer*, September 1979.

214   "The *National Law Journal* reported": *National Law Journal*, September 6, 1982.

214   "In 1983": Interview with Constance Charles Willems, September 28, 1983.

215   "In 1972 Elizabeth Anderson Hishon": Information about Elizabeth Hishon obtained from the following sources: Connie Bruck, "The Case No One Will Win," *American Lawyer*, November 1983; New York *Times*, November 1, 1983; *Wall Street Journal*, December 20, 1983.

217   "Corporate lawyer Barbara M. Levi": Interview with Barbara M. Levi, October 25, 1985.

9. WOMEN ON THE BENCH

218   "When O'Connor became": Statistics supplied by Hon. Joan Dempsey Klein in interview July 8, 1983. Justice Klein was President of the National Association of Women Judges.

219   "It was not until 1949": Larry Berkson, "Women on the Bench: A Brief History," *Judicature*, December–January 1982, pp. 292–293.

219   "When President Richard Nixon": Bella Abzug, *Gender Gap*, p. 8.

219   "Although Morris had not been trained": McHenry, *Liberty's Women*, p. 293.

219   "At the time of her appointment": Levenson, *Women of the West*, p. 60.

219–220 "To his amazement": Mae Urbanek, "Justice of the Peace," *The Women Who Made the West* (Garden City: Doubleday, 1980), p. 200.

220   "Things hadn't been too peaceful": Ibid., p. 201.

220   "Justice first": Ibid.

220–221 "Of herself": Ibid.

221   "Judge Harker": *Chicago Legal News*, June 25, 1881.

221   "It was reported": Robinson, "Women Lawyers," p. 20.

221–222 "performed the duties": Ibid.

222   "Ricker 'was said' ": Ibid.

222   "It noted": *Foster's Daily Democrat*, November 12, 1920.

222   "Each time": New York *Times*, November 12, 1920.

223   "Let your hopeful bosom": *Case and Comment*, October 1914.

223   "Orphaned at the age of eleven": New York *Times*, June 30, 1909.

223   "After her terms as master": Robinson, "Women Lawyers," p. 29.

224   "In *State of Washington*": *Case and Comment*, September 1913.

224   "With all due veneration": Grace I. Rohleder, *Women on the Bench* (Washington D. C.: Fairview Publishing, 1920), p. 1.

224–225   "Our courts as presently organized": Ibid., p. 11.

225   "We are told all occupations": *Women Lawyers Journal*, May 1914.

225   "Judge Kelley": Eldon F. Roark, Jr., *Holland's Magazine of the South*, September 1931.

226   "Judge Kelley was joined": Kogan, *The First Century*, p. 106.

226   "In 1933": New York *Times*, July 26, 1954.

226–227   "Grace Rohleder wrote": Rohleder, *Women on the Bench*, p. 21.

227   "But the *DeSena* case": Schlosser, *Lawyers Must Eat*, pp. 213–226.

230   "Wren had practiced law": *Women Lawyers Journal*, July 1928.

230   "One newspaper noted": Ibid.

230   "The New York *Times* however": New York *Times*, March 24, 1958.

231   "Her appointment": *Women Lawyers Journal*, July 1928.

231   "Members of the association": New York *Times*, May 16, 1928.

231   "I do want to say": New York *Times*, June 7, 1928.

231–232   "Her mother": Unless otherwise indicated, information about Florence Ellinwood Allen is from her autobiography, *To Do Justly* (Cleveland: The Press of Western Reserve University, 1965); the archives of Case Western Reserve University; and from Beverly B. Cook, "The First Woman Candidate for the Supreme Court," *U.S. Supreme Court Historical Society Yearbook*, 1981, p. 19.

232   "Allen remembered that interviewers": Jeanette E. Tuve, associate professor of history, Cleveland State University, unpublished biography of Florence Ellinwood Allen, p. 50.

234   "In 1928 Allen was reelected": Information obtained from James B. Casey, head reference librarian, The Western Reserve Historical Society, Cleveland.

235   "Later Truman told Edwards": Myron Waldman, "A Female Justice Is Not a New Idea," *Newsday*, September 29, 1981.

235   "At issue": *Johnson v. Darr*, 272 Southwestern Reporter 1098.

236   "The courtroom was filled": "Women on Texas Supreme Court Bench," *Law Student*, April 1, 1925.

236   "After two years of teaching": Information about the late Judge Sarah T. Hughes was obtained from a written interview with her in November 1982. The Hon. Barefoot Sanders, judge of the U.S. District Court in Texas, delivered my written questions to her, and since Judge Hughes was convalescing from a stroke, the answers were recorded for her.

236	"State Senator": *Women Lawyers Journal*, February 1935.
236	"No firm would hire her": Zimmerman, *75 Year History*, p. 440.
237	"The appointment went through": Joseph C. Goulden, *The Benchwarmers* (New York: Weybright and Talley, 1977), p. 55.
237	"Then I read the oath": Merle Miller, *Lyndon* (New York: Putnam, 1980), pp. 318–319.
237	"The New York *Times*": New York *Times*, November 23, 1963.
237–238	"Among the firsts": Berkson, "Women on the Bench," p. 287.
238–239	"The announcement": Washington *Post*, February 8, 1968.
239	"Only three women": Berkson, "Women on the Bench," p. 293.
239	"Every Federal judge": Elaine Martin, "Women on the Federal Bench: A Comparative Profile," *Judicature*, December–January 1982.
240	The first woman chief justice: Information about Hon. Lorna Lockwood obtained from the following sources: Arizona *Republic*, January 8, 1965; Arizona *Republic*, May 15, 1975; Arizona *Republic*, July 20, 1975.
241	"In 1975": Interview with Hon. Susie M. Sharp, July 12, 1983.
242	"Her immediate reaction": Zimmerman, *75 Year History*, p. 434.
243	"In 1977": Information about Hon. Rose Bird obtained from Shawn D. Lewis, *Barrister*, Spring 1983, p. 26.
244	"One of the most interesting": Interview with Hon. Moria Krueger, June 27, 1983.
245	"Simonson was out": New York *Times*, October 17, 1982.
245	"Krueger currently": Francis J. Flaherty, "Women Judges Acclaim Recent Gains," *National Law Journal*, October 25, 1982.
245	"Despite the appointment": "A Look at the Honorable Gladys Kessler," *District Lawyer*, March/April 1983, p. 39.
245	"At NAWJ conventions": New York *Times*, October 17, 1982.
245–246	"Appellate division": Interview with Hon. Geraldine Eiber, January 16, 1982.
246	"Appellate judge": Interview with Hon. Joan Dempsey Klein, July 9, 1983.
246	"And fondly recalled": Interview with Hon. Betty Ellerin, February 6, 1983.
246	"It found": Susan Carbon, Pauline Holden, Larry Berkson, "Women on the State Bench: Their Characteristics and Attitudes About Judicial Selection," *Judicature*, December–January 1982, pp. 295, and Elaine Martin, p. 307.
246	"Historian Beverly Cook": Beverly Blair Cook, "The Path to the Bench: Ambitions and Attitudes of Women in the Law," *Trial*, August 1983.
246–247	"I think that we have": *District Lawyer*, March/April 1983.

INDEX

Morrison, R. F., 60, 61, 63
Mory's, 116n
Motley, Constance Baker, 156–59, 170,
   212–13; judicial appointments of,
   161–62, 239; and NAACP Legal Defense
   Fund, 159–61, 212
Mott, Lucretia, 10
Motto case, 233
Mount Holyoke College, 105
Mulkey, Anita, 215
Murphy, Betty Southard, 217
Murphy, Frank, 115
Mussey, Ellen Spencer, 73–74, 75
"Mussey Act," 75

NAACP, 153, 155, 157; Legal Defense Fund,
   159–60, 161, 212
Napier, J. C., 146
Napton, William B., 45
Nash, Clara H., 37
Nation, Carrie, 112
National Association of Black Lawyers, 167
National Association of Black Women Attor-
   neys, 154, 156
National Association of Women Judges
   (NAWJ), 245
National Association of Women Lawyers,
   126, 127, 186n, 204
National Bar Association, 156
National Bar Journal, 148
National Commission on the Causes and Pre-
   vention of Violence, 172
National Conference of Law Women, 86
National Judicial Education Program to Pro-
   mote Equality for Women and Men in
   the Courts, 188
National Labor Relations Board (NLRB), 99,
   214, 217
National Law Journal, 195, 196, 214
Naitonal League of Women Voters, 96
Naitonal Organization for Women (NOW),
   115–16; Legal Defense Fund, 188
National Prohibitory Amendment Guide, 110
National Review, 140
National University Law School, 31, 71–73
National Women's Conference, 239
National Women's Party, 238
Nebraska, first woman lawyer, 37
Nebraska's *State Journal*, 110–11
Neff, Pat, 235, 236
Nevada, first woman lawyer, 37

New England School of Law, 70
New Hampshire, first woman lawyer, 37
New Hampshire Daily Democrat, 222
New Haven Register, 91
New Jersey, first woman lawyer, 37
New Jersey Supreme Court, 244
Newsweek magazine, 196, 243
Newton, Watson J., 73
New York, first woman lawyer, 37
New York Call, 128
New York City Commission on Human
   Rights, 211, 212, 213
New York Continental, 79
New York Daily Register, 95
New York Evening Post, 200
New York Herald, 10–11, 77–78, 92n
New York Journal, 81
New York Law Journal, 95
New York School of Social Work, 98
New York Sun, 175–76, 184
New York Times, 79, 116, 180, 204–5, 207;
   and *Hishon* v. *King & Spalding*, 216; on
   Sarah Hughes, 237; on Barbara Jordan,
   171; and Dorothy Kenyon, 134–35; on
   Carrie Kilgore, 223; on Belle La Follette,
   128; on Amy Wren, 230
New York Tribune, 197–98, 199
New York University (NYU), 77, 78, 80, 159,
   209, 211
New York University Law School, 77, 78,
   198, 201, 208, 232; admission of women
   to, 80–87; radical women lawyers gradu-
   ating from, 131–33; Women's Rights
   Committee, 86, 210
New York Women's Bar Association, 206
New York World, 122, 179
Nixon, Richard M., 170, 189, 207, 208, 219
Nolan, M. Eleanor, 237
Norris, Jean H., 227–30
North Carolina, first woman lawyer, 37
North Carolina Supreme Court, 242
North Dakota, first woman lawyer, 38
Northeastern School of Law, 166
Northwestern University, 185
Norton, Eleanor Holmes, 86, 167, 211–12
Nott, Charles, 32, 33
Noyes, Walter C., 202
Nuremberg trials, 184

Oakland Daily Democrat, 59
Oakland Raiders case, 243

ABOUT THE AUTHOR

Karen Berger Morello is General Counsel of the Metropolitan Assistance Corporation in New York City and Historian of the Women's Bar Association of the State of New York. She has written numerous articles on women and the law for such publications as the *National Law Journal*, the *New York Law Journal* and the *Harvard Law School Record* and was a contributing author to *Gerry*, a biography of vice-presidential candidate Geraldine Ferraro. Ms. Morello is a resident of New York City and Westhampton, Long Island.